Crete

Hints for using the Guide

F ollowing the tradition established by Karl Baedeker in 1844, sights of particular interest and hotels and restaurants of especially high quality, are distinguished by one ★ or two ★★.

To make it easier to locate the various places listed in the "A to Z" section of the Guide, their co-ordinates on the large map of Crete are shown in red at the head of each entry: e.g., Chaniá B 5.

Coloured strips along the outside edge of the right-hand pages makes it easy to find the different sections of the guide. Blue indicates the introductory material, red the descriptions of sights and yellow the practical information at the end of the book.

Only a selection of hotels and restaurants can be given; no reflection is implied therefore on establishments not included.

In a time of rapid change it is difficult to ensure that all the information given is entirely accurate and up-to-date, and the possibility of error can never be entirely eliminated.

Although the publishers can accept no responsibility for inaccuracies and omissions, they are constantly endeavouring to improve the quality of their Guides and are therefore always grateful for criticisms, corrections and suggestions for improvement.

Preface

This guide to Crete is one of the new generation of Baedeker guides.

These guides, illustrated throughout in colour, are designed to meet the needs of the modern traveller. They are quick and easy to consult, with the principal places of interest described in alphabetical order, and the information is presented in a format that is both attractive and easy to follow.

This guide to Crete – an island famed for its many beautiful beaches, the excavated remains of the unique Minoan culture, its scenic beauty and its interesting monasteries and churches – is in three parts. The first part gives a general account of Crete, its topography, climate, flora and fauna, environmental problems, population, mythology, religion, economy, famous people, history, art, music and dances. A number of suggested routes for

visitors provide a lead-in to the second part, in which the principal sights are described; and the third part contains a variety of practical information designed to help visitors to find their way about Crete and make the most of their stay. Both the sights and the practical information are listed in alphabetical order.

Vái Beach, the famous palm-fringed beach on the north-eastern coast of Crete

The new Baedeker guides are noted for their concentration on essentials and their convenience of use. They contain numerous specially drawn plans and colour illustrations; and at the end of the book is a large map making it easy to locate the various places described in the "A to Z" section of the guide with the help of the co-ordinates given at the head of each entry.

Contents

Baedeker Specials

Crete –

The charm of the myth-laden island of Crete reveals itself only to those who allow themselves time to discover those parts of the island, particularly in the north, which lie remote from the popular tourist resorts on the coast. Its unique features are the extraordinary Minoan culture, still represented by numerous fascinating remains, and its scenic beauties, "never overcharged", in the words of the famous Cretan writer Nikos Kazantzákis.

The gamut of its landscapes runs from expanses of barren waste to forest-covered hills with great stretches of chestnuts, oaks and cypresses. Groves of olive-trees are prominent features of the countryside. Steep and rugged rocky coasts alternate with beaches of soft sand or shingle worn smooth by the sea. Inland there are mountains with deeply indented gorges, the best known of which is the Samariá Gorge, and fertile plains like the Mesará and Lassíthi. Here too can be found the roots of Greek mythology: Zeus, father of the gods, is believed to have been born and grown up on Crete. The legend that Zeus, in the form of a bull, carried off the Phoenician princess Europa and brought her to Crete suggests that this was the cradle of European culture. In Crete, too, one of the

Knossós

the largest and most impressive Minoan palace in Crete

Áyios Nikólaos

the picturesque little town on Lake Voulisméni

Samariá Gorge

Europe's longest gorge

Island of Myth

world's great civilisations, the Minoan culture, came into being and developed. Among the impressive remains of this culture are the large palace complexes of Knossós, Phaistós, Mália and Káto Zákros. Among the outstanding showpieces of this culture are its pottery, its vase-painting and its frescos, the finest examples of which are to be seen in the Archaeological Museum in Iráklion and in museums at Chaniá, Réthymnon,

Lassíthi Plain

the plain of windmills

Áyios Nikólaos and Sitía. The Byzantine period is represented by numerous old churches with beautiful frescos, the Venetian period by port installations and fortifications, the Turkish period by mosques and minarets. Added to all this are the attractions of the island's many beaches and beautiful bays, with a guaranteed 300 days of sunshine in the year. The relatively flat north coast in particular, with its sandy beaches and attractive bays, draws many visitors. Here too are the popular tourist centres such as Chersónisos, Mália and Áyios Nikólaos and the island's larger towns. The south coast, with its much indented coastline and steep cliffs, attracts fewer visitors; but here too are found a number of beautiful beaches, though some of them are accessible only from the sea.

Spouted jug

a 4000-year-old masterpiece with reed decoration

Gulf of Mirabéllo

the beautiful bay in north-eastern Crete

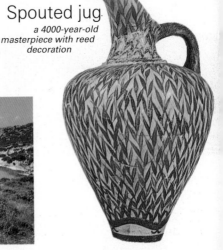

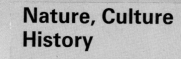

Nature, Culture History

Facts and Figures

The spelling of Greek names always gives rise to difficulty, since there is no generally accepted system for the transcription of modern Greek into English, and neither a mere transliteration nor an exact phonetic rendering seems satisfactory. Even in Greece and in Greek publications there are variations and inconsistencies in the way Greek words and names are reproduced in the Latin alphabet.

In this guide we have sought to retain the accepted orthography of classical names of people and places and to give modern Greek terms in a form reflecting their pronunciation, with an acute accent to mark the stressed syllable. Where necessary alternative versions of names have been given; but visitors must be prepared to encounter many other variations.

General

Size

With an area of 8261sq.km/3186sq. miles, Crete (in modern Greek Kríti) is the largest Greek island (disregarding the independent island of Cyprus in the eastern Mediterranean) and the fifth largest island in the Mediterranean, after Sicily, Sardinia, Corsica and Cyprus.

The island extends for 260km/160 miles from west to east, varying in breadth between 12 and 60km (7½ and 37 miles). It has a total coastline of 1046km/650 miles.

◀ The beautiful Gulf of Mirabéllo in eastern Crete, with the island of Spinalónga

Crete, the most southerly outpost of Europe, lies some 100km/63 miles south-east of the Peloponnese on the southern edge of the Aegean. It is the principal element in the arc of islands which links southern Greece with Asia Minor. Lying in latitude 35°, it reaches farther south than Tunis.

Crete is divided into four administrative regions (Greek *nomós*, plural *nomí;* chief towns in brackets): at the west end Chaniá (Chaniá), then Réthymnon (Réthymnon) and Iráklion (Iráklion), and to the east Lassíthi (Ayios Nikólaos). The island's capital is Iráklion (Herakleion). The *nomí* are in turn divided into provinces (eparchies). These administrative divisions were originally introduced by the Venetians.

The regions are headed by prefects (*nomárkhes*) appointed by the Greek government. Each town and commune elects its mayor (*dímarkhos*) or chairman (*próedros*).

The island, which is traditionally "green" (socialist), is represented in the Greek Parliament in Athens by, on average, twelve locally elected deputies.

Topography

Crete is the main element in the arc of islands which extends from the south of Greece to Asia Minor. It lies on the shelf of the Aegean Plate, under which the African Plate thrusts northward. In this zone of geological tension there are occasional earthquakes (see Baedeker Special), whose effects on the earth's surface can sometimes be of catastrophic proportions. In geologically recent times western Crete was thrust upwards by tectonic processes while the eastern part of the island sank. The tension in the earth's crust in this area is reflected in the fact that there is a difference of more than 7000m/23,000ft between the highest point on Crete and the deepest point in the sea off the island.

The geological substructure of Crete is formed by slates, phyllites and crystalline rocks laid down in the Palaeozoic period. Between the Carboniferous and the Tertiary era, but particularly in the Mesozoic period, these were overlaid by calcareous sediments. In the course of geological history there were upthrusts and subsidences of varying intensity in the earth's crust, mainly through the drifting of the continental plates against one another, and as a result of the high pressure thus produced the outcropping rocks were melted or otherwise altered. These changes affected the slates exposed at many places at the west end of the island as well as the metamorphic dolomites, chlorites and serpentinites at its eastern end and the gypsums and anhydrites at the foot of some of the ranges of hills. At the extreme west end of the island there are small deposits of iron ore, and at some points there are also deposits of lignite.

The relief pattern of Crete has largely been formed since the Pleistocene era: that is, over the last two million years, during which there

Chaniá

CHANIÁ

Réthymnon

RÉTHYMNON

Iraklion

IRAKLION

Ayios Nikólaos

LASSITHI

© *Baedeker*

Crete

—— District boundaries

11

Africa versus Europe

Crete lies in one of the most seismically active zones in the whole of the Mediterranean region, at the point where the African Plate, drifting north-ward at the rate of some centimetres a year, thrusts under the Aegean Plate, on the southern edge of the European Plate. This process operates discontinuously, without producing tensions. But the rocks have only a certain degree of elasticity, and rock masses of varying size become in-volved with one another; then tensions build up on the surfaces in contact and on reaching a certain point are violently discharged. The Athens Ob-servatory records anything up to 500 seismic shocks of varying intensity every month in the Aegean.

The earth's crust is divided into several large continental plates of var-ying size, which float on the viscous magma of the earth's mantle, drifting against one another or scraping alongside one another. When the rock can no longer resist the resultant tensions cracks open up, the energy is dis-charged in the hypocentre and causes an earthquake on the surface, radi-ating from an epicentre.

Over the last six thousand years Crete has been devastated by severe earthquakes several times. Catastrophes of this kind are believed to have contributed to the collapse of Minoan civilisation. In the 3rd century B.C. there was a massive shock in which the western part of the island was thrust upwards. Since the 13th century Crete has suffered at least six severe earthquakes, which destroyed many of the island's once splendid build-ings of the Byzantine and Venetian periods. Heavy damage was caused by an earthquake in June 1926. The last spectacular event of this kind took place on May 24th 1994, when an earthquake rated 6.1 on the Richter scale devastated the island. On that Monday morning, at ten minutes before ten, the island's population was seized by panic. At many places electricity supplies and telephones were cut off; many houses were destroyed, and children rushed in panic from their classrooms. Fortunately, however, no lives were lost.

were a number of ice ages. The island's hills, solid in appearance, have suffered much karstic action and are broken up by gorges and valleys. The effects of erosion have been particularly spectacular on the south side of the Lefká range (the White Mountains), with the Samariá Gorge, now one of Crete's major tourist attractions. The alternations of cold and warmer periods led to variations in sea level, which have left their mark particularly on the coasts of eastern Crete. More recent changes in level can also be detected in the landscape pattern. As a result of tectonic processes western Crete has risen by almost 10m/33ft since ancient times, and ports in the south-west of the island which were active in ancient times are now cut off from the sea. On the other hand subsidence resulting from tectonic action has led to ancient port towns in eastern Crete disappearing under the sea.

Mountains

Three surprisingly high ranges of mountains form the backbone of Crete. In the west of the island the Lefká Ori (White Mountains), often covered with snow, rise to 2452m/8045ft above sea level. In central Crete the Mount Ida or Psilorítis range, also frequently snow-capped, reaches a height of 2456m/8058ft in Mt Psilorítis, Crete's highest moun-tain. In eastern Crete there is the Díkti range (the Lassíthi Hills), its

The snow-capped summits of Mount Ida

highest peak rising to 2148m/7048ft. At the eastern tip of the island –
beyond the Ierápetra isthmus, which is only 12km/7½ miles wide – are
the hills above Sitía (the Thriptis range), rising to 1476m/4843ft. The
Cretan hills, now largely deforested, have been much eroded and
dissected by karstic action, offering scope only for modest pastoral
agriculture. Agriculture and horticulture are possible only in poljes
(depressions) containing fertile soil. On the south coast of the island
the Asteroúsia range, whose highest peak is Mt Kóphinas
(1231m/4039ft), borders the fertile Mesará plain. To the north of the
Psilorítis range the Tállion (Kouloúkouna) uplands extend westward to
the outskirts of Réthymnon. To the east the limestone dips into the Gulf
of Iráklion.

Caves

Crete has several thousand caves, many of them containing magnificent stalactitic formations. For the most part they are the result of
chemical erosion in the permeable limestone. Surface water pene-
trates into the rock through clefts and crevices and flows away underground. Before seeping into the rock the water absorbs carbonic acid
from the air and then, slightly acidic, dissolves the limestone, forming
hollows in the rock which in the course of time are enlarged into caves.
As water continues to drip into a cave its lime content is separated
out again as a result of evaporation, and stalactites form on the roofs of the
cave. Where the water drips more rapidly it forms stalagmites on the
floor of the cave. Frequently the stalactitic formations join up to form
stone organ-pipes or even "waterfalls".

Swallow-holes, poljes

When the roof of a cave falls in this creates a dish- or funnel-shaped
depression on the surface known as a doline or swallow-hole. When
the roofs of an entire cave system fall in or chemical erosion extends
more widely or deeply this can give rise to whole fields of swallow-
holes, poljes and karstic plains.

The rocky south coast of Crete, near Ayía Rouméli

Plains

Between the high ranges of hills extend fertile plains offering scope for profitable agriculture and horticulture. Particularly famed is the extensive and very fertile Mesará plain in the south of the island. Here the water of the Ieropotamos makes possible a highly productive horticulture, yielding a great variety of fruit and early vegetables. The Omalós (White Mountains), Nida (Mt Ida range) and Lassíthi (Díkti range) plateaux are enclosed by ranges of hills. The Lassíthi plain is particularly impressive. Lying at a height of around 800m/2625ft above sea level, it is almost exactly circular, with an area of some 45sq.km/17sq. miles. An elaborate watering and drainage system established centuries ago provides the basis for profitable agriculture and horticulture. Characteristic of the Lassíthi plain is the network of windmills with white cloth sails which bring groundwater to the surface. The main crops in this area are potatoes, cucumbers and cereals.

On the north side of the island is a fertile coastal plain which has been cultivated since ancient times and is well provided with roads.

Rivers, lakes

A striking feature of the topography of Crete is its dense network of valleys, large and small. Most of the rivers and streams flow only during the rainy winter months or when the snow is melting; at other times they are mostly dry.

To the west of Réthymnon is a small freshwater lake, Lake Kournás, which is fed by an underground river and has an underground outlet. Lake Voulisméni at Áyios Nikólaos, well stocked with fish, was originally a freshwater lake but was linked up with the sea by a channel dug in the 19th century and now has a mixture of salt and fresh water.

Almyrós

Underground rivers carry the abundant quantities of water which seep down from Crete's three high mountain ranges south-eastward to near the coast, where it mingles with salt water coming in through underground channels from the sea. The resultant mixture of salt and fresh water comes to the surface at some places on the island – for example to the west of Iráklion, on Yeoryioúpolis Bay and to the east of Áyios Nikólaos – in the spring pools known as *almyrós*.

While long stretches of the south coast, with its few bays and inlets, plunge down to the sea in steep and rugged cliffs, the north coast is flatter and much more broken up. As a result the island's largest settlements have developed along the north coast, and most of the main tourist resorts are on the more sheltered and flatter beaches on this coast. There are a number of beautiful beaches on the south coast, but access is difficult; some of them, indeed, can be reached only from the sea.

The main island of Crete is surrounded by over two dozen small islands, most of them fairly barren and uninhabited. The islet of Día off Iráklion has an area of 12sq.km/4½sq. miles, with its highest point rising to 265m/870ft. Off the south coast, in the Libyan Sea, is the little island of Gávdos, the most southerly point in Europe.

Flora and Fauna

The vegetation of Crete, much of which was originally covered by sparse oak, cedar and pine forests and groves of cypresses, is closely related to climatic conditions. The upper tree line lies at around 1700–1800m (5600–5900ft), with a predominance of kermes oaks and holm oaks (*Quercus ilex* and *Quercus coccifera*). Large areas of the island are covered by the rocky heathland known as *phrýgana* and macchia-type scrub. These are expanses of Mediterranean shrub vegetation growing up to 2m/6½ft high in varying degrees of density, including kermes oaks, dwarf oaks, myrtle, mastic, various other sclerophyllous evergreens and spurges, as well as a variety of aromatic shrubs – origano, marjoram, lavender, rosemary, thyme, sage – and various species of orchid.

To many who know the island, its characteristic tree is the cypress (*Cypressus sempervirens*), which is found in situations with a southern exposure at heights of up to 1200m/3940ft. The architectural feature known as the "Minoan column" is modelled on the trunk of a cypress, turned upside down.

A characteristic feature in the present-day Cretan landscape is the undemanding olive-tree, which has long been one of the island's most important economic crops. In still drier situations the carob tree, Agave and prickly pear flourish.

Other important economic crops, in addition to the olive, are vines (yielding both wine and table grapes, raisins and sultanas), citrus fruits (particularly oranges and mandarines) and cereals. Other crops which have flourished in recent years are vegetables (including early potatoes, cucumbers, tomatoes and onions), fruit (apricots, peaches, apples, melons, sweet chestnuts, bananas, figs, almonds, etc.) and flowers.

The fauna of Crete presents a comparatively limited range of species. Domestic animals have long displaced the island's original wild species, though it is still possible in the more remote areas to encounter the celebrated Cretan wild goat, the kri-kri (*Capra aegagrus cretensis*), as well as wild sheep, wild cats, badgers and weasels. The numbers of birds and reptiles are now much reduced. In the mountains peregrine falcons and hawks can still be found, and the lammergeier can occasionally be seen hovering watchfully overhead. During the winter, terns and black-and-white oystercatchers forage for food along the coasts. Among Crete's most beautiful birds are the brightly coloured bee-eaters and the common roller, which is most at home on the

Thyme, perfuming the countryside of Crete

Cretan wild goats, now rarely to be seen

island's cliff-fringed coasts. More frequently to be seen are various species of bunting and above all, magpies.

Typical of the Mediterranean area, and accordingly well established on Crete, is the cicada, whose chirping, when there are large numbers of them, can be almost deafening.

Particularly in scrubland, but not only there, visitors should be wary of vipers, which are both aggressive and poisonous, and also of scorpions which are found in many areas on the island and of the poisonous rogalida spiders.

Endangered species are tortoises and turtles, certain birds (including song thrushes, nightingales and quails) and the seals which used to be seen at certain points on the coast.

Several species of fish of the gurnard family live in the waters off Crete. Particularly sought after is the white and very tasty flesh of *Trigla lineata*. Other denizens of the sea found in large numbers round Crete are tunny, grey mullet, mackerel, smelt, various species of bream (including bass and dentex), the reddish barbel, hake, cod and anchovy.

Climate

Crete lies in the Mediterranean climatic zone, the particular characteristics of which are a marked dry period in summer with subtropical temperatures and a relatively mild rainy period in winter.

The Cretan spring is famous for its magnificent displays of spring blossom, after abundant rainfall during the winter months (December to March).

Spring

Summer in Crete begins at the end of April or in early May and lasts until October. During this period there is only sporadic rainfall. From June to September there is practically no rain, and this is a period of marked drought. It is only in the second half of September or in October that there are showers – locally very heavy – of the longed-for rain.

Summer

The water of the Mediterranean, which is relatively warm until late autumn, gives Crete comparatively agreeable temperatures even during the cooler part of the year. It is only in December that the weather becomes disagreeable and sometimes decidedly cool. The rainy period lasts from November to March.

Autumn/winter

The coldest months are January and February. At Iráklion the average maximum temperature in the afternoon is around 16°C/61°F. During this period there can be quite warm days with temperatures above 23°C/73°F and also very cold days when temperatures fall below freezing point. At higher levels in the mountains there will be snowstorms. In March the cool period comes to an end, and temperatures will occasionally rise above the 30°C/86°F mark. In May it becomes really warm and sometimes even hot, when average day temperatures rise above 25°C/77°F and maximum temperatures can pass the 40°C/104°F mark.

Temperatures

From June to September it is decidedly hot. During this period temperatures seldom fall below 20°C/68°F. Long periods of heat, with temperatures of up to 42°C/109°F, are trying for both man and beast. Then in autumn, thundery showers at last begin to cool the atmosphere.

As already noted, most of Crete's rain falls between November and March. Three-quarters of Iráklion's annual rainfall occurs between the end of November and February. The amount of rain varies considerably, however, with altitude and exposure (on the windward or

Rainfall

Climatic table	Temperature in °C (°F)			Hours of sunshine per day	Days with rain per month
Months	Average maximum	Average minimum	Seawater		
January	15.6 (60.1)	8.7 (47.7)	16 (61)	3.4	12
February	16.2 (61.2)	8.8 (47.8)	15 (59)	4.7	7
March	17.1 (62.8)	9.6 (49.3)	16 (61)	5.7	8
April	20.1 (68.2)	11.6 (52.9)	16 (61)	8.1	4
May	23.7 (74.7)	14.8 (58.6)	19 (66)	10.3	2
June	27.5 (81.5)	19.1 (66.4)	22 (72)	11.6	1
July	29.0 (84.2)	21.3 (70.3)	24 (75)	12.7	0
August	29.2 (84.6)	21.7 (71.1)	25 (77)	11.7	0
September	26.6 (79.9)	19.1 (66.4)	24 (75)	9.7	2
October	23.5 (74.3)	16.2 (61.2)	23 (73)	6.5	6
November	20.8 (69.4)	13.5 (56.3)	20 (68)	5.7	6
December	17.4 (63.3)	10.8 (51.4)	17 (63)	4.0	10

lee side of the hills). While the north coast has only 450–600mm/17¾–23½in, the south coast has 700–750mm/27½–29½in and at higher levels up to 1200mm/47in. During autumn thunderstorms there may be deluges which account for anything up to a quarter of total annual rainfall and may give rise to catastrophic flooding.

Winds

During the summer months the trade winds, the *meltemi*, almost continually blowing north winds, make the heat a little more tolerable. These winds have been harnessed from time immemorial to power the island's windmills.

There is also the *sirocco*, a strong hot wind which blows over the sea from Africa, particularly in spring.

Sunshine

Iráklion has something like 2900 hours of sunshine over the year. Between April and September there are more than 8 hours of sunshine per day.

When to visit Crete

The best time to visit Crete is between May and September. In May the days are long and the humidity of the air increases. In September, after the two very hot months of July and August, the temperature again becomes tolerable, so that more strenuous trips become possible. Most visitors come to Crete, however, at Easter and Whitsun and during the summer holiday period. In consequence there tends to be pressure on hotel accommodation and overcrowding on the beaches and at the main tourist sights.

Water temperatures

Bathing is possible as early as May. At the beginning of the month water temperatures are around 18°C/64°F, but by the end of the month they have risen to around 20°C/68°F. In August temperatures are over 25°C/77°F; and thereafter they fall gradually to around 21°C/70°F by the middle of October.

Protection of the Environment

Over-exploitation

Since ancient times the natural equilibrium on Crete has suffered continual and enduring damage from the activities of man. In order to obtain timber for building houses and ships, or as a source of energy, and to clear land for agriculture (particularly arable farming) the forests of cedars and pines and the stands of cypresses have by now been reduced to a small percentage of their original area. In recent times much of the secondary vegetation (*phrýgana, macchia*) has also been cleared to provide land for cultivation. As a result, the soil has been exposed to the destructive forces of erosion, and in the course of time there have been significant climatic changes. There have been isolated efforts to remedy the situation, at least on a local basis, by re-afforestation.

The development of agriculture, and in particular the intensive cultivation of fruit and vegetables, involving the heavy use of fertilisers and pesticides, has led in some areas to an alarming deterioration in the quality of the soil and the groundwater.

In addition, continually developing industrialisation and the rapidly growing tourist trade have aggravated existing ecological problems. A very visible sign of this trend is the alarming decline in plant and animal species in the coastal regions.

Over-exploitation of the natural landscape and over-development over the last thirty years or so have greatly aggravated the problem of water supply. The island's natural resources of fresh water are regularly over-used, particularly during the very dry summer months. In the densely populated areas on the north coast, with their large numbers of visitors, the supplies of ground and spring water have, in some places, been almost completely exhausted, with the result that the water table is steadily sinking. In the immediate proximity of the coast, too, there has been some penetration of seawater into the subsoil.

Water shortage

In recent years an attempt has been made to tackle these problems, with strict regulations on building and land use. Thus all hotels of any size are required to have their own sewage plant with provision for biological treatment. The water thus produced is used for the watering of gardens and fields, and only thereafter does it re-enter the natural cycle.

The complicated geological structure of Crete considerably increases the difficulties of water supply. Nevertheless, great efforts are being made to develop a decentralised water supply system.

Population

The population of Crete rose steadily between the middle of the 19th century and 1960 in spite of a wave of emigration around the turn of the century. It then fell during the 1960s as a result of the movement of population away from the land. The small areas of arable land were no longer sufficient to provide a living, and large number of men left to seek work in Germany. Many also moved to Athens or Iráklion.

Since then the population has increased again and now stands at 750,000. The flight from the land continues, with people continually moving into the towns and tourist resorts.

The distribution of the population between the island's four administrative districts is roughly as follows: half the population live in Iráklion, a quarter in Chaniá on the north and an eighth in each of the other two districts, Réthymnon and Sitía. Over all there are 72 people to the sq. kilometre (186 to the sq. mile). The largest town is Iráklion, followed by Chaniá, Réthymnon, Áyios Nikólaos, Sitía and Ierápetra. Most of the population thus live on the north coast; only a quarter live in the south, mostly concentrated in the Mesará plain. The rest of the south coast and the mountain regions are thinly populated or uninhabited. Half the population still live on the land.

Distribution of population

Ethnically the Cretans are not a homogeneous group, since over the last 8000 years there have been many incomers and immigrants who

Population development

Market women, who make a considerable contribution to the family income

have mingled their blood with that of the native inhabitants. The population structure has also been changed by emigration from the island. After the coming of the Minoans and Mycenaeans there was a movement of the Aegean population around 1200 B.C. during which many Cretans moved to the Levant and the island's population withdrew from the coastal regions to the mountains. Thereafter the Dorians moved into the island. After the Arab conquest of Crete in 824 Moslem refugees began to settle there and the still existing original population of the island emigrated. Then in 961 Crete was recovered by the Byzantine Empire, and there was a fresh immigration from elsewhere in the Empire. Later arrivals were Italians and Turks – the last of whom were expelled in 1923 – and finally Greek refugees from Asia Minor.

Family structures

Cretan society is still patriarchal. The patriarchal system has survived for so long partly because there have been no social reforms in the course of Cretan history, and also because industrialisation, which brings women more economic independence, has made less progress in Greece than in other European countries. Moreover the patriarchal order offers more social security than the state, of which Cretans are by nature suspicious.

There is a strict distribution of roles in the Cretan family. The husband is head of the family – a position recognised by law – while the wife is responsible for running the household and bringing up the children. She also plays a major part in agriculture, and thus earns most of the family income and controls its spending. But as a result of the increasing use of machinery in agriculture – the man's province – the wife is now losing influence and independence.

Leisure time, too, is spent separately. While the husband goes to the coffee-house the wife sits out in the street with other women discussing the events of the day.

These firm family structures have a very positive side. When the old are no longer able to look after themselves they are cared for in the family home. The crime rate is very low in country areas, where the close family bond still survives.

During the 1980s the Greek Parliament introduced major changes in the laws regulating marriage, the family and divorce. Women have now an equal share in deciding on the education of children and are entitled to receive the same pay as men for the same work. In the event of divorce the wife receives a third of the increase in value of the family property during the marriage.

Family policy

The birth rate has fallen steadily since 1951, and is lower in the towns than in the country. Contraceptives are obtainable on a medical certificate, and the law allows the termination of pregnancy within the first three months.

There is a strict moral code governing relations between the sexes, though there is now a steadily growing gulf between the towns, where western standards are increasingly accepted, and the country areas. When a man expresses admiration for a woman that is still taken, particularly in the country, as a promise of marriage. The man is allowed to gain experience before marriage, at the hands of a prostitute, a "dishonourable" wife or a widow; but great importance is still attached to the virginity of a woman. When a woman loses her good name she is expelled from the village community, for to the Cretans, honour is a matter of great importance.

Relations between the sexes

When a girl reaches marriageable age her parents and relations look for a suitable bridegroom, taking into account such pragmatic considerations as the origins, property and influence of the young man. The eldest daughter is the first to be provided for. To remain unmarried is, for both sexes, an unfortunate fate. According to the traditional view a girl can enjoy a full life only as wife and mother.

Marriage

Although the obligation to provide a dowry was abolished by law in 1983, women must still bring a rich dowry when they marry; and accordingly daughters, being "expensive", are less prized than sons. The bride is expected to bring with her a house, or land, or livestock, or a good profession. The dowry is partly a matter of prestige, but it also provides for the maintenance of the bride in her new family and gives her a degree of economic independence. Since this imposes a heavy financial burden on families, they now tend to substitute an "intellectual" dowry, giving their daughters a good education at school and university (where half the students are now women). These educated women, however, are no longer prepared to submit to the patriarchal structures of Cretan society. (This trend is mainly to be observed in the towns.)

A wedding is also an expensive item for the family. The celebrations will often last several days, and the whole village will be invited.

After the wedding the new bride usually goes to the husband's house. Her position in the new family will only be fully established, however, with the birth of children, particularly of boys.

Cretan hospitality, based on an ancient tradition, is proverbial. It is rooted in the need to establish contact with people outside the family, with an expectation that the attitude will be reciprocated. Great importance is attached to hospitality – as is shown by the fact that the Greek word *xénos* means both "stranger" and "guest". With the increase in tourism this attitude has encountered problems, for it was not possible to offer hospitality to all visitors. Unfortunately, too, some visitors abused the hospitality of local people. The Cretans, however, found an ingenious solution: they labelled holiday visitors *touristas*, and were thus relieved of the obligation to offer hospitality.

Hospitality

The Kafeníon – for Men Only

The man's domain in Crete is the kafeníon or coffee-house, where he spends his time discussing politics (international, national or local) and the latest village gossip. Here everyone can say what he thinks. Here too they can play cards or *távli* or read the newspapers. Or, in a practice taken over from Islam, they may merely let their *kombolóyion* ("worry beads" of olive-wood, amber, silver or precious stones) slip through their fingers. There is no obligation to order anything to drink. Business, too, can be transacted in the kafeníon, deals being settled by a handshake, which is absolutely binding – dishonesty is inconceivable in the village. The men still wear their old partisan garb, with baggy breeches, high boots and a fringed scarf round their head. Every village has at least one kafeníon. Where there is more than one the men go to the one whose host shares their political views. The kafeníon exemplifies the patriarchal order of Cretan life. Women are not banned from entering a kafeníon, but they have other places for meeting their friends – sitting outside their houses or when shopping.

The kafeníon, *where the men of the village exchange gossip and discuss politics*

In the remoter parts of the island, however, visitors can still find themselves being invited to a meal. They should then take care to express their thanks to their hosts by sending them copies of photographs taken during the visit, or perhaps a picture postcard, after their return home. In this way it may be possible to preserve the old tradition of hospitality between local people and visitors.

Mythology

Many of the legends of Greek mythology are concerned with Crete – indicating that the Greeks of later periods believed the roots of their culture to lie there. These myths still surround the island with a mysterious radiance and a special magic.

Zeus

A central part in Cretan mythology is played by Zeus, father of the gods, who features in numerous legends. Cronus (Kronos), lord of the earth, swallowed his children Hades, Poseidon, Hera, Hestia and Demeter because it had been prophesied that he would be stripped of power by a son of his. Accordingly his wife Rhea gave birth to her son

Zeus, for his own safety, in a cave in Crete (perhaps the Dictaean Cave at Psykhró) and gave Cronus a stone wrapped in swaddling clothes to eat instead of her son. In order to drown the baby's crying she ordered the Curetes to make a noise so that Zeus should hear nothing. The child was brought up by nymphs and spent his early years in the Idaean Cave. Later Zeus, acting as his father's cupbearer, gave him an emetic so that he brought up his children. The children then appointed him their leader, and Zeus took over the lordship of the world. He created a state or community of the gods, each with his particular province, and appointed Mount Olympus to be the seat of the gods.

A Cretan legend has it that Zeus was buried on Mt Yioúkhtas, near Iráklion, where he was committed to the earth every year and at once reborn. The silhouette of the mountain as we see it today is said to represent the face of the sleeping god.

Zeus, who had innumerable amorous adventures, fell in love with a Phoenician princess named Europa and, in the form of a handsome bull, carried her off to Crete. Arriving on the beach at Mátala, he transformed himself into an eagle and flew with her to Górtys. Here he took her by force and fathered three sons, Minos, Rhadamanthys and Sarpedon, founders of the Minoan ruling dynasty. This happened under a plane-tree, which thereafter preserved its leaves throughout the year.

Europa

There is in fact an evergreen species of plane on Crete. At Górtys visitors are shown the actual tree under which Europa's three sons were conceived.

Zeus soon left Europa for other amours. Europa then married Asterius, king of Crete, who adopted her three sons, whose dynasty became known as the Asterids. Europa's second marriage produced a daughter called Krete, who gave her name to the island.

For nine years Minos was instructed in the art of governing by his father Zeus in the Idaean Cave, from which he brought a code of laws for his future kingdom. To establish his authority as king of Crete (with the palace of Knossós as his principal seat) Poseidon presented him with a magnificent bull as a sacrificial offering. When Minos used an inferior animal for the sacrifice Poseidon punished him by causing his wife Pasiphae to fall violently in love with the bull. The universal genius Daedalus made a bronze cow for Pasiphae in which she concealed herself and mated with the bull. She then gave birth to the Minotaur, a man with a bull's head. Appalled by this creature, Minos hid it in the Labyrinth, also constructed by Daedalus, which has been equated with the palace of Knossós because of the palace's complicated layout.

Minos;
the Minotaur

After his death in Sicily (see below) Minos, who was greatly esteemed for his justice, became one of the three judges in Hades along with his brother Rhadamanthys.

Minos gave his name to a whole epoch in Cretan history. So far, however, no historical ruler of that name has been identified: it is now believed, therefore, that Minos was a general term for a ruler.

When Androgeos, one of his sons who had been staying in Athens to compete in the games, was killed Minos avenged his death by compelling the Athenians to send him seven virgins and seven young men every nine years to be devoured by the Minotaur. On the third occasion Theseus, son of King Aegeus of Athens, sailed to Crete along with the sacrificial victims with the intention of killing the Minotaur. Ariadne, Minos's daughter, who had fallen in love with Theseus, promised to help him if he would take her back to Athens as his wife. She gave Theseus the proverbial thread which enabled him to find his way through the Labyrinth and kill the Minotaur. Then, on Daedalus's advice, Theseus knocked the bottom out of Minos's ships to prevent any pursuit and escaped to Naxos along with Ariadne and the young

Theseus and
Ariadne

The famous Labyrinth of King Minos, depicted on a gold coin

Athenians whom he had saved. There he abandoned Ariadne, on the ground that she had been promised to Dionysus as a bride, and returned to Athens. On the way home, however, he forgot to hoist the white sail which he had agreed with his father would indicate the successful completion of his enterprise. When Aegeus saw the black sail of mourning he concluded that his son had been killed and thereupon threw himself into the sea which since then has been known as the Aegean. Theseus later married Phaedra, Ariadne's sister.

This story can be seen as a mythic recollection of the liberation of the Greeks from the Minoan overlordship in the eastern Mediterranean.

Daedalus and Icarus

Minos then imprisoned Daedalus and his son Icarus in the Labyrinth to punish them for the help they had given to Theseus; but Daedalus, the skilled craftsman, contrived wings for himself and his son which enabled them to escape. When Icarus, intoxicated by altitude and the speed of their flight, flew too close to the sun the wax in his wings melted and he plunged down into the sea near an island, which thereafter the island was known as Icaria while the sea became the Icarian Sea. Daedalus flew on to Sicily, where he was hospitably received by King Cocalus. Minos's thirst for revenge, however, was not yet satisfied. Seeking to find Daedalus, he travelled from one royal court to another, promising a reward to anyone who could insert a thread into the spirals of a snail's shell. When he came to Cocalus's court the puzzle was solved by Daedalus, who tied the thread to an ant and with honey as a bait induced it to draw the thread through the shell – and Minos knew that he had found his man. In order to save Daedalus, however, Cocalus's daughters scalded Minos to death in his bath.

Archaeologists have found artifacts from the Aegean in Sicily, and Sicilian place-names such as Heraclea Minoa may point to the presence of Minoan refugees.

Heracles performed his seventh labour on Crete, capturing the Cretan Bull which Minos had received from Poseidon. He compelled it to swim with him to the mainland, where he released it. It was later killed by Theseus.

Heracles

Britomartis, also known as Dictynna, goddess of purity and chastity, was particularly venerated on Crete. She is said to have been born at Kainó in the Samariá Gorge. Pursued by Minos, she threw herself into the sea but was caught in fishermen's nets and rescued. She then became the goddess of fishermen.

Britomartis

Talos (or Tauros) was a bronze giant constructed for Minos by Hephaestus, god of smiths, to serve as guardian of Crete. His body was invulnerable except for one spot on his ankle. He drove off intruders with large stones or killed them by making himself red-hot in a fire and pressing them to his breast. He tried by this means to prevent the Argonauts from landing on the island, but met his end when Medea, using magic, made him mad and then wounded him on his one vulnerable spot so that he bled to death.

Talos

Religion

Minoan Religion

The study of Minoan religion depends on the interpretation of scenes in Minoan paintings and seeks to establish links with later mythological conceptions and with contemporary cultures or the earlier phases of Aegean culture.

The principal divinity of the Minoans is believed to have been the great mother goddess, goddess of the earth and of fertility, whose name is not known. A characteristic feature of representations of the goddess is the emphasis given to the breast and buttocks. She was worshipped in cult buildings, hilltop shrines and caves, which were associated with the act of giving birth. Sacred to her were trees, mountain goats, birds, snakes and ships. As symbols of rebirth and immortality these may indicate that the goddess was also mistress of the underworld.

The Great Goddess

The worship of the goddess was essentially a vegetation and fertility cult concerned with birth, death and growth and dying down in nature. The shrines of the cult were places where the great nature goddess appeared, summoned by ecstatic ceremonies (dances), prayer and sacrifice. Poppy-seed, which was grown to produce opium, may have been taken by devotees for its intoxicating effect.

The bull cult played a central part in Minoan religion, though its significance is still not clear. The bull is also of central importance in mythology, and bulls' horns, along with the double axe, were important cult symbols. Bulls served mainly as sacrificial animals.

The bull cult

An extraordinary custom, found only on Crete, was bull-leaping – perhaps a ceremony held to secure protection against the primal powers of nature. Most of the bull-leapers are likely to have paid for this cult action with their lives, for it is difficult to see how the leap could have been successfully executed. At the end of the ceremony the bull was offered as a sacrifice, possibly as a symbol of the final victory over the primal forces.

Bull-leaping

The famous bull's-head *rhyton*, like other *rhytons* (libation vessels), points to one element in the cult: the ceremonial pouring out of consecrated fluids such as water, oil, wine and the blood of sacrificial victims.

The bull's-head rhyton

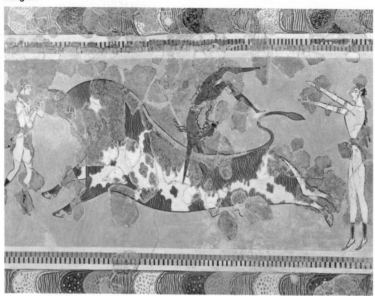

Acrobats engaged in the religious rite of bull-leaping

The Greek Orthodox Church

Almost the whole population of Crete belongs to the Greek Orthodox Church, whose influence in both private and public life has remained unshaken. Church and state are closely associated with one another, as they were even during the period of rule by the military junta. The present socialist government, however, is anxious to make this relationship less close. The church is always represented at great public occasions, and private ceremonies like weddings and burials are hardly conceivable without the blessing of the church – even though civil marriage was introduced in 1982.

History

At times when the state was weak the church not only preserved the national culture but exercised the authority of the state. During periods of foreign rule it fought for liberation with intellectual and spiritual means but also on occasion with arms. Particularly during the Turkish occupation churches and monasteries were centres of resistance and places of refuge for the oppressed and persecuted. Accordingly many monasteries have a fortress-like aspect: for example Toploú monastery, whose name means "Cannon Monastery". Many local saints are neomartyrs: that is, Christians who died for their faith during the Turkish period. This historical development explains the high standing which the Cretan church has preserved down to the present day.

Church structure

The Cretan church does not belong to the autocephalous church of Greece headed by the Metropolitan of Athens but, along with the monkish republic of Athos and the islands of the Dodecanese, is directly subordinate to the Oecumenical Patriarch of Constantinople (Istanbul). With its semi-autonomous status, however, it occupies a special position: the ecclesiastical province is administratively independent and the metropolitan is appointed by the Patriarch. This difference between the churches in mainland Greece and in Crete results from the fact that the Greek church cut its link with Constantinople in 1850 as a consequence of the war for liberation from the Turks, while the Cretan church did not, even after its reunion with Greece in 1913.

The Cretan church has six bishoprics headed by metropolitans: Chaniá, Réthymnon, Kalyviáni, Neápolis, Sitía and Iráklion, which is the seat of the archbishop.

An ordinary priest must be married, and the marriage must take place before he is ordained. If his wife dies he is permitted to remarry. Married priests may not, however, enter a monastery or be appointed to higher church dignity.

Priests

Cretans have a close relationship with their *papas,* who participate in everyday life. The priests, who are paid by the state, are available to help when any matter of consequence has to be discussed and settled. Accordingly they are also to be encountered in the *kafeníon.*

On the island there are just under 800 communes, each with its church, and almost the same number of priests. There are also 30 monasteries and some 3000 smaller churches and chapels.

Some monasteries on Crete, such as Arkádi monastery, are directly subordinate to the Patriarch of Constantinople. The monasteries have lost much of their importance, and many have been abandoned. Some are occupied only by a few monks or nuns, since there is a lack of new recruits.

Monasteries

Economy

The main sources of income for the islanders are agriculture and, increasingly, tourism. In recent years Crete's gross domestic product has been increasing at an annual rate of 10%.

Agriculture

Agriculture is the most important branch of the Cretan economy, providing employment for roughly half the population. The agriculture of Crete, thanks to its fertile soil and good climate, is highly productive. The island's farming land, which accounts for 41% of its total area, is worked mainly by small farmers and their families. Although the average holding on Crete is smaller than elsewhere in Greece the income from agriculture is above the Greek average.

General

Thanks to improvements in the road network and ferry services much of the island's agricultural produce, which formerly served to meet local needs, is now exported to Athens and Central Europe. The main export products are oranges and lemons.

Crete requires to import cereals, mainly because its main crops are now fruit and vegetables.

Olives are the most important agricultural crop in Crete, yielding an annual 120,000 tons of excellent quality olive oil. The olive is now believed to have come to Crete from Phoenicia. Most of the crop serves to meet local needs. Cretan olive oil, the only cooking oil used by the islanders, whose consumption is twice as high as in Italy, is highly esteemed all over Greece. It is pressed in oil mills, most of which are run on a co-operative basis.

Olives

Wine-growing is also of great importance in Crete. In addition to wine (including retsina), table grapes, raisins and sultanas are produced. Cretan wines, which have no chemical additives, are of good quality and very palatable. Important wine-growing areas are the Iráklion

Grapes

Olives: Crete's most important product

region (with the famous Rosaki grapes grown round Arkhánes) and eastern Crete. The growing of raisins was introduced in recent years by settlers from Asia Minor, and Crete is now the world's fourth largest exporter of raisins. Little of the crop is consumed in Crete; the main purchaser is Germany. As a result of high production costs and increasing competition from cheaper foreign – particularly Turkish – producers the export market is in a state of crisis.

Vegetables and fruit

An element of great importance in Cretan agriculture is vegetable growing, mainly practised in the northern coastal plains of western Crete, round Iráklion, in the Mesará (the most important vegetable-growing area on the island) and on the Ierápetra plain. The principal products are tomatoes, melons, cucumbers, beans, artichokes, aubergines and avocados. On the Lassíthi plateau the main crops are potatoes, cucumbers and cereals. The main growing areas for citrus fruits (oranges, mandarines, lemons) are in the south of the island and round Chaniá in western Crete. Other crops of some importance are carobs and bananas, which grow round Mália and Árvi.

Irrigation systems are increasingly being developed in agricultural areas, with motor pumps replacing the traditional windmills. There are now also huge numbers of hothouses made of plastic sheeting, making it possible to grow crops throughout the year. As a result there has been a very large increase in the export of vegetables.

Livestock

Stock farming is also an important branch of the economy. The livestock consists mainly of goats, sheep, pigs and poultry. In summer the shepherds – a predominantly male profession – drive their flocks of goats and sheep to pasture in the mountain regions. Roughly half the soil of Crete is grazing land. The animals eat trees and bushes as well as grass, and as a result of this farming pattern the land has suffered from over-grazing and has increasingly been eroded by karstic action. Action to deal with the problem has been slow to develop.

Cretan sheep- and goats'-milk cheeses (*anthótyro, kephalotýri*), which are of excellent quality and taste, are highly esteemed.

Industry

Industry is of no great importance in Crete, which has little in the way of raw materials. These are imported, processed and re-exported. Almost Crete's only industries are foodstuffs and consumption goods (soap factories, oil presses, wineries, soft drinks, furniture), mainly in Iráklion.

Apart from gypsum, Crete's minerals (iron, copper, zinc, lead, magnesium, chalk, brown coal) are not much worked. | Minerals

Craft workshops, mostly employing only a few workers, play a more important part than industry. Among the principal crafts are metalworking, spinning, weaving, embroidery and pottery. Their products are mainly aimed at the tourist market. | Crafts

Numerous Cretans are engaged in commerce, though many of their businesses are not particularly profitable. | Commerce

In recent years tourism has enjoyed a considerable upswing, thanks to the island's mild, sunny climate and numerous archaeological sites. After agriculture it is the most important branch of the Cretan economy, attracting just under 2 million visitors annually. | Tourism

The island's hotel resources have been vastly increased. The main tourist development has been on the stretch of coast between Iráklion and Mália Bay and Áyios Nikólaos. There is now, however, a ban on

Hand-weaver at work

29

new hotel building in these towns. Places which have no hotels of any size offer a wide range of guesthouses (pensions) and accommodation in private houses.

But tourism also beings problems. Young people prefer to work in restaurants rather than on the land, and as a result the villages are being abandoned and, in the longer term, Cretan agriculture is threatened with ruin. For visitors the most obvious change is the decline in traditional Cretan hospitality.

Famous People

This section contains brief biographies of notable people who were born, lived or worked in Crete or died there.

Little is known about the life of Michael Damaskinós (Michele Damas-ceno), the principal representative of Creto-Venetian painting. It is known only that he came from Iráklion and studied in the university run by the monks of Mount Sinai in the church of Ayía Aikateríni. In 1577 the Greek community in Venice commissioned him to work in the church of San Giorgio dei Greci. Later, on the basis of a legacy from his fellow-countryman Giacomo Carvelà, he was given the task of carrying out the decoration of the whole interior of the church. After living for some time on Corfu he returned to Crete.

Some of his best-known works can be seen in the Icon Museum in Iráklion.

Michael
Damaskinós
(1535–91)

The poet Odysseus Elytis (original surname Alepoudelis), was born in Iráklion and spent his early years in Athens, where he studied law. He was a member of the group centred on Yeoryios Seferis, who led a renaissance of modern Greek poetry in the 1930s. In 1979 he was awarded the Nobel Prize for Literature.

Elytis wrote surrealist poems inspired by nature, whose charac-teristic feature is a daring new use of metaphor. His principal work is "To axion esti" (1959), a volume of poems which was set to music by Mikis Theodorakis.

Among his other works are "To ro tou erota" ("Songs of Love", 1972), "Maria Nepheli" (1978) and "Imeroloyion enos atheatou Apri-liou" ("Diary of a never-seen April", 1984).

Odysseus Elytis
(1911–96)

The prophet and priest Epimenides is believed to have been an actual historical figure. His assertion that all Cretans were liars – he himself being a Cretan – became a celebrated example of a logical paradox; for if Epimenides was telling the truth not all Cretans were liars, while if he was telling a lie his statement was wrong.

Epimenides was also credited with remarkable longevity, and was said to have fallen asleep for 57 years.

Epimenides
(7th c. B.C.)

The British archaeologist Arthur Evans was described by C. W. Ceram as "a little man, incredibly short-sighted, who used a stout stick to feel his way ahead".

As correspondent of the "Manchester Guardian" in the Balkans, Evans supported the Greek fight for independence from Turkish rule. He went to Greece and was fascinated by the discoveries of Heinrich Schliemann, with whom he established personal contact. The dis-covery of seals with pre-Phoenician hieroglyphic signs took him to Crete in 1893. With his inherited fortune he purchased the site of the legendary palace of Knossós, where some digging had already been done, and from 1900 onwards carried out excavations at his own expense. These led to the discovery of the palace of King Minos and 2800 clay tablets in ancient Cretan script. Evans was obsessed with Knossós. In his four-volume work "The Palace of Minos" (1922–35) he described life in the palace of the Minoan kings. On the basis of his many years of excavation he established a chronology of Minoan culture. He also carried out much restoration and reconstruction work on the palace, though the accuracy of this is now disputed. His researches won wide scholarly recognition, and he was knighted in 1911. He was also appointed to a chair in Oxford. In the last 40 years of his life, however, he failed to decipher the clay tablets he had found.

Sir Arthur Evans
(1851–1941)

Famous People

El Greco
(c. 1541–1614)

El Greco (Spanish for "the Greek") was born Doménikos Theotokópoulos about 1541, probably in Phódele, to the west of Iráklion. While still a boy he learned the art of icon-painting; then he went as a young man to Venice, where he was taught by Titian, Tintoretto and other artists, and later to Rome. Since the Italians found it impossible to pronounce his name he became known as Il Greco. In 1577 he went to Toledo, where he worked for King Philip II and the Church. His paintings were mainly on religious themes, though he also produced vivid portraits and landscapes. His work belongs to the high Mannerist school. Characteristic features are the elongated, contorted figures, the unnaturally pale colouring and the unreal light effects, which combine to create an impression of transcendence and spirituality. It has been suggested that the distorted proportions in his paintings were due to an eye disease; but against this it has been noted that Tintoretto's Spanish pictures show the same characteristic.

El Greco died in Toledo in 1614.

Nikos Kazantzákis
(1883–1957)

Nikos Kazantzákis, a native of Iráklion, is one of the leading representatives of modern Greek literature. With a wide range of intellectual interests from his earliest youth, he began by studying law in Athens, taking his doctorate in 1906, and then went to Paris to study philosophy (Henri Bergson being one of his teachers) and political science. Returning to Greece, he became head of a government department and in 1945–46 was briefly a minister, but resigned after a party-political disagreement. Thereafter he lived mainly in the south of France. He died in 1957 at Freiburg in south-western Germany and was buried on the Martinengo Bastion, on the old town walls of Iráklion.

Kazantzákis travelled extensively in Britain, Spain, Russia, Japan and China, recording his experiences and impressions in a number of remarkable travel books. In addition he wrote lyrical and epic poetry ("Odyssey", 1938), short stories, novels, tragedies on ancient Greek, early Christian and Byzantine themes and philosophical works. His works are notable for their vivid descriptive power, fresh and inventive language, lyrical abundance and philosophical profundity. In his novel "Zorba the Greek" (1946; see Baedeker Special), which achieved world fame, particularly in its film version, Kazantzákis displayed the two sides of his Cretan personality, his civilised erudition and his fresh and original power and vitality. Other well-known novels are "O Kapetan Mikhalis" ("Freedom and Death", 1953), in which he gives a stark account of the 1889 rising against Turkish rule, and "O Teleftaios Pirasmos" ("Last Temptation", 1954), which was filmed by the French director Jules Dassin in 1957 in the village of Kritsá near Áyios Nikólaos. Kazantzákis also translated into Greek works by Homer, Dante, Goethe, Shakespeare, Darwin, Nietzsche, Rimbaud and García Lorca.

Yeóryios
Khortátzis
(end of 16th c./
beginning 17th c.)

The dramatist Yeóryios Khortátzis lived in Réthymnon around the turn of the 16th and 17th centuries. He is credited with the authorship of the comedy "Katzourbos", the love drama "Erophile" (written in the early 17th century, published in Venice in 1637) and the pastoral drama "Panoria". "Erophile" was one of the works which established the fame of Cretan writing in the 17th century. Although the Cretan plays of this period were influenced by French and Italian models their lyrical passages gave them a distinctive character of their own.

The poet and dramatist Vitzéntzos Kornáros, a native of Sitía, was the author of one of the leading works in 17th century Greek literature, the novel-like epic poem "Erotokritos", a work of some 10,000 lines in rhyming couplets. The poem was strongly influenced by French and Italian knightly romances and dramas. Kornáros is believed also to have been the author of the religious drama "Abraham's Sacrifice".

Vitzéntzos
Kornáros
(d. 1677)

The writer Pantélis Prevelákis studied philology in Paris and Salonica. From 1939 to 1975 he was professor of the history of art in the Athens Academy of Art, but remained attached all his life to his home town of Réthymnon.

Pantélis Prevelákis
(1909–86)

Prevelákis made his name with a new approach to history, "myth-history", a mingling of historical account and subjective and mythic impressions. An example of this is his novel "Chronicle of a Town" (1938), in which he describes Réthymnon. The theme of his novel "The Sun of Death" (1961) is the blood feud.

Prevelákis, in contrast to Kazantzákis, has been unjustly forgotten; but both writers are essential reading for those who want to understand the Cretan way of life and thought.

The Greek composer Mikis Theodorákis was born on the island of Chios, but his parents came from Crete, giving him a particular attachment to the island.

Mikis Theodorákis
(b. 1925)

Theodorákis studied in Athens and in Paris under Messiaen. He was several times a member of the Greek Parliament and was imprisoned after the colonels' coup; he had previously been imprisoned some years earlier.

His works, all reflecting his political commitment, included orchestral works, ballets, oratorios, songs and music for the stage and films (including "Zorba the Greek", 1964). They achieved wide popularity with their use of Greek folk songs and their catchy tunes and rhythms. Theodorákis himself has said that Cretan music was of decisive importance to his development as a composer.

The lawyer, politician and statesman Elefthérios Kyriakos Venizélos, born at Mourniés near Chaniá, was a charismatic personality, still greatly revered in Crete, who fought for the union of the island with Greece.

Elefthérios
Kyriakos
Venizélos
(1864–1936)

To achieve this aim he led an armed rising in Thériso, a small hill village near Chaniá, the only result of which was the removal of the governor of Crete. A further attempt, when Venizélos proclaimed the reunion of Crete with Greece, was also unsuccessful.

As the founder of the Greek Liberal Party, Venizélos became prime minister of Greece for the first time in 1910. His party sought to re-establish a Greater Greece including Constantinople and the coastal regions of Asia Minor.

With his wide-ranging domestic reforms (land reform, recognition of trade unions, social insurance) Venizélos created the modern Greek state. In foreign policy his aims were the union of all Greeks and territorial expansion by military means. Two Balkan wars (1912/13) brought substantial territorial gains and the final union of Crete with Greece, but other expansion plans were frustrated by Turkish resistance under the leadership of Mustafa Kemal Pasha (Atatürk). After an unsuccessful attempt to overthrow the Tsaldáris government Venizélos went into exile in Paris, where he died in 1936.

Venizélos's greatest achievements were his domestic reforms. His expansionist foreign policy had catastrophic consequences for the Greeks.

33

History

Neolithic (6500–3500/3100 B.C.)

The earliest traces of human settlement in Crete date from the Neolithic period, when the island had a population of hunters and gatherers.

Settlers, probably coming from Anatolia and/or Africa, take to a sedentary life; beginnings of agriculture and stock farming; production of domestic pottery.

Houses are built of undressed stone or sun-dried mud.

Developing social structure of village type; religion predominantly of fertility cults.

Prepalatial Period (3300/3100–2100 B.C.)

During the Prepalatial period (Early Minoan I–III), from the 3rd millennium onward, the production and use of bronze articles and the introduction of the potter's wheel, on which the stylish spouted jugs and other vessels were made, are developments of major importance. In

Chronology of the Minoan Period

according to	Niemeier	Evans	Levi	Hood
Sub–Minoan	1050–990			
SM IIIC	1200–1050		1100	1200–1150
SM IIIB	1360/30–1200			1310–1200
SM IIIA2	1420/10–1360/30			1375–1310
NEOPALATIAL PERIOD				
LM IIIA1	1460/50–1420/10	1400	1350	1400–1375
LM II	1520/10–1460–50	1450–1400	1350	1450–1400
LM IB	1620/10–1520/10			
LM IA	1700–1620/10	1550–1450		1550–1450
MM IIIB		1700–1550	1500	1600–1550
MM IIIA	1800–1700	1700	1500	1700–1600
PROTOPALATIAL PERIOD				
MM IIB				
MM IIA	1900–1800			1800–1700
MM IB	2000–1900	1900		1900–1800
MM IA	2100–2000	2100–1900	1800	2100/2000–1900
PREPALATIAL PERIOD				
EM III	2250–2100	2400–2100	1800	2200–2100/2000
EM IIB	2700–2250			
EM IIA		2800–2400		2480–2200
EM IB	3300/3100–2700			
EM IA		3400–2800	2000	2740–2480
Neolithic	8000–3300/3100		2000	3000/2740

34

The Phaistós Disc: the world's oldest printed script

addition to modest buildings of mud-brick there are also palace-like buildings of one or two storeys. The dead are buried in chamber tombs, in some of which (e.g. at Mókhlos) gold filigree jewellery in stylised leaf and flower forms has been found.

Protopalatial Period (2100–1800 B.C.)

Around 2000 B.C., at the beginning of the Protopalatial period (Middle Minoan I–III), Crete consolidates its predominance in the Aegean. At Knossós, Phaistós, Mália and other sites palaces of several storeys are built, with spacious courts and numerous rooms. Kamáres-style pottery is notable for its ornamental painting (delicate spiral patterns, etc.). Seal-cutting also flourishes. A linear script (Linear A) slowly develops out of the original hieroglyphic script, which some scholars believe was an independent Minoan achievement, while others regard it as an Egyptian import. Around 1800 B.C. this phase comes to an abrupt end, probably as a result of devastation caused by a severe earthquake.

Neopalatial Period (1810–1410 B.C.)

The rebuilding of the palaces marks the beginning of the Neopalatial period (Late Minoan I–IIIA), which leads to the apogee of Minoan culture. Long-distance trade reaches as far afield as Sicily, Egypt and the Near East. Palaces of several storeys, lavishly appointed, with large inner courts, are built at Knossós, Phaistós, Mália and Zákros; they serve as administrative, economic and cultural centres. The population of the island rises to an estimated 200,000–250,000 – evidently living at peace with one another, for there are no fortified structures. Large

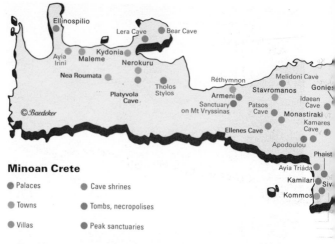

Minoan Crete

- ● Palaces
- ● Towns
- ● Villas
- ● Cave shrines
- ● Tombs, necropolises
- ● Peak sanctuaries

towns, with houses containing several rooms, grow up round the palaces; farms and country houses are established all over the island. An adequate food supply is provided by intensive arable farming, goat and sheep rearing and food storage facilities. Metalworkers, using smelting furnaces and advanced casting and forging techniques, produce bronze articles of outstanding quality. The potter's art flourishes, producing a great variety of forms with elaborate painted decoration and applied plastic ornament. Timber is used in the construction of houses and ships. A large merchant fleet carries on a busy import and export trade. The main imports are metals such as gold and silver, copper and tin, which are exchanged for the island's products (oil, wine, honey, pottery, weapons). Well trained craftsmen and competent officials, using the Linear A script, guarantee the quality of the products and ensure efficient administration. In the religious field the earth-bound belief in the forces of nature, celebrated in hill and cave shrines, at first predominates, but is increasingly overlaid by snake and bull cults.

Around 1625 B.C. there is a volcanic eruption on the island of Thera (Santorin) which devastates some areas on Crete with tidal waves and showers of ash.

Mycenaean Rule (1410–1200 B.C.)

Social conflicts and a decline in trade weakens the Minoan civilisation, enabling Mycenaeans from mainland Greece to capture and control parts of the island (Late Minoan IIIA–C). Some of the palaces are destroyed and abandoned, but Knossós remains the centre of government under Mycenaean rule. There is a general decline in craft and artistic products. Building is concentrated on fortified strongholds and dwellings centred on a megaron. A particular achievement of the Mycenaeans is the development of a new script, Linear B, a forerunner of the Greek alphabet.

The Minoan civilisation comes to an end with the final destruction of the palace at Knossós – whether as a result of a natural catastrophe or by foreign conquerors is not known.

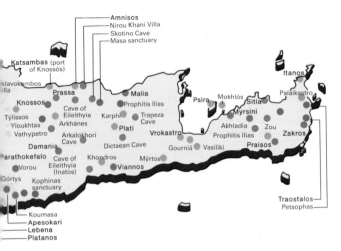

Postpalatial Period (1200–1000 B.C.)

Migrations and the movement of refugees lead to great social and economic changes. Aeolian and Ionian tribes penetrate for a time into the Aegean islands, wreaking destruction and driving out the native populations.

Protogeometric and Geometric Periods (1000–700 B.C.)

Dorian incomers to Crete bring new customs and usages. A strict military hierarchy is introduced in social and political life. Many new settlements are established on hillsides and summits with separate harbours. The metalworkers work mainly with iron, which is used to make weapons, while bronze continues to be used for smaller articles. Pottery is decorated with geometric patterns consisting of concentric rings and cross forms. Burial practices change, inhumation giving place to cremation. The older natural religion is increasingly replaced by the worship of personalised gods. Tales and poems centre on Greek/Cretan myths and legends: King Minos, the Minotaur and the Labyrinth, Ariadne and Theseus, Zeus in the Idaean Cave.

Orientalising Period (700–620 B.C.)

A new political structure develops in Crete, with a number of city-states competing with one another. Trade and shipping connections with Rhodes, Cyprus and the coast of Asia Minor bring Oriental art forms to Crete. A new script is taken over from the Syrian/Phoenician area and developed into the Greek alphabet – though a written language known as Eteo-Cretan (still not deciphered) long continues in use in eastern Crete.

Archaic Period (620–480 B.C.)

Crete is still divided into numerous small city-states, probably organised essentially on the model of the Greek *polis*. Górtys, Knossós and

Crete – Where Women Held Sway

Our continent is named after Europa, the Phoenician princess whom Zeus, taking on the form of a bull, carried off to Crete, and by whom he had three sons, founders of the Minoan ruling dynasty. Zeus himself, father of the gods, was born and brought up on Crete. This legend and other mythological tales set in Crete indicate that the roots of European culture are to be found on the island. The fact that Europa came from the Near East suggests that Crete also received cultural influences from there.

Around the 2nd millennium B.C. there developed on Crete, lying at the point of intersection of the advanced cultures of Egypt and Mesopotamia, a new "European" culture, for which the island's temperate subtropical climate offered propitious conditions. The Minoan civilisation became the earliest advanced culture in Europe, extending its influence to the Greek mainland and beyond. This culture is so fascinating because the Minoans are still a mystery for us. Their culture was destroyed and only a few broken walls and myths which are difficult to interpret remain to bear witness to it. Since it had no direct successor it remains alien to us. It is scarcely possible to establish any link between our western traditions, so strongly influenced by the Greco-Roman world, and the Minoans. A visit to the Minoan sites on Crete raises many questions in the visitor's mind, and frequently the archaeologists cannot give him any adequate answers. He admires many evidences of this culture – the enchanting wall paintings for example – but their meaning is hidden from him. But it is just this incomprehensibility and this strangeness that creates their extraordinary fascination. What was the nature of this mysterious culture?

The famous Snake Goddess

It is now well established that women played a prominent part in Minoan religion and society. The religious beliefs of the Minoans centred on the Great Goddess. Other indications of a matriarchal society are the unusually peaceable nature of Minoan society and the dominance of "feminine taste" (plants, animals). Men played a rather subordinate role. It is even possible that the kingdom may have been ruled by a priestess-queen.

What makes the greatness of Minoan culture? It is not massive buildings, nor material treasures, nor military exploits, nor political successes. Rather it is a culture rich in creative force, imagination and intellectual capacity: in other words, a culture in the true sense of the term.

Cydonia (Chaniá) are among the most powerful of these states. Trade with the rest of the Mediterranean world gradually ceases. In parallel with developments in Greece, the first plain rectangular temples are built (notably at Priniás), vase-painting shows increased delight in decoration and monumental sculpture and reliefs are vigorous and expressive.

Classical Period (480–330 B.C.)

Crete plays no significant part either in political events in the Greek world or in the flowering of art in the Classical period. The Cretans do not join the other Greeks in their conflict with the Persians, nor do they take sides in the Peloponnesian War between Athens and Sparta. Instead they exhaust themselves in endless petty wars among themselves. They do, however, establish relations with the Argolid and with Sparta. The Greek legal tradition finds a home at Górtys, where a code of twelve laws, very progressive for its time, written in a Creto-Doric dialect, is inscribed on stone blocks dating from the 5th century B.C.

In 386 B.C. the island is devastated by an earthquake. In 330 B.C. there is a great famine.

Hellenistic Period (330–67 B.C.)

The Cretans regard Alexander the Great's victorious campaigns with some scepticism, and actually allow his opponents (e.g. the Persian fleet and the king of Sparta) to seek refuge on their island. Changing alliances, particularly between the cities in western Crete and foreign rulers, lead to repeated but usually only temporary interventions by foreign rulers on the island. Only with Sparta do some of the Cretan cities in course of time establish more intensive relations.

The two rival cities of Knossós and Górtys seek to agree on a division of the island into two spheres of influence, among them Lyttos, which is defeated and destroyed after violent fighting. These Cretan conflicts lead to the intervention of the great powers of the day; but the Greek world has been much weakened by the Social War. King Philip V of Macedon briefly succeeds in incorporating Crete in his kingdom. — *220–217 B.C.*

The Macedonian king's attempts to establish hegemony lead Rome to intervene, and Philip is compelled in 197 B.C. to submit. In 184 B.C. the Roman Senate sends a commission to Crete to settle the conflicts on the island. The Romans are now increasingly seeking to extend their authority into the eastern Mediterranean and regard Crete as an important naval and commercial base. The Cretans achieve a modest degree of prosperity as dependants of Rome and do well out of piracy. — *c. 200 B.C.*

In order to pursue the Roman policy of expansion in the Mediterranean and to repress piracy the Roman consul Mark Antony tries to occupy the island, which has hitherto been independent, but is defeated by the fierce resistance of the Cretans. — *74 B.C.*

Roman Period (67 B.C.–A.D. 337)

In 69–67 B.C. the Roman general Quintus Caecilius Metellus, surnamed Creticus, conquers Crete, which is incorporated in the Roman Empire as Provincia Creta.

After the Roman Civil War the province of Crete falls to Mark Antony and in the reign of Augustus is given the status of a senatorial province — *42 B.C.*

The Laws of Górtys: the oldest known European law code

in which Cyrenaica is combined with Crete. The new capital of the island and seat of the Roman governor is Górtys. Temples, aqueducts, houses and country villas are built in various parts of Crete. At Knossós land holdings are granted to Roman veterans, creating the thriving new settlement of Colonia Julia Nobilis Cnosus.

A.D. 59   The Apostle Paul is believed to have landed at Kali Liménes and brought Christianity to the island. Thereafter the faith is propagated by Titus (possibly the recipient of Paul's Epistle to Titus), Crete's first bishop.

c. 250   During the persecutions of Christians in the reigns of the Emperors Decius and Valerian Crete is the scene of the martyrdom of the "Holy Ten" (Ayii Déka), ten bishops who according to tradition were executed after refusing to attend the consecration of a pagan temple. It is not known with certainty how many bishops there were in Crete in Early Christian times. The earliest known bishops were at Górtys (where the basilica of St Titus was built), Knossós and Cydonia (Chaniá). There is firm evidence for twelve bishops only in the 8th century.

311   An edict issued by the Emperor Gallienus in Salonica grants official recognition to Christianity, which in Crete is more closely associated with the eastern half of the Empire, though still under the authority of the Pope in Rome.

First Byzantine Period (337–826/827)

In 330 the Emperor Constantine moves his capital to Constantinople, and in 337 institutes a new organisation of the Roman provinces under which Crete becomes part of the praetorian province of Illyricum, Italy and Africa. When the Roman Empire is finally divided into two in 395 Crete falls to the East Roman (Byzantine) Empire, which uses the island as a military base and administers it through governors. During the 5th and 6th centuries numerous churches are built – large aisled basilicas – but these are mostly destroyed during the Arab occupation. In the 7th century the Arabs expand into the Mediterranean, and trade is endangered by the activities of pirates, though the Arabs are unable to establish any permanent settlement in Crete. The island's links with the Eastern church are strengthened in 731, when the Cretan bishops are brought under the authority of the Patriarch of Constantinople.

Arab Occupation (826/827–961)

An Arab force led by Abu Hafs Omar lands on the south coast of Crete and destroys the ancient city of Górtys. The Arabs found the town of Al Khandaq (later known as Candia) on the site of present-day Iráklion.

The people of Crete are exploited and oppressed by the occupying forces. A number of unsuccessful attempts are made by the Byzantines to recover the island.

Second Byzantine Period (981–1204)

The Byzantine general Nicephorus Phocas reconquers Crete after a six-month-long siege of Iráklion.   981

The church is reorganised, and those inhabitants who had abjured their Christian faith are re-Christianised. Settlers from mainland Greece, the islands and Asia Minor come to Crete. Feudal rule is established. The island now enjoys a period of prosperity. At the end of the 12th century Genoese merchants establish themselves in Crete and build fortifications to protect their trade.

Venetian Period (1204–1669)

After the destruction of the Byzantine Empire in the fourth Crusade Boniface of Montferrat, who has been granted Crete, sells it to Venice.   1204

The new owners call the island and its capital Candia (in English Candy). Large estates are granted to Venetians and later to Greek archons, who are also given residences in the capital. The rural population are compelled to pay heavy taxes and to work on Venetian fortifications and man Venetian galleys. The Roman Catholic faith predominates, at least in the towns, but the Orthodox church is tolerated.

Soon there are risings by the rural population, including some Venetians, against foreign rule. The Venetian authorities react by expelling the population of the rebellious areas, particularly Sphakía and Lassíthi, but also institute reforms.

Over the centuries Venetian rule becomes less oppressive and the island begins to prosper. This prosperity is reflected in the monasteries and in the flowering of the arts, particularly literature and painting, and learning. The famous painter Doménikos Theotokópoulos, better known as El Greco (see Famous People), is probably a native of Crete.

Crete is increasingly subjected to raids by Turkish pirates. Among them is the famous Khaireddin Barbarossa, who in 1538 plunders 80 ports and townships. In response to these attacks the island's coastal fortifications are strengthened.   16th century

In 1645 the Turks capture their first town on Crete, Chaniá, and in 1646 take Réthymnon. With the fall of Iráklion in 1669 after an eleven-year-long siege Creta finally falls under Turkish rule.   17th century

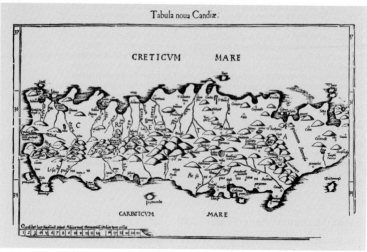

Tabula noua Candiæ.

Crete in 1522: a historic map

Turkish Period (1669–1898)

The period of Turkish rule is a time of even harsher oppression. The population are converted to Islam, and the Orthodox faith survives only in remote mountain regions. The Turks frequently attempt to gain control of these areas, to which many refugees withdraw. The people of Crete are forced to pay heavy taxes and are exposed to the harsh rule of the janissaries. Turks become large landowners in prosperous agricultural areas.

1692	The Venetians attempt to recover Crete, but are able only to hold on to Soúda, Gramvoúsa and Spinalónga until 1715.
18th century	A number of risings – notably one led by Daskaloyánnis in 1770 – are repressed.
1821	The Cretans join in the unsuccessful rising in mainland Greece against the Turks, who are supported by Egypt.
1832	With the establishment of an independent Greek state Crete is assigned by the great powers (Britain, Russia and France) to Egyptian administration.
1840–98	After full Turkish authority over Crete is restored there are a series of hard-fought and bloody rebellions (1858, 1866–69, 1878, 1889, 1896–98) aimed at achieving union with Greece. The most celebrated rising, which came to a bloody end, is in Arkádi monastery in 1866. The 1889 revolt, which took on the proportions of a civil war, is the setting of the novel "Freedom and Death" (1953) by the famous Cretan writer Nikos Kazantzákis (see Famous People). Finally in 1898, after a number of unsuccessful attempts, the great powers compel the Turks to withdraw from Crete. The island is given independent status under a High Commissioner, Prince George of Greece, but remains under Turkish sovereignty.

Arkádi monastery, the scene of a bloody rising against the Turks

20th Century

Following a further rising led by the Liberal politician Elefthérios Venizélos (see Famous People) and aimed at the union of Crete with Greece Prince George is compelled to resign.	1906
Venizélos becomes prime minister of Greece.	1910
Crete is united with Greece (May 30th).	1913
During the First World War King Constantine I observes strict neutrality. Since Venizélos hopes to win territory from Turkey with the help of the Entente he compels the king, with Entente support, to abdicate. Although Greek forces take little active part in the war, Venizélos is able to obtain extensions of Greek territory under the treaty of Sèvres between the Ottoman Empire and the Entente powers.	1914–20
The war between Greece and Turkey ends with a Greek defeat. Greece loses territory in Asia Minor which has been occupied by Greeks for thousands of years as well as the islands of Imbros and Tenedos. There is a massive exchange of populations: all Turks leave Crete and refugees from Asia Minor settle on the island.	1920–23
Greece is declared a republic.	1924
A period of government by the Liberals, headed by Venizélos, leads to stabilisation in domestic and foreign affairs.	1928–32
Following the world economic crisis, which hits Greece like other countries, the monarchy is restored under King George II (reigns 1922–23 and 1934–46).	1935
General Ioánnis Metaxas dispenses with the Greek Parliament and, with the king's approval, establishes a dictatorship supported by secret police, censorship and a nationalist ideology.	1936

History

May 20th 1941 to October 1944	After the German conquest of Greece British troops withdraw to Crete. German paratroops land at Máleme and elsewhere in Crete and the bloody "Battle for Crete" begins (see Operation Mercury).

The people of Crete suffer for three and a half years under a harsh occupation, enforced by terror, torture and informers. In 1941 and 1942 there is a severe shortage of food. Many Cretans fight as partisans along with British agents on the islands, leading to the imposition of forced labour and reprisals by the Germans.

1945–49	Civil war in Greece between the government, supported by Britain and later by the United States, and communist resistance groups.

Operation Mercury

British troops came to Crete on October 29th 1940, the day after the Italian attack on Greece, to honour the guarantee given to Greece in 1939 and to secure this strategically important island: whoever holds Crete controls access to the Dodecanese and the rest of the eastern Mediterranean. To Britain Crete, with its natural harbour in Soúda Bay, offered an important supply base for the Mediterranean fleet, which had to provide reinforcements for British forces in Egypt, to protect Malta and to keep the Italian fleet in check.

After the German occupation of Greece, which was concluded by April 29th 1941, the king, the government and part of the army fled to Crete. When the Germans invaded the island some 28,000 Commonwealth troops (mainly New Zealanders, with some Australians and British) and just over 10,000 Greeks were stationed there. They were inadequately equipped – in particular they had far too few aircraft – but they had the great advantage of exact information, through radio intelligence, about German intentions.

On May 20th 1941, at 7.15am, was launched Operation Mercury, the largest airborne operation in history, involving a paratroop division and a division of mountain troops (some 23,000 men), almost 500 transport aircraft, more than 100 sailing cargo vessels and over 600 fighter aircraft. The paratroops landed at three points – at Máleme airfield in western Crete, between Chaniá and Soúda Bay and in the Iráklion area – where they were later reinforced by mountain troops. Everywhere they met bitter resistance from the Allied forces and suffered heavy losses. It was only by throwing in fresh troops and equipment, regardless of losses – some 170 transport aircraft were lost on the first day – that the Germans were gradually able to drive the Allies back. The battle reached its climax on May 23rd, and on May 26th the order was given to evacuate the Commonwealth and Greek forces. Most of the defenders withdrew to the Sphakiá area on the south coast, from where the Royal Navy were able, from May 29th onwards, to evacuate 16,500 men to Egypt. 4000 others were evacuated from Iráklion. 18,000 Commonwealth soldiers remained in Crete.

By June 1st 1941 Crete was under the control of German forces and the Italians who had in the meantime landed in the east of the island. The Allies lost 15,000 men, including 2000 sailors from British ships sunk by the Luftwaffe. The Germans lost some 7000 men on Crete itself and an unknown number of mountain troops drowned when a German convoy was sunk by the British.

The German success was proclaimed by Goebbels's propaganda machine to be one of the most glorious military achievements of the war. In fact, however, losses during the battle for Crete were among the heaviest the German army had ever suffered, depriving it of one of its most effective units; for the paratroop division which had been sent into action with such reckless disregard of the cost never recovered from its losses on Crete, and their conquest of Crete played no significant part in the further conduct of the war.

Peter I (reigns 1947–64) becomes king.	1947
Greece becomes a member of NATO.	1952
Greece signs a treaty of association with the European Economic Community.	1962
King Constantine II (reigns 1964–67) succeeds his father Paul I.	1964
A coup d'état led by Col. Yeóryios Papadópoulos leads to a military dictatorship. The king flees to Rome and later to London.	1967
A plebiscite decides in favour of a democratic republic.	1974
Conservative government of the Néa Dimokratía party, headed by Karamanlís.	1974–81
A new constitution of the Hellenic Republic is promulgated.	1975
Karamanlís becomes President of Greece and is succeeded as prime minister by Rállis (May).	1980
On January 1st Greece becomes the tenth member of the European Community (in Greek EOK). In a parliamentary election on October 18th the Panhellenic Socialist Movement (PASOK) wins an absolute majority. Papandréou becomes prime minister.	1981
The Greek Parliament ratifies an agreement on the stationing of American troops in Greece.	1983
Conference in Athens in January on making the Balkans a nuclear-free zone (Greece, Yugoslavia, Bulgaria, Romania, Turkey).	1984
After a controversial selection process Khristós Sartzetákis becomes President of Greece. In a parliamentary election brought forward to June 2nd PASOK again wins. Greece declares the state of war with Albania which has existed since 1940 to be at an end.	1985
An amendment to the constitution restricts the powers of the President (March 7th).	1986
The introduction of value-added tax on January 1st sparks off three general strikes in January and February.	1987

On the occasion of an economic conference held at Davos (Switzerland) at the end of January the Greek prime minister, Andréas Papandréou, and the Turkish head of government, Turgut Özal, declare that their two countries will in future strive to maintain peaceful relations. In June Özal visits Athens for political discussions.
  An attack by terrorists (unidentified) on the excursion ship "City of Poros" during its return from the island of Hydra to Athens kills eleven people (July 11th).
  Greece terminates the 1983 agreement on American bases.
	1988

In a parliamentary election on June 18th PASOK loses its majority. A contributory factor in its defeat is the Koskotas scandal: Yeoryios Koskotas, director of the Bank of Crete, accused of taking bribes, declares that the prime minister and other members of his government have also accepted bribes. None of the other parties, however, can assemble enough votes to form a government. In order to get round	1989

45

the stalemate the Néa Dimokratía party joins with the "United Left" in an unlikely alliance to form a transitional government led by the Conservative politician Tsánnis Tsannétakis. Tsannétakis calls an early election, but soon resigns (October 7th) and is succeeded by Ioánnis Grivas. After the election, held on November 5th, an all-party coalition is formed under the leadership of Xenophón Zolóthas (November 21st).

1990

A general strike paralyses public life (January 25th). The all-party government falls apart (February 12th) and Zolóthas forms a transitional government of independent politicians. Parliament is dissolved (March 12th).

In an election on April 8th the conservative Néa Dimokratía party falls short of an absolute majority by one vote. A member of the Democratic Renewal party (DEANA) goes over to Néa Dimokratía and thus gives it a majority. The new government, headed by Konstantinos Mitsotákis, seeks to deal with the country's catastrophic economic problems – high inflation, public debts equal to a year's gross domestic product, widespread tax evasion, loss-making state enterprises, costly privileges of government officials – by a policy of drastic economies. In view of the government's slender majority, however, it is unable to carry through this policy against the resistance of the trade unions, the socialists and the communists, who respond with general strikes.

A terrorist organisation calling itself "November 17th" justifies its bomb attack on an industrialist as part of its campaign against privatisation and foreign (particularly German) investment ("de-Hellenisation").

Konstantinos Karamanlís is elected President of Greece (May 4th). A new agreement is reached on American bases in Greece for another eight years (July 8th). In the Gulf War Greece contributes a warship to the multi-national naval forces.

1992

Greece opposes the recognition of Macedonia, formerly a republic within Yugoslavia, as the sovereign Republic of Macedonia, since this might lead to territorial claims on the northern Greek region of Macedonia; a huge demonstration is held in Athens on December 10th.

1993

The socialist opposition puts forward a motion of no confidence in Mitsotákis, but is defeated.

A private visit to Greece by the exiled ex-King Constantine and his family gives rise to political controversy. In a parliamentary election brought forward to October 10th PASOK wins an absolute majority; its leader, Andréas Papandréou, becomes prime minister.

1994

Greece takes over the presidency of the Council of the European Union.

The Greek government puts a trade embargo on the republic of Macedonia, much of whose trade passes through Salonica, and closes the Greek consulate in the Macedonian capital, Skopje (mid February), as a means of putting pressure on Macedonia to change the name of the state and the preamble in its constitution which might imply a claim to Greek territory and to eliminate the sixteen-pointed star of Veryina – which is regarded as a purely Greek symbol – from its national flag.

Greece mourns the death (in New York on March 6th) of the actress, singer and socialist politician Melina Merkouri (b. 1925 in Athens), who was deprived of her Greek citizenship by the military junta between 1967 to 1974 and was Greek minister of culture from 1981 to 1989 and again from the autumn of 1993.

1995

Prime Minister, Papandreou becomes ill and is replaced by Konstantinos Simitis.

1996

Death of Papandreou.

Art and Culture

Minoan Civilisation

Only a small selection of Crete's great range of works of art can be discussed in detail here. Unless otherwise indicated, the works mentioned – including the frescos, of which there are only copies at Knossós itself – are in the Archaeological Museum in Iráklion.

The large palaces of the Minoans, remains of which can be seen at Knossós, Phaistós, Mália and Káto Zákros, are among the most important Bronze Age buildings in the eastern Mediterranean, and indeed in the whole of Europe. Although the palace architecture reflects cultural and artistic influences from the Near East, their layout and aspect are determined by the specific conditions of life on Crete. The first palaces were built between 2100 and 1700 B.C., the Protopalatial period, also known as Middle Minoan. This was followed by the Neopalatial or Late Minoan period, with even more elaborate palaces; this period was brought to an abrupt end by the arrival of the Mycenaeans around 1420/1410 B.C.

Architecture
Palaces

The changing form of the palaces reflected profound political and economic changes on the island. The development of a central authority headed by a priest-king led to the establishment of a hierarchical administrative structure and a centrally directed economy, with the palace as the focal point of all decisions and activities. Thanks to the intensive use of the island's resources, combined with efficient arrangements for the storage of supplies, division of labour and exchange of goods, merchants, craftsmen and artists were freed from concern with gaining their subsistence and could concentrate on their own particular tasks. In this system the ruler and his court occupied key positions as patrons and purchasers of their products. Thanks to their carefully directed promotion and control of production the rulers of the island acquired ever more economic and political power, which was given expression in their palaces. In the modest architecture of the Protopalatial period (3100–2100 B.C.) the central inner court was an important feature, with numerous rooms, grouped according to their function, laid out round it. From the time of the earliest palaces the layout was usually centrifugal, with the state apartments and cult rooms at the centre and the more modest structures which served as workshops or store-rooms in the outer regions of the palace. From the outset, too, the palaces were not surrounded by any enclosure wall and had no defences; often, indeed, the palace buildings merged almost imperceptibly into the ordinary houses of the town. Evidently the Minoans had no reason to fear attack from without or rebellion within. The Neopalatial period also attached particular importance to the rectangular central court, from which radiated the many passages leading to the different sections of the palace, marked by their varying façades. The masonry was of dressed stone, later faced with plaster. Timber frames and beams were used to reinforce the walls and form the roof structure, the ceilings being strengthened with brushwood and beaten earth. Some of the rooms were floored with marine limestone, glistening with something of the effect of mother-of-pearl. Many of the pillars and columns, which served to divide up rooms as well as to decorate passages, staircases and verandas, were of wood, ornamented with stucco and painted.

Façade of the palace of Knossós

A comparison of the plans of the principal Cretan palaces shows considerable similarities in layout. As a rule the groups of buildings were laid out round the rectangular central court on a longitudinal axis running north–south. The main entrance, usually at the north end, was a monumental gatehouse or hall with rows of columns or pillars. Subsidiary entrances gave access to the different sections of the palace. Outside the façade of the west wing there was often a spacious paved court traversed by slightly raised processional ways. Since the west wing was usually designed for sacred rituals it contained numerous dark cult rooms which depended on artificial lighting, resembling the cave shrines elsewhere on the island in which the Minoan earth and fertility cults were celebrated. Other features were ritual basins, altars, votive offerings and treasure chambers. The west wing, which was two-storeyed, also contained magnificently decorated state apartments designed for cult ceremonies and official occasions, among them a so-called "throne room". There was also a series of store-rooms – plain rectangular cells in which various foodstuffs were stored in large terracotta jars (*pithoi*).

The east wing, on the opposite side of the central court, contained the ruler's residence and state apartments, beyond which were rooms for servants and more store-rooms, and near them the workshops of craftsmen and artists. An elaborate system of channels brought water from nearby springs and supplied numerous fountains, lustral basins and cisterns, while waste water drained away in separate channels.

A characteristic feature of the Minoan palaces was that they were laid out on different levels, linked by large indoor and outdoor stair-cases, long corridors, verandas and ramps. The façades consisted of a number of irregular elements, some projecting and some recessed, and the flat roofs were sometimes decorated with bulls' horns in the

A beautiful spouted jug in Kamáres style ▶

manner of battlements. The entrances to the various wings were usually at the corners of the court. Numerous flights of steps, rows of columns, light-wells and ventilation shafts relieved the weight and massiveness of the structure. In all the major palaces – at Mália, Káto Zákros and above all at Phaistós – remains of monumental staircases have been found. The massive steps may have served as benches from which the Minoans watched theatrical performances or cult ceremonies. They may also have been processional routes to the cult rooms in the interior of the palace. At Knossós, on the Royal Road outside the north entrance, is the so-called Theatral Area, with two monumental staircases meeting at right angles which may have served as platforms on ceremonial occasions. Some archaeologists believe that the bull games took place in this area; others see them as taking place in the central court, others again in an area outside the palace, watched by an audience on the verandas.

In the Neopalatial period the palaces took on increasingly monumental dimensions both in plan and in elevation, with a complex layout which gave them a labyrinthine character, although the planners followed certain rules. A further enrichment of the palaces resulted from the provision of numerous small regularly laid out inner courts which gave the rooms more light and air. Now, too, columns and pillars increasingly replaced the massive walls of the interior. This frequently produced a pattern in which the wall between two adjoining rooms was opened up by a number of gate-like openings (*polythyron*), giving a more open and airy character to the structure.

In general the palaces – which at Knossós and Phaistós, for example, were built on a slope – fitted inobtrusively into the landscape; laid out on many levels, they sloped down to the plain in terraces. Broad access roads led to the palace from the harbour, the necropolises and the interior of the island. The town, with the houses of the citizens, the more modest dwellings of the poorer inhabitants and the elegant mansions of the nobles, ran up close to the palace, which was not set apart by any enclosing wall. This close relationship of the palace with its surroundings reflected both the economic dependence of the outer districts on the centre and the unchallenged authority of the ruler.

Villas

In the country round the great palaces archaeologists have discovered the remains of handsome villas, for example Vathypetro and Tylissos near Knossós and at Ayía Triáda near Phaistós. Although it is not known with certainty what the function of these villas was, most scholars believe that they may have been summer residences or sub-centres with economic, political and religious functions similar to those of the palaces. The layout of a villa was similar to that of a palace but on a smaller scale, with suites of state and private apartments, cult rooms, store-rooms and workshops. Only the Ayía Triáda villa shows an unusual ground-plan, with two courts, one facing north towards the sea – perhaps serving the purposes of trade – and the other facing south, perhaps designed for ceremonies and cult rituals. No explanation has been suggested for this unique duplication, both wings being identical in ground-plan.

Cult buildings and tombs

Apart from the crypt-like rooms in the palaces designed for cult ceremonies the Minoans seem to have had no separate temple buildings. This reflects the chthonian (earth-bound) character of the Minoan cult of the gods which was celebrated in cave shrines. Only summit sanctuaries on Mt Yioúkhtas and at Petsophás and a rock shrine at Anemóspilia have yielded remains of simple walled rectangular structures with a court and a raised cult area. Minoan sepulchral architecture is also represented by numerous necropolises round the larger settlements. The commonest types of tomb are shaft, passage and chamber tombs, in which the dead were deposited either directly or in a sarcophagus. Princely tombs had a number of underground rooms, as in the Khrysólakkos necropolis to the north of the palace at Mália. Among the most elaborate tombs are the two-storey temple tomb and the royal tomb at Isopata near Knossós, a forerunner of the Mycenaean tholos tomb.

The Minoan towns grew up round the great palaces, following no unified plan, though they were always adapted to the topography of the site and took account of economic and social considerations. As a rule they were traversed by a network of streets leading from the palace towards the sea, the town's hinterland and its necropolises. In the centre of the town there was originally a square surrounded by benches which was used for assemblies of the inhabitants, but as the palace developed into the sole centre of authority this feature disappeared. Gourniá in eastern Crete gives a vivid picture of a Minoan town, situated on a sloping site near the sea, which was occupied from around 3300 to 1100 B.C. The low houses formed irregular blocks served by narrow winding lanes. In the centre, on higher ground, was a grander house, presumably the seat of a governor, with many features modelled on the great palaces.

Town layout

Evidence on Minoan houses is also provided by a series of small faience plaques depicting house-fronts which were found elsewhere in Crete. They show that the houses were rectangular in plan, were of one or two storeys and had a flat roof which was also used as a terrace. In the principal room, which was sometimes surrounded by columns, was the hearth, and there was an open inner court providing light and air.

In contrast to the monumental sculpture found in Mesopotamia at this period, Minoan sculpture was small-scale – on pottery vessels, jewellery, gems, seals and votive figures.

Sculpture

Among early ceramic products of the Prepalatial period are the "Goddess of Myrtos" (2400–2200 B.C.; in Archaeological Museum, Áyios Nikólaos; illustration, p. 86), a spouted vessel in anthropomorphic form, and the hourglass-shaped chalices with delicate surface ornament in the Pýrgos style. With the help of the potter's wheel, probably introduced from Anatolia, and new firing techniques Minoan potters produced the distinctively mottled spouted jugs in the Vasilikí style and later barbotine ware decorated with dotted patterns. At the beginning of the Protopalatial period (2100 B.C. onwards) the Kamáres style predominated, with ornamental patterns consisting of spiral, disc and leaf forms which enliven the surface. Other ceramic products are thin-walled cup-like vessels, eggshell ware, frequently with black and white decoration, and male and female idols. A unique example is the Phaistós Disc (illustration, p. 35), with hieroglyphic signs inscribed on both sides, in an early script which has not yet been deciphered.

Pottery

Two decorative techniques predominated in pottery – painting and relief ornament, sometimes in the form of appliqué work – which were frequently combined. Beautifully shaped vases, often with over-ornate decoration, were produced in great variety, particularly during the Neopalatial period, when the Floral and Marine styles flourished, as in the jug with reed decoration illustrated on page 7. Masterpieces of naturalism are two snake goddesses (illustration, p. 38).

The final phase in ceramic art, found exclusively at Knossós during the transition to the Mycenaean period in Crete, is the palace style with its naturalistic representations of the island's flora and fauna. Products during the Postpalatial period included pottery idols with raised hands and what looks like a hoop skirt, representing women worshippers or goddesses. Minoan ceramic art reached its final climax with a group of small female figures performing a round dance, a model of a circular temple and a rhyton in the form of an ox-cart.

Among other products of Minoan potters were bathtub-shaped sarcophagi, frequently decorated with naturalistic animal and flower

Sarcophagi

motifs. The only stone sarcophagus found on Crete was one recovered from a grave at the Ayía Triáda villa, with unusually rich painted decoration (c. 1400 B.C.; illustration, p. 138).

Cut stones

The art of cutting stone developed in Crete due to influences from the Near East resulting from the island's trading connections. An early work of great beauty, dating from the Prepalatial period, is the stone pyxis from Zákros with delicate hatched decoration and a handle in the form of a recumbent dog (illustration, p. 126). A masterly rhyton (illustration, p. 1) is the unusually realistic bull's head in steatite from Knossós. From the same period are the relief-decorated steatite vases found in the Ayía Triáda villa. Among the finest of these are the Harvester Vase (illustration, p. 133) and the Chieftain's Cup, with lively decoration showing great artistic skill and refinement. Another particularly fine item is a rhyton of rock crystal with a handle of crystal beads. A notable rarity is the limestone *kernos* (a circular libation table) in the Mália palace.

Seal-cutting

The cutting of seals in semi-precious stones or ivory is another field of art in which Minoan craftsmen were influenced by models from the East. Before the introduction of writing the seals had a very practical use as a means of establishing the ownership of property and were used to seal chests, caskets and other containers. Since the pattern of the seal had to be easily distinguishable and also distinctive to the owner, they were made in a great variety of forms. Originally they were modelled on cylinder seals from Mesopotamia, stamp seals from Syria and scarab seals from Egypt, but the Minoans soon developed their own types, for example in the form of flattened cylinders with small handles, lens-shaped, ring-shaped and even fourteen-sided. In comparison with Eastern seals, the patterns showed from the outset greater freedom in the choice of motifs, usually taken from nature (landscape features, animals) but also including hunting scenes, divine apparitions or ritual dances, and finally developing purely heraldic motifs.

Goldsmith's art

Among the oldest items of jewellery on the island are the gold filigree chains and pendants from Prepalatial tombs at Mókhlos, many of them in delicate leaf and flower patterns (Archaeological Museum, Áyios Nikólaos). A necklace from Arkhánes shows an unusual combination of gold, ivory and faience. There were also numerous gold rings with figure motifs and necklaces of gold and glass paste, gold pendants and amulets in the form of animals, gilded sword hilts, gold ceremonial double axes and gold cups with impressed spiral ornament. The great technical skill of Minoan goldsmiths is demonstrated in such famous items as the bee pendant found in the Mália necropolis. Two bees with their heads and abdomens joined, forming a ring, hold a drop of honey with their legs. Their extended wings are of striking artistic effect, an effect enhanced by the contrast between the smooth and granulated surfaces.

Bronze-working

Although the craft of metalworking was known on Crete it was little used for the production of bronze sculpture. The few statuettes and animal figures that have been discovered are of poor quality. Minoan weapons, however, were much esteemed; they were usually produced for export. Bronze double axes were also made for cult purposes.

Ivory

Ivories of the Neopalatial period – including small panels with relief decoration, fragments of a footstool and handles from a piece of furniture – have mainly been found as grave goods. A particularly lively piece is the figure of a bull-leaper (illustration, p. 130).

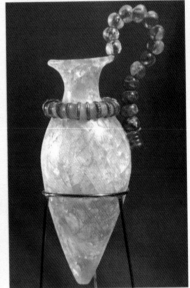

Bee pendant

Rhyton *of rock crystal*

The walls of state apartments, processional corridors and cult rooms in the palaces were covered with magnificent paintings. Although most of the surviving frescos are later than 1600 B.C., it seems likely that as early as the Protopalatial period the walls, which were faced with gypsum, were decorated with paintings, probably under the influence of Egyptian art. Most wall paintings are from the palace at Knossós; some were also found in villas and houses near the palaces. While the paintings in the palaces frequently show figures, floral patterns predominate in the villas.

The oldest paintings are described as miniature frescos, since they are much smaller than life size. Scenes at the court are frequently depicted, for example a ceremony taking place in front of a shrine decorated with bulls' horns and double axes, watched by ladies of the court or perhaps priestesses seated on a veranda and surrounded by a crowd of people looking in different directions and thus creating a very lively effect. A particularly striking figure is the "Parisienne" (illustration, p. 137), who features in a scene depicting the offering of a libation. This priestess with luxuriant black hair, a ritual knot on the nape of her neck, painted red lips and rich clothing was evidently seen as the epitome of female beauty.

In the Neopalatial period frescos in relief became more popular. The best example of this is the relief of a bull's head, part of a large composition which decorated the wall of the north entrance to the palace at Knossós. This depicted the capture of a wild bull in a forested landscape, the attitude of the bull at bay being represented in a very lively way. Some frescos also show life-size figures with remarkable realism. A famous example is the "Prince of the Lilies" fresco, which depicts a male figure with a loincloth and codpiece, wearing an elaborate headdress of flowers and peacock feathers and walking through a landscape with large stylised lilies; the young man is holding

Painting

53

a cord, which may have secured a griffin, now missing. Another striking scene is the bull-leaping fresco from the east wing of the Knossós palace (illustration, p. 26), which depicts three young acrobats performing a ritual game with a bull, one of whom is actually leaping over the bull. But scenes from court life, cult games, festivals and processions were not the only themes of the frescos: there were also landscapes with highly naturalistic representations of animals and plants. Apart from the realism of detail, however, it was the aim of the Minoan artists to conjure up the image of a paradisiac natural landscape. Thus they painted scenes with marvellous blue birds and scented flowers such as lilies and roses. In another fresco blue monkeys frolic against a background of grey, turquoise, yellow and pink rocks and lotus blossoms, mingling exotic and Cretan features. Other scenes depict partridges, cats chasing pheasants, dolphins (in the queen's chamber) and a frieze of griffins (in the throne room). Great sensibility to nature and exact observation of movement are displayed by the Minoan artists, who can depict with equal skill the swaying of grasses in the wind, the rustling of leaves, the bull's sharp changes of direction, the flight of birds, the gambolling of dolphins and the movements of dancers. These lively scenes are a favourite means of relieving the long corridors, staircases and halls of the palaces. Thus the processional frescos accompany the worshippers carrying offerings on their way to the shrine. The illusionist landscapes brighten the rooms of the palace and make them seem bigger. They bring something of nature into the palaces, providing a charming link between the natural world outside and the man-made world within.

Greco-Roman Period

After the fall of Minoan civilisation Crete lay on the margins of artistic activity in the eastern Mediterranean, during the period, between 1000 and 500 B.C., when architecture and sculpture in Greece were developing into the classical style, with splendid temples and idealised human figures.

One of the earliest Greek towns to be founded in Crete was Lato (8th/7th century), situated on a sloping site, whose remains are still impressive. From the town gate a stepped street winds its way up past shops to the agora, the central meeting-place in a Greek city, with its public buildings and temples. The temples were rectangular buildings with a grand staircase leading up to the entrance at one end. Another example of early Greek temple-building can be seen at Rizeniá near Priniás. Temple A at this site, with a pronaos and cella, is similar in ground-plan to the Greek temple in antis but has pillars rather than columns at the entrance. Temple B has an irregular plan with an opisthodomos at the west end. The first temple of Dictynna on the Rodopoú peninsula was built in the 7th century B.C. and converted in the 2nd/1st century B.C. into a Doric peripteral temple. When the Emperor Hadrian visited Crete in A.D. 123 he built a new temple at this site, amphiprostyle in form with Ionic and Corinthian columns.

In Roman times Górtys was the most important town on Crete and capital of the province of Creta et Cyrene. Although there are scanty remains of the acropolis and theatre of the Greek period, the site as we see it today is essentially Roman. Excavation has revealed the foundations of the praetorium with its long peristyle hall, administrative offices and private apartments, the residence of the Roman governors. The temple of Isis and Serapis, a rectangular building with a small crypt and niches for statues, was built after the incorporation of Egypt into the Roman Empire. The temple of Apollo Pythios dates from the 6th century B.C. but was converted in Roman times into a three-aisled

Architecture

◀ *The Prince of the Lilies, with a headdress of flowers and peacock feathers*

55

structure with a central apse and a pronaos of six Doric columns. There are also remains of nymphaeums, aqueducts and an amphitheatre.

Sculpture

The archaeological museums in Crete have small collections of Greco-Roman sculpture, but the works they display cannot compare with the great achievements in other parts of the Greco-Roman world during this period. The Protogeometric and Geometric periods (1000–725 B.C.) produced pottery decorated with circles, spirals and chequerboard patterns. During the Orientalising and Archaic periods (725–550 B.C.) vases notable for their beauty of form were produced, for example the three-handled hydria decorated with bees (Archaeological Museum, Áyios Nikólaos).

Examples of figural clay sculpture are the female protome (Archaeological Museum, Áyios Nikólaos) and the Archaic female heads with their enigmatic smiles (Archaeological Museum, Réthymnon).

Minoan bronze-workers produced breastplates and weapons. Other outstanding examples of their work are the bronze reliefs, for example the bronze ship with oarsmen from the Idaean Cave.

Of notable quality is the relief frieze of a procession of horsemen from the Archaic temple at Rizenía.

Sculpture of the Classical period includes the finely carved funerary stele of a young archer and the metope of Heracles and the Erymanthian boar from a temple at Knossós.

From the Roman period date the bronze figure of a richly apparelled young man, a marble statue of Aphrodite and the bearded figure of a philosopher. Among the various portrait heads of the Roman Imperial period the portrait of Marcus Aurelius wearing a laurel wreath is outstanding (Archaeological Museum, Chaniá). There are also numerous small bronzes, perfume and ointment bottles, oil lamps, domestic pottery, bronze vessels and relief-decorated sarcophagi.

Mosaics

Numerous Roman floor mosaics give some idea of the decoration of town houses and country villas. There are some particularly fine mosaics in the Archaeological Museum in Chaniá, including one with motifs from a comedy by Menander.

Vase-painting

Since no wall or panel paintings of the Greek period have survived, only vase-painting remains to give some impression of the variety of motifs. Black-figured vase-painting, which originated in Corinth, was succeeded by red-figured painting in Athens around 530 B.C., and from Attica passed to Crete. It displays great variety of form, including storage vessels (amphoras, pelike, stamnos), jars for mixing water and wine (hydrias), jugs (oinochoe), drinking vessels (kylix, kantharos) and ointment bottles (alabastron, aryballos).

Byzantine Period

The foundation of Constantinople in A.D. 330 and the division of the Roman Empire into a western and an eastern (Byzantine) empire in 395 brought a new flowering of art and culture to the eastern Mediterranean which lasted until the fall of the Byzantine Empire in 1453 and also spread to Crete. In spite of the Arab occupation from 826/827 to 961 and the period of Venetian rule which began in 1246 artistic activity on the island was influenced by the various developments in Byzantine art: the art of the Justinianic period (527–565) of Iconoclasm (726–843), art under the Comneni (1081–1185) and the art of the Palaeologue period (1261–1453).

Architecture

When Christianity was recognised by the state in the 4th century the first Christian churches were built in basilican form. From the second half of the 5th century date the foundations and the beautiful mosaic pavement of the basilica at Oloús/Eloúnda. The basilica of St Titus

Byzantine cross-in-square church
(Kyr Yiánnis, Alikianós)

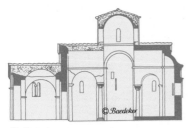

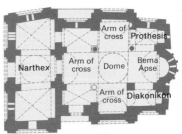

Section   Plan

(probably 6th c.) at Górtys, a three-aisled structure with a dome over the crossing and transepts, is a masterpiece of Early Byzantine church architecture.

In the course of time the rectangular type of church increasingly gave place to a centralised structure, and in the 10th century the domed cruciform (cross-in-square) church developed alongside the barrel-vaulted cruciform plan. The commonest type is the church with four columns supporting a central dome, four barrel-vaulted arms of a cross, usually of the same length and height, and four areas in the angles between the arms. At the east end, on either side of the apse, are two rooms, the prothesis and the diakonikon, which serve liturgical purposes (the preparation of the bread and wine and the robing of the priest); at the west end there is frequently a porch or narthex. The external walls were of undressed stone and brick, frequently in elaborate patterns; the interior was covered with frescos.

In the country areas of Crete the predominant type of church is a simple one-room chapel decorated with frescos which are often of remarkable quality.

In the interior of the church the chancel area containing the altar (bema) was originally separated from the main part of the church, the naos, by a low stone screen, which later developed into the tall iconostasis.

As a result of destructions by the Arabs in the 9th and 10th centuries only a few examples of painting have survived from the Early Byzantine period, particularly from the period of Iconoclasm when images representing saints were banned by imperial edict. Among such paintings with aniconic motifs (floral and geometric patterns) some fragments, painted in vigorous colours, can be seen in the church of Áyios Nikólaos in the town of Áyios Nikólaos. Masterpieces of monumental painting in the Comnenian style are the frescos (1230–36) in the church of Áyios Nikólaos in Kyriaskosélia, with finely contrived compositions, elegantly modelled bodies, delicate lines and rich colour.

Most frescos of the 14th and 15th centuries, however, are in variants of the Palaeologan style. The frescos devoted to the Archangel Michael (1315/16) in the church of the Archangel Michael at Asómatos (a one-room chapel) are expressive and lively examples of this style. The high point of church decoration in Crete is reached in the magnificent frescos (1250–1350) in the church of the Panayía Kera at Kritsá. Here vigorous and lifelike figures alternate with thin-limbed figures in a mannered style. They include the naked figure of Christ in the Baptism scene, apostles and saints clad in garments falling in elaborate folds, and knights in armour taking part in the Massacre of the Innocents. Charming, too, are the backgrounds, almost like stage settings, with landscape and architectural detail.

Painting

57

In paradise: a fresco from the church of the Panayía Kera, Kritsá

In the Late Byzantine period two brothers, Manuel and John Phokás, were famed for their paintings. The paintings in churches at Émbaros (1436/37) and Avdoú (1449) are notable for their delicate linear style, their changing colours (in spite of some schematisation) and their architectural backgrounds.

In panel painting the main emphasis was on icons, usually for display on the iconostasis (see Baedeker Special, p. 140).

The iconographic programme

The paintings in an Orthodox church are arranged in accordance with a strict iconographic programme laying down the disposition of the various themes in different parts of the church, so as to give expression in the structure of the church to the idea of the universal divine creation. Particular importance was attached to the paintings in the dome, seen as a symbolic representation of heaven: here was depicted the figure of Christ Pantokrator, Ruler of All, surrounded by angels and prophets. Important, too, was the apse, symbolically forming a bridge between earth and heaven, where the Deesis, with the Mother of God and John the Baptist interceding with Christ for mankind, is commonly found. The sanctuary (*bema*) was painted with liturgical themes expressing the mystical conception of heaven, and the Ascension and the Descent of the Holy Ghost were frequently represented on the upper part of the walls.

Along the side walls of the naos martyrs and saints bear witness to the Christian faith. Higher up, symbolically in an intermediate situation between heaven and earth, are New Testament scenes or representations of the festivals of the Orthodox church, including the Annunciation, the Nativity, the Presentation in the Temple, the Baptism, the Entry to Jerusalem, the Crucifixion, the Descent into Hades and the Dormition (Death) of the Mother of God. The west wall is usually occupied by a Last Judgment.

Since there was no monumental sculpture, largely on religious grounds, attention was concentrated on smaller-scale works. Among notable products of the Byzantine period are precious fabrics, including liturgical vestments, and goldsmith's and silversmith's work, notably liturgical utensils such as chalices and patens.

Minor arts

Creto-Venetian Period

The occupation of the island by the Venetians in 1204 led to new developments only in secular architecture: church-building remained mainly under Byzantine influence.

In the coastal towns – Iráklion, Chaniá, Réthymnon and Sitía – the Venetians built imposing ports to serve as naval and commercial bases, with long quays, lighthouses, arsenals, custom houses and defences. Iráklion has a massive fortress, the Koúles (see below), defending its harbour, with reliefs of the lion of St Mark, and a rampart with gates, bastions and outworks designed by the famous Veronese architect and military engineer Michele Sanmicheli (1550–60).

Port installations and fortifications

Among the handsomest Venetian buildings in Crete are the loggias in the towns, in High Renaissance style, which were designed as meeting-places for the Creto-Venetian nobility. The most magnificent of these is in Iráklion: a two-storey building in Palladian style with arcading and a balustrade fronting the roof (1626–28).

Public and residential buildings

Members of the nobility and prosperous citizens built numerous town palaces in the late medieval period and the Renaissance. Some of these can still be seen in the old Venetian quarters of Chaniá and Réthymnon.

The Venetian fort defending Iráklion's harbour

Fountains

Crete has a number of charming fountains dating from this period. In the centre of Iráklion are the handsome Morosini Fountain (1628), with relief decoration on its scalloped outer basin and a central basin borne by lions, and the Bembo Fountain of 1558.

Churches

The finest Roman Catholic church in Crete is the church of San Marco in Iráklion, a three-aisled basilica with lean-to-roofed lateral aisles which dates from 1239 and from then until 1669 was the seat of the Latin archbishop of Crete. Among monastic churches there is the church of San Francesco in Chaniá (16th c.; now the Archaeological Museum), also a three-aisled basilica, with a pointed barrel vault over the raised nave and ribbed vaulting over the lateral aisles.

The Venetian Renaissance style also influenced Orthodox church building in the 16th and 17th centuries, particularly in the design of the façade. The west front (1587) of the Arkádi monastery, for example, has paired Corinthian columns and a massive entablature.

Alongside the cross-in-square type trilobate churches on a cloverleaf ground-plan were now frequently built in western Crete. An example is the monastic church at Goniás (1634).

Painting

During the medieval period only a few saints (e.g. St Francis) and the theme of the Trinity were taken over from the Latin church into Byzantine iconography.

In the 16th century the Renaissance style was brought to Crete by the Venetians. In panel painting Michael Damaskinós (see Famous People) created some outstanding works in the second half of the century. His icons of the Last Supper and the Adoration of the Magi (both in the Icon Museum in Iráklion) are notable for their lively figures, movement, use of perspective and rich colouring.

The most celebrated Cretan painter, Doménikos Theotokópoulos, better known as El Greco (see Famous People), one of the great masters of European Mannerism, left no works on his native island.

The panel paintings of Emmanuel Skordilis, including a Christ in Majesty and a Last Judgment in the Ayía Triáda monastery, date from the first half of the 17th century. The old cathedral of St Minas in Iráklion contains some fine works by George and Zacharias Gastrophilákos, including a "Creation of Eve" in a beautiful landscape setting. Around 1770 Ioánnis Kornáros painted a number of icons of great narrative richness, with numerous figures, in Toploú monastery.

Sculpture and minor arts

The Historical Museum in Iráklion has a large collection of sculpture and the minor arts, including Gothic reliefs, Venetian tombstones, works of sculpture from churches, carved coats of arms, architectural fragments, gold and silver coins, jewellery, tiles, pottery, carved wooden crosses and bishops' crosiers.

Turkish Period

Dring the Turkish occupation (1169–1898) a number of Christian churches were converted into mosques. In Iráklion, for example, the metropolitan church of St Titus became a mosque, a centralised structure oriented towards Mecca with a central dome and four subsidiary domes. In 1925 it was converted back into an Orthodox church with three apses, but the Turkish period is still recalled by two Islamic prayer niches with stalactitic vaulting. In Chaniá, Réthymnon and Sitía there are still many wooden houses with enclosed balconies as well as bath-houses and fountains dating from the Turkish period.

19th Century

In the second half of the 19th century and around the turn of the century, after Crete achieved independence in 1898, new residential quarters and public buildings' in the variety of old architectural styles then favoured in Europe, ranging from Neo-Renaissance by way of Neo-Baroque to Neo-Classicism, were built. The Historical Museum in Chaniá occupies a handsome Neo-Classical villa dating from the turn of the century. A notable industrial building is Chaniá's market hall (1908), on a cruciform ground-plan.

In church-building the Cretans remained true to the traditional forms of Byzantine architecture, including interior decoration in accordance with the established iconographic programmes. The metropolitan church of St Minas in Iráklion, completed in 1895, is a five-aisled domed structure in that tradition.

Glossary of Technical Terms (Art and Architecture)

The upper of the capital of a Doric column, a square slab above the echinus.	**Abacus**
The highest part of a Greek city; the citadel.	**Acropolis**
The market square of a Greek city, the main centre of public life.	**Agora**
An unguent bottle.	**Alabastron**
A raised pulpit or lectern in a Christian church.	**Ambo**
(Temple) with columned portico at both ends.	**Amphiprostyle**
A two-handled jar of bulbous form, used for the storage of oil, wine, honey, etc.	**Amphora**
A pillar-like projection at the end of the side wall of a temple. A temple in antis has columns between the antae at the front end.	**Anta**
A projection (usually semicircular) at the end (normally the east end) of a church.	**Apse**
A horizontal stone lintel resting on the columns of a temple.	**Architrave**
A spherical oil flask.	**Aryballos**
1. Originally a royal hall, usually divided into aisles, used for commercial or judicial purposes. 2. A standard form of Christian church developed in the 4th century, with three or five aisles.	**Basilica**
1. A platform used by orators in classical times. 2. The sanctuary of a Christian church.	**Bema**
A bulbous, double-handled, cup or jug.	**Cantharos**
The top of a column or pillar, supporting the architrave.	**Capital**
The semicircular auditorium of a Roman theatre.	**Cavea**
The enclosed chamber of a temple; the Latin equivalent of the Greek naos.	**Cella**
(Divinities, etc.) of the earth.	**Chthonian**
The half-dome of an apse.	**Conch**
See Orders.	**Corinthian order**

61

Glossary of Technical Terms (Art and Architecture)

Cross-in-square church
A church with a central dome over the crossing-point of four arms of equal length.

Crypt
An underground tomb below the choir of Romanesque and Gothic churches.

Deesis
The "Intercession": the Mother of God and John the Baptist interceding with Christ for the world.

Diakonikon
A room in the right-hand lateral apse of a Byzantine church.

Doric order
See Orders.

Dromos (plural dromoi)
A passage; specifically, the massage leading to a Mycenaean tholos (domed) tomb.

Echinus
A convex moulding under the abacus of a Doric temple.

Exedra
A recess, usually semicircular, containing benches.

Frieze
A decorative band above the architrave of a temple.

Horns of consecration
Stylised bull's horns, a feature of Minoan shrines.

Hydria
A water jar.

Iconostasis
A screen for the display of icons in a Byzantine church, between the sanctuary and the main part of the church.

Ionic order
See Orders.

Kernos (plural kernoi)
A cult vessel with a number of receptacles for offerings.

Krater
A two-handled jar for mixing water and wine.

Larnax (plural larnakes)
A small sarcophagus or urn.

Megaron
The principal room in a Mycenaean palace, regarded by many scholars as the basic form of the Greek temple.

Metope
A rectangular panel between the triglyphs in the frieze of a Doric temple, either plain or with relief decoration.

Naos
1. The enclosed chamber of a temple: the Greek equivalent of the Latin cella.
2. The main part of an Orthodox church.

Narthex
The entrance hall or porch of a Byzantine church.

Necropolis
Cemetery ("city of the dead").

Odeon, odeion
A hall (usually roofed) for musical performances, etc.

Oinochoe
A wine jug.

Opisthodomos
A chamber at the rear end of a temple.

Orchestra
A circular or semicircular area between the stage and the auditorium of a theatre in which the chorus danced.

Orders
In Greek architecture three orders are distinguished:

In the Doric order the columns are fluted and show a slight swelling known as entasis. They stand directly on the stylobate, without a base. The capital has a square abacus. On the architrave is a frieze with alternating triglyphs and metopes. — Doric

The columns of the Ionic order, which stand on a base, are slender, with the flutings separated by narrow ridges. The capitals have volutes. The architrave has a continuous frieze decorated in relief. — Ionic

The Corinthian order is similar to the Ionic except that the capital has two rings of acanthus leaves and small volutes. — Corinthian

An urn containing human remains. — **Ossuary**

A plate containing the consecrated bread used in communion. — **Paten**

A storage jar similar to an amphora. — **Pelike**

(Temple) surrounded by a peristyle. — **Peripteral**

A colonnade surrounding a building. — **Peristyle**

A pillar engaged in a wall. — **Pilaster**

A large storage jar. — **Pithos** (plural pithoi)

A pillared hall. — **Polythyron** (plural polythyra)

A vestibule at the entrance to a temple. — **Pronaos**

Gateway. — **Propylon**

A room in the left-hand lateral apse of a Byzantine church. — **Prothesis**

A three-dimensional representation of the head and forepart of an animal, or the head and upper part of a human figure, used as decoration on buildings or vases. — **Protome**

Office of the *prytanes* (city councillors) — **Prytaneion**

A small lidded box in pottery, stone, etc. — **Pyxis** (plural pyxides)

A drinking or libation vessel, often in the form of an animal's head. — **Rhyton**

The stage building of a theatre. — **Skene**

A two-handled jar with a very narrow neck. — **Stamnos**

A domed Mycenaean tomb. — Tholos (plural tholoi)

The spiral scroll of an Ionic capital. — **Volute**

Music and Dance

Music

Music played an essential part in the life of the Cretans. During the period of Turkish rule songs were a form of resistance and helped to

When Zorba Dances the Syrtáki

"**A** stranger of about sixty, very tall and lean, with staring eyes, had pressed his nose against the pane and was looking at me. He was holding a little flattened bundle under his arm. The thing which impressed me most was his eager gaze, his eyes, ironical and full of fire. At any rate, that is how they appeared to me. As soon as our eyes had met – he seemed to be making sure that I was really the person he was looking for – the stranger opened the door with a determined thrust of his arm. He passed between the tables with a rapid, springy step, and stopped in front of me. 'Travelling?' he asked. 'Where to? Trusting to providence?' 'I'm making for Crete. Why do you ask?' 'Taking me with you?'" So begins the encounter between a young English writer and the Cretan, Alexis Zorba – two men who could hardly be more different from one another: one educated, introverted, more at home in his books than in real life, and the other full of vigorous life and impetuous passion in all that he does, a man who lives by his belly and with his heart. It is the story of a friendship between two men, set against the background of everyday Cretan life in all its harshness, but also all its poetry and unspoiled, archaic beauty. The author of the story, Nikos Kazantzákis, came from Crete but, closely bound as he was to his native island, was a thoroughly cosmopolitan spirit and a sharp critic of his fellow-countrymen. The publication of "Zorba the Greek" in 1946 made Kazantzákis, already known in Greece as a writer, world-famous at a stroke. Within a few years the novel was translated into English and German.

What is little known, however, is that Alexis Zorba was not a pure invention: there really was such a man. The real Zorba was not called Alexis, but Yeóryios, and was a miner. In 1916 Kazantzákis's and Zorba's ways crossed. In that year the writer spent some months in the Peloponnese with the Macedonian miner, working lignite: the mining project in the novel thus had a basis in real life. After the time they spent together Kazantzákis apparently heard only occasionally from his friend, who died in Skopje in 1942, never having set foot on the island of Crete. No one – and certainly not the man himself – could ever have imagined that Yeóryios Zorba, or rather the Zorba which Kazantzákis had made of him, would feature in literary history as the hero of a novel. The novel's success, however, was merely the prelude to the still greater popularity which the story of these two men was to achieve when the book was turned into a film. The film "Zorba the Greek" (1964), directed by Michael Cacoyannis, drew huge audiences and attracted great critical acclaim. "Zorba the Greek" quickly became a film classic. The film was shot in Crete, particularly in the little fishing village of Stavrós on the Akrotíri peninsula near Chaniá. But much in the film that looks authentically Cretan or authentically Greek is revealed on closer inspection to be a (very skilful) cheat. An example is the syrtáki which Anthony Quinn dances so magnificently. Since there was not enough time during the shooting of the film for him to learn the complicated Cretan folk dances, a simpler dance was devised for him to the music of Mikis Theodorákis – who at least was a Greek. As a result most visitors to Crete now think that the syrtáki is a traditional Cretan dance.

The fact that Cacoyannis's film simplifies or schematises the novel will not surprise anyone who has seen other film versions of novels, nor will it diminish the fame of the film. Cacoyannis, of course, created characters who were on the very verge of being overdrawn and cliché-like figures; but the film's convincing effect was due to the excellent cast. In addition to Anthony Quinn as Zorba, Alan Bates played the young pale-skinned writer, Lila Kedrova the ageing Bouboulina and Irene Papas the austerely beautiful widow.

The success of the film, however, was principally due to the fine

Anthony Quinn and Alan Bates, stars of the film "Zorba the Greek"

performance by Anthony Quinn. The character of Zorba seemed so exactly made to measure for Quinn that the actor and the character became one figure for viewers of the film: Quinn did not act Zorba, he *was* Zorba. The additional element in the figure of Zorba in the film as compared with the character in the novel is the vigorous, free and boundlessly optimistic aura which radiates from this man and sends the audience out into reality with a positive feeling. Who can forget the magnificent scene at the end of the film when Zorba, after the collapse of his cableway, says "Boss, did you ever see anything crashing so beautifully?"

(Quotations from the novel are in the translation by Carl Wildman).

preserve the island's cultural identity. In spite of the pop music which predominates today the old songs are still sung.

Cretan tunes have become popular in the west thanks to the music of Mikis Theodorákis (see Famous People).

Instruments

The most important Cretan instrument is the *lyra*, a three-stringed fiddle played with a bow, which sometimes has bells attached. The *santoúri*, which is played by Alexis Zorba, is another important stringed instrument. Other instruments used in a small orchestra are the *laoúto*, which was introduced in Venetian times, and the *askomantoúra*, a wind instrument.

Mantinádes

Mantinádes are impromptu verses, sung to a musical accompaniment on family occasions, teasing the various members of the family with jokes and allusions to their behaviour.

Dance

Dance, as an expression of the delight in being alive, is deeply rooted in Cretan society. The Cretans dance readily and on any occasion.

Most Cretan dances have developed in a particular region but have then spread to other regions in an altered form. There are dancing societies and folk dance groups. In addition to the dances described below there are many others that are no longer danced.

Visitors to Crete may get the erroneous impression that it is only the men who dance; but women also like dancing and do so frequently, on religious festivals and occasions such as christenings and weddings.

When a visitor comes on a group of Cretans dancing he should not think that he cannot join in because he doesn't know the steps. The local people would not understand why he shouldn't.

Dancing in Crete gives expression to both positive and negative feelings. This is clear from the words of Alexis Zorba in Kazantzákis's novel: "Boss, I've dozens of things to say to you. I've never loved anyone as much before. I've hundreds of things to say, but my tongue just can't manage them. So I'll dance them for you!" (From Carl Wildman's translation).

Syrtáki

Many people think that the syrtáki is an old Cretan dance, but it is not. It is a product of the Hollywood dream factory, created in 1964 for the film "Zorba the Greek". Since the Cretan dances were too difficult for Anthony Quinn, who played Zorba, a simpler dance was devised for him, to the music of Mikis Theodorákis. This was the syrtáki.

Siganós

The siganós ("slow"), also known as the "dance of Theseus", forms the introduction to the pentosális. It is a slow dance, accompanied by the lute and the lyra.

Pentosális

The pentosális ("five-step dance"), which like all Cretan dances is of Minoan origin, is a spirited dance to lively music, consisting of five basic steps. It offers scope for improvisation and extraordinary leaps by the principal dancer.

Syrtós

The light syrtós ("round dance"), also known as the khaniótikos, is the most natural and original Cretan dance. Originally from Chaniá, it is now danced all over the island. It is danced by both men and women, with gliding steps.

Soústa

The soústa ("feather dance"), originally peculiar to Réthymnon, is the only Cretan pair-dance. It is an erotic dance in which the man and woman dance up to each other with light hopping steps and then draw apart.

The name of the kastrinós is derived from Megalo Kastro (Iráklion); it is also known as the maleviziotikos, after the district of Malevízi. It is danced by men, who perform great leaps in the course of the dance.

Kastrinós

The pidikto originated in the Iráklion area. Like the other dances, it has many variants.

Pidikto

Quotations

Homer
(8th c. B.C.)

Crete is a land amid the wine-dark sea,
Fair and rich and sea-girt; it is well peopled,
With great numbers living in ninety cities,
Each speaking a different language. They are a mixed people:
There are Achaeans and high-hearted Eteo-Cretans,
Dorians with flying hair, Cydonians and noble Pelasgians.
Among the cities is Knossos, with Minos as king,
Who took counsel with Zeus, the mighty, every nine years.

From the "Odyssey", Book 19

William Lithgow
(1582–1645?)

The women generally wear linen breeches, as men do, and boots after
the same manner, and their linen coats no longer than the middle of
their thighs, and are insatiably inclined to venery; such is the nature of
the soil and climate. The ancient Cretans were such notable liars, that
the heathen poet Epimenides, yea, and the apostle Paul, in his epistle
to Titus, did term them to have been "ever liars, evil beasts, and slow
bellies"; whence sprung these proverbs, as *Cretense mendacium* and
Cretisandum est cum Cretensibus.

The Candiots are excellent good archers, surpassing all the oriental
people therein, courageous and valiant upon the sea, as in former
times they were; and they are naturally inclined to singing, so that
commonly after meat man, wife and child of each family will, for the
space of an hour, sing with such an harmony as is wonderful melo-
dious to the hearer; yea, and they cannot forgo the custom of it.

From "Rare Adventures and Painfull Peregrinations", 1614–32

Baedeker's
"Greece" (1904)

To the Cave of Zeus on Mount Ida (3–4 days) . . . From Anogia it takes 6
hours of a stiff ascent (on foot or horseback) to a plateau on the eastern
slope of the main peak of Ida which preserves in its name *Kampos tes
Nidas* the old name of the mountain. It extends for 2–2½ miles from
east to west, is watered by a number of springs and in summer is
inhabited by shepherds with whom one can spend the night. The cave
(about 5000ft above sea-level) in which Zeus was cared for during his
childhood by nymphs and curetes and which was still held in veneration in Roman times, lies on the west side of the plateau, some 500ft
higher up on the slopes of Mount Ida, where the path from the summit
comes down. The entrance, above which the rock face rises vertically,
faces west. To the left is a crag at the foot of which the rock has been
hewn into a large square altar (16 by 7ft). The interior of the cave is
divided into a high main chamber some 100ft in diameter and a smaller
annexe about 100ft long. Excavations in the cave and in front of it have
shown it to be the Cave of Zeus and have yielded a quantity of clay
votive offerings and fragments dating back to Archaic times and
closely related to the bronzes found at Olympia.

The Dictaean Cave, with which the legend of the birth of Zeus is
associated, lies above the village of *Psychró* (rather more than a day's
ride from Candia), on the northern slopes of the principal peak in the
Lassithi range. The interior has recently been more closely examined.
The upper cave is connected by a shaft about 150ft long with an
underground stalactitic cave, the adyton. Here were found many votive
offerings of the Mycenaean period and the Geometric period which
followed it, including small bronze double axes.

To portray here the individuality of Crete, this island which, till the beginning of the twentieth century, had been "700 years in perpetual revolt", is scarcely possible. Our visit was a reconnoitre, a prelude, perhaps, to further exploration. At first we remained in the capital, Canea. The buildings of this town epitomise the whole history of the Levant. Across the mouth of the harbour, as the rowing-boat enters, runs a mole ending in a Turkish lighthouse, a truncated minaret delicately embroidered with stone ornament. Nearer in, on the east, stands the earliest mosque on the island, a tiny building with a dome that resembles three-quarters of a doughnut and is supported by flying buttresses that might have been borrowed from St George's, Windsor. Look now across to the west. It is Venice. High, multi-coloured houses, each black window reflected in the sunlit water, jumble along the quay; and reveal, on closer view, that it was Venice, and that the lions of St Mark still cry a weatherbeaten echo from the bellying walls. Behind, up the slope from the sea, it is the same. Twisting narrow streets, the houses so tall as to exclude all sun, display Renaissance porticoes, escutcheons of the Venetian nobility, and even basrelievo portraits of the generals of the Republic in plumed helmets. On one such there appeared also the stone fez of a later tenant. And above, as if to complete the tale, the cornice had been furnished with a row of Greek *acroteria*. Adjacent lies the old Turkish quarter, to-day the centre of commerce, where lanes of windowless shops are piled with the importations of the West, side by side with the traditional clothing and commodities of the island.

Robert Byron (1905–41)

From "The Station" (1931)

Dawn was hardly peeping through when I started out. I went past the gardens, followed the edge of the sea, hurriedly made my acquaintance with the water, earth and air of the spot, picked wild plants, and the palms of my hands became redolent with savory, sage and mint.

Nikos Kazantzákis (1882–1957)

I climbed a hill and looked round. An austere countryside of granite and very hard limestone. Dark carob and silvery olive trees, figs and vines. In the sheltered hollows, orange groves, lemon and medlar trees; near the shore, kitchen gardens. To the north, an expanse of sea, still angry and roaring as it came rushing from Africa to bite into the coast of Crete. Nearby, a low, sandy islet flushing rosy pink under the first rays of the sun.

To my mind, this Cretan countryside resembled good prose, carefully ordered, sober, free from superfluous ornament, powerful and restrained. It expressed all that was necessary with the greatest economy. It had no flippancy, or artifice about it. It said what it had to say with a manly austerity. But between the severe lines one could discern an unexpected sensitiveness and tenderness; in the sheltered hollows the lemon and orange trees perfumed the air, and from the vastness of the sea emanated an inexhaustible poetry.

From "Zorba the Greek" (1946). Translation by Carl Goldman

Next morning I took the bus in the direction of Knossus. I had to walk a mile or so after leaving the bus to reach the ruins. I was so elated that it seemed as if I were walking on air. At last my dream was about to be realised. The sky was overcast and it sprinkled a bit as I hopped along. Again, as at Mycenae, I felt that I was being drawn to the spot. Finally, as I rounded a bend, I stopped dead in my tracks; I had the feeling that I was there. I looked about for traces of the ruins but there were none in sight. I stood for several minutes gazing intently at the contours of the smooth hills which barely grazed the electric blue sky. This must be the spot, I said to myself, I can't be wrong. I retraced my steps and cut

Henry Miller (1891–1980)

through the fields to the bottom of a gulch. Suddenly, to my left, I discovered a bald pavilion with columns painted in raw, bold colours – the palace of King Minos. I was at the back entrance of the ruins amidst a clump of buildings that looked as if they had been gutted by fire. I went round the hill to the main entrance and followed a little group of Greeks in the wake of a guide who spoke a boustrophedonous language which was sheer Pelasgian to me.

There has been much controversy about the aesthetics of Sir Arthur Evans' work of restoration. I found myself unable to come to any conclusion about it; I accepted it as a fact. However Knossus may have looked in the past, however it may look in the future, this one which Evans has created is the only one I shall ever know. I am grateful to him for what he did, grateful that he had made it possible for me to descend the grand staircase, to sit on that marvellous throne chair, the replica of which at the Hague Peace Tribunal is now almost as much of a relic of the past as the original.

Knossus in all its manifestations suggests the splendour and sanity and opulence of a powerful and peaceful people. It is gay – gay, healthful, sanitary, salubrious. The common people played a great role, that is evident . . .

Greece is what everybody knows, even *in absentia,* even as a child or as an idiot or as a not-yet-born. It is what you expect the earth to look like given a fair chance. It is the subliminal threshold of innocence. It stands, as it stood from birth, naked and fully revealed. It is not mysterious or impenetrable, not awesome, not defiant, not pretentious. It is made of earth, fire and water. It changes seasonally with harmonious undulating rhythms. It breathes, it beckons, it answers.

Crete is something else. Crete is a cradle, an instrument, a vibrating test tube in which a volcanic experiment has been performed. Crete can hush the mind, still the bubble of thought.

From "The Colossus of Maroussi" (1941)

Johannes
Gaitanides
(1909–88)

Crete is in truth a continent on its own and should be seen as such by visitors . . .

Crete, the oldest Europe, has its youngest people, bursting with vitality and originality, as insatiable in its thirst for life as it is unhesitating in squandering itself. So many sediments of history weigh down on Crete, and yet it shows no weariness, no trace of exhaustion: an air of wisdom – such wisdom that it can commit every kind of folly.

From "Das Inselmeer der Griechen" (1962)

Suggested Routes

The following routes are intended merely as suggestions to guide visitors in planning their trip to Crete, leaving them free to select and vary the routes in accordance with their particular interests and preferences.

The suggested routes take in all the main tourist sights in Crete; but not all the places of interest described in this guide lie directly on the routes, and to see them it will be necessary to make side trips from the main routes. The descriptions in the A to Z section of the guide, therefore, contain numerous suggestions and recommendations for trips to these other sights.

The suggested routes can be followed on the map enclosed with this guide, which will help with detailed planning.

In these routes the names of places which are the subject of a separate entry in the A to Z section of the guide are given in **bold** type. Most of the places mentioned – towns and villages, regions, mountains, rivers and isolated features of interest – are included in the Index at the end of the guide, making it easy to find the description of any sight.

The distances given at the head of each route are rounded figures for the main route. The additional distances involved in the various side trips and excursions are indicated in each case.

1. Iráklion via Knossós to Arkhánes

From ★★**Iráklion** the route runs south, signposted to Arkhánes, and in a few kilometres comes to ★★**Knossós**, the most celebrated and most visited Minoan palace in Crete. From here the main road continues south, passing an impressive Venetian aqueduct (17th c.) which brought water to Iráklion. Soon after this a road goes off on the right to **Arkhánes**, a town famous for its grapes, situated in a productive wine-growing region.

Distance: 17km/10½ miles

To the north of the town are two interesting archaeological sites, the necropolis of Phoúrni, one of the most important Bronze Age burial grounds in the Mediterranean area, and the sanctuary of Anemóspilia, where evidence of human sacrifice was found. Just to the south of Arkhánes is the church of Asómatos, with frescos dating from 1315. From the road running south from Arkhánes a rough and stony side road goes off on the right to Mt Yioúkhtas (811m/2661ft), from which there are magnificent views extending as far as Iráklion. The road to the south continues to the Minoan villa of Vathýpetro, finely situated on a ridge of hill above a beautiful valley.

2. Iráklion via Górtys and Phaistós to Mátala

The road south from Iráklion to the fertile Mesará plain runs through country of great scenic beauty, passing a number of interesting monasteries and important excavation sites.

Distance: 75km/47 miles

Leaving Iráklion by the Chaniá Gate, the road runs south, signposted to Mires. It passes through the island's main sultana-growing area and begins to climb gently in wide curves. The village of Sivá marks the beginning of one of Crete's most important wine-growing areas, which produces the famous Malvasia (Malmsey). A whitewashed rock in Ayía Varvára marks the geographical centre of Crete.

Suggested routes

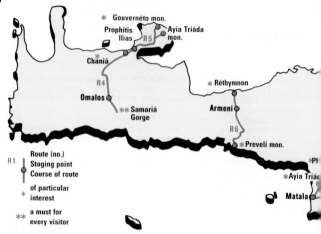

Route (no.)
Staging point
Course of route
of particular interest
a must for every visitor

Side trip to Rizenía

From here it is worth making a side trip (6km/4 miles) to the remains of ancient Rizenía, from which there are spectacular views of the sea and the surrounding area.

Side trip to Kamáres and Mount Ida

A rather longer side trip (29km/18 miles) from Ayía Varvára is to Kamáres in the Mount Ida range, well worth it for the sake of its scenic beauties and interesting monasteries. The road runs through Yéryeri, where there is a memorial commemorating the shooting of hostages by the Germans in 1944, to Zarós, which is famed for its trout hatchery.

From the monastery of Áyios Nikólaos above this village there are wide views over the southern foothills of the Mount Ida range and the Mesará plain. Also above the road, farther west, is the Vrondísi monastery, with a church, containing fine frescos, which is a jewel of Byzantine architecture.

At the village of Vorízia is the third monastery on the route, ★Valsamónero, which has a magnificent situation and contains frescos of outstanding quality. From Kamáres, the end-point of this trip, it is possible to climb to the Kamáres Cave, a Minoan sanctuary, and Mt Psilorítis, the highest peak in the ★**Mount Ida** range.

Soon after Ayía Varvára the main road climbs to the Vourvoulitis pass (650m/2130ft), from which there are superb views over the Mesará, Crete's largest plain. Then, shortly before Ayii Déka, the road turns west and soon comes to the ruins of ★**Górtys**, the one-time Roman capital of Crete.

Side trip to Léntas

The side trip from Górtys to Léntas (33km/21 miles south) will be of particular interest to those interested in archaeology. At Plátanos are two important Early Minoan circular tombs, and at Léntas, on the south coast, are the remains of the Greco-Roman town of Lebena.

The main road, continuing west, offers fine views of the Mesará plain with its vineyards and olive trees. ★Vóri, 2km/¼ mile north of the road, has the finest and most interesting folk museum in Crete. From here a road runs south to the beautifully situated ★**Phaistós**, the most important Minoan palace in Crete after Iráklion.

Just under 3km/2 miles west is the large Minoan villa of ★**Ayía Triáda**.

The main road south now winds its way down into the Mesará plain. Almost at once it comes to the village of Áyios Ioánnis, at the far end of

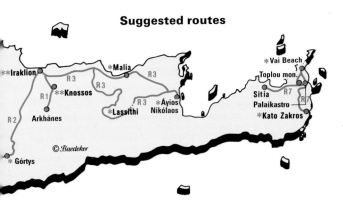

Suggested routes

©Baedeker

which, in a churchyard, is the architecturally interesting church of Áyios Pávlos. The road then runs through a magnificent olive grove to the charming village of Pitsídia, round which artichokes are grown. From there a track leads to the excavation site of Kommós, once one of the ports serving Phaistós. Just beyond the village, from the summit of a pass, there is a beautiful view of Mesará Bay. The road comes to an end at Mátala, which has an attractive little beach edged by limestone cliffs riddled with caves. This is a good place to enjoy a rest from sightseeing.

3. Iráklion to Áyios Nikólaos and Back

Leave Iráklion on the coast road to the east (E75), and at Káto Goúrnes take a road which runs south-east to the Lassíthi plain, passing through some of the most beautiful scenery in Crete. At Potamiés is the monastic church of the Panayía Gouverniótissa, and in the next village but one, Avdoú, there are several interesting Byzantine churches. The road now runs up, with many bends, through a beautiful upland region. Off the road on the left are two villages which offer the opportunity for a restful pause, Mokhós and Krási, which has one of the oldest plane-trees in Crete. Beyond this is the picturesque little monastery of Kardiótissa-Kera, with beautiful frescos.

Distance 175km/109 miles

From the Ambelos pass (900m/2950ft), where the ruins of a number of grain mills can be seen, there is a magnificent view of the beautiful ★Lassíthi plain with its many windmills. Beyond this a road goes off on the right to the village of Psíra, above which is the much visited ★Diktaíon Antron (Dictaean Cave), in which Zeus is supposed to have been born.

The road over the plain continues to Áyios Yeóryios, which has an interesting folk museum. The road which runs east to join the coast road is also very beautiful. 8km/5 miles along the coast road, on the beautiful Gulf of Mirabéllo, is the picturesque little town of ★Áyios Nikólaos.

From Áyios Nikólaos a side trip to ★Kritsá (11km/7 miles south-west) is a must. Just before the village is the famous ★★church of the Panayía

Side trip to Kritsá

Kera, which has the finest frescos in Crete. Beyond this a road goes off
on the right to the impressive remains of the Dorian city of ★Lató, from
which there are superb views.

The pretty village of Kritsá, picturesquely situated on a hill, is famed
for its weaving and its needlework.

4km/2½ miles south of Kritsá is the village of Kroustás. Half way there
is the church of Áyios Ioánnis, with a very fine iconostasis, and 4km/2½
miles south of the village is another church with the same dedication,
with frescos of 1347.

Detour
via Eloúnda

On the way back to Iráklion a detour (23km/14 miles) can be made via
★Eloúnda, situated in a beautiful bay on the coast road to the north,
with the remains of ancient Oloús. From the coast road there are
superb views of the beautiful ★★Gulf of Mirabéllo. From Eloúnda a
boat trip can be taken to the rocky island of Spinalónga, with a ruined
Venetian fortress.

From Eloúnda a road runs north and then west to the very beautiful
village of Kastéli and then continues to rejoin the main road (E75).

On the road to Iráklion a stop should be made at the remains of the
Middle Minoan palace of Mália, the most important Minoan site in
Crete after Knossós and Phaistós.

4. Chaniá to the Samariá Gorge

Distance:
42km/26 miles

From ★**Chaniá** the road runs south-west and then south to Omalós and
the famous Samariá Gorge, one of Crete's scenic high points. 15km/9½
miles from Chaniá it comes to Phournés.

Side trip
to Mesklá

6km/4 miles south-east of Phournés is Mesklá, with the church of
Sotiros Christoú, which has frescos of 1303.

The road continues south through an impressive rocky landscape to
the fertile Omalós plateau. 6km/4 miles south, at the Xylóskalo pass, is
the start of the magnificent ★★Samariá Gorge, 18km/11 miles long.
The walk down the gorge to the coast takes 6 hours. From the village of
Ayía Rouméli, at the mouth of the gorge, a footpath runs 4km/2½ miles
east to the church of Áyios Pávlos, strikingly situated on the sea.

5. Chaniá to the Akrotíri Peninsula

Distance:
24km/15 miles

The road from Chaniá to the Akrotíri peninsula runs past Mt Prophítis
Ilías, on which is the national memorial to the Cretan statesman Elefthérios Venizélos (see Famous People) and his son Sophoklis. The
route eastwards follows the main road to the airport and then turns
north, coming in a few kilometres to the Ayía Triáda monastery, one of
the most important in Crete.

4km/2½ miles farther north on a very beautiful road is the ★Gou-
vernéto monastery, impressively situated on a ridge of hill, from which
there are superb views. From there it is a pleasant walk to the abandoned Katholikó monastery.

6. Réthymnon via Arméni to Préveli Monastery

Distance:
38km/24 miles

From ★**Réthymnon** the road to Ayía Galíni runs south to Arméni,
where there is an interesting necropolis. From there the road continues
south through beautiful scenery. In 12km/7½ miles a side road goes off

A landscape of austere beauty near Zákros

on the right and runs south to Préveli monastery, through striking scenery, passing the grandiose Kourtaliótiko Gorge, to which a path leads down.

A few kilometres beyond the village of Asómatos, with a picturesque Turkish bridge, and a short distance farther on are the ruins of the Kato Moní Préveli (Lower Préveli Monastery). 1km/¾ mile beyond this, in the gorge to the left, is the chapel of Ayía Photiní, which has frescos of around 1500. Then the road comes to the thousand-year-old ★Piso Moní Préveli, in a magnificent situation.

There is good bathing on the palm-shaded Préveli beach.

Sitía via Vái Beach to Káto Zákros

From **Sitía** a road runs east, coming in a few kilometres to Ayía Photiá, where there is an interesting Minoan necropolis. From there the route continues north-east through an austere and barren landscape which has a charm of its own. The fortress-like monastery of Toploú was a centre of resistance to the Turks. In another 6km/4 miles the road comes to a junction from which a road runs north. A short distance along this road a side road on the right runs east to ★Vái Beach, with Crete's only palm grove, which attracts large numbers of visitors.

Distance:
55km/34 miles

2km/1¼ miles north of the junction with the Vái road are the remains of the once powerful ancient city of Itanos.

Side trip
to Itanos

From here the road runs south to Palaíkastro, with the scanty remains of Roussolákkos, the largest Minoan town in Crete after Gourniá. The road ends 25km/15 miles farther south at the remains of Káto Zákros, an important Minoan palace.

Sights
from A to Z

Arkhánes

Arkhánes

D 11

Αρχάνες

Nomós: Iráklion
Chief town of nomós: Iráklion
Population: 4000

Situation and characteristics

The little town of Arkhánes, situated amid vineyards 16km/10 miles south of Iráklion (bus service), is famed for its wine and table grapes, in particular the Rosáki grape.

In the centre of the town is a triangular platía, with a number of coffee-houses.

History

In the Early Minoan period (4th/3rd millennium B.C.) this was an important cult and administrative centre with a residential area and a necropolis outside the town, at Phourní.

The site was excavated by Arthur Evans in 1909, when remains dating from all phases of Minoan civilisation were found.

Sights in Arkhánes

Panayía church

In the platía is the church of the Panayía, which contains a number of valuable and richly carved icons, including the Mother of God and Child, the Dormition of the Mother of God, Christ and disciples in a vineyard and St Nicholas, with scenes from his life.

Minoan excavations

150m/165yd from the entrance to the town (coming from Iráklion) a road goes off on the left, and 100m/110yd along this a side road on the right leads to the Minoan excavations, which are not of great interest.

The partially excavated building, either a palace or a villa, is dated to the Late Minoan period, around 1500 B.C. Something like a dozen rooms have been preserved; in one of them are two column bases and remains of a paved floor.

Surroundings of Arkhánes

Phourní necropolis

On a hill to the north of the town is the Phourní necropolis, one of the largest and most important Bronze Age cemeteries in the Mediterranean area. Since the site is locked and the way there is difficult to find, you should enquire for the custodian (*phýlakas*), who holds the key, at the *kafeníon* in the *platía*. At the near end of the town (signpost) a road runs down on the right, crosses a bridge and comes to a quarry, from which a path (15 minutes) runs up the hill to the site.

Tour of site

The entrance is on the east side of the site. Just beyond the entrance, well to the left, is a Mycenaean tholos, Tholos D (*c.* 1300 B.C.), with a woman's tomb, richly appointed. The tour continues in a northerly direction. Above Tholos D is Tholos E, which is 1000 years older and contained numerous sarcophagi and two *pithoi* (ash-urns). The tombs still higher up date from 2000–1700 B.C.

Beyond this is an enclosed burial area with two tholoi, G and B, and other tombs. Tholos G contained mainly Cycladic material, suggesting that there was a Cycladic settlement here. Away to the left is a rocky area in which votive offerings and animals' bones were found. In the ossuary to the north-east (3rd millennium) numerous skulls and seals, some of them inscribed with hieroglyphs, were found. Another ossuary to the right (4th/3rd millennium) contained mainly secondary burials in *pithoi* and

◀ *The Venetian Harbour, Chaniá: a favourite meeting-place*

Vineyards round Arkhánes

larnakes. The next tholos tomb, B (2000 B.C.), which consists of a dromos, the tomb chamber and a number of other chambers, has a bench running round it; it contained large numbers of skulls, pottery vessels and fragments of frescos.

The next building, in which the finds included a loom and a wine-press, evidently housed working quarters. The artificial cave sanctuary is the only one of its kind on Crete. Tholos A (*c.* 1400 B.C.), an unrobbed Mycenaean tomb, consists of a dromos approaching it from the east, a circular structure over 5m/16ft in diameter and 5m high and a tomb chamber on the south side. The numerous grave goods, including many bronze vessels, valuable jewellery and fine pottery, indicate that this was the tomb of a rich woman.

At the end of the site are seven Mycenaean shaft tombs.

The sanctuary of Anemóspilia ("Caves of the Winds") also lies to the north of Arkhánes, on the northern slopes of Mt Yioúkhtas. Some 200m/220yd beyond the junction with the one-way street in the town a poor gravel road goes off on the right and comes in 3km/2 miles to the excavation site, above the road on the left. Since the site is fenced in you should enquire in Arkhánes for the custodian (*phýlakas*).

Anemóspilia
(Ανεμόσπηλια)

The sanctuary (2100–1800 B.C.) is, visually, not particularly interesting, but it was an archaeological sensation when it was discovered. It consists of three adjoining chambers preceded by a transverse hall, in which numerous vessels were found. In the central chamber there was evidently a monumental wooden cult figure, of which only two feet survived. In the chamber to the east were found numerous vessels and votive offerings.

The sensation was caused by the discovery, in the chamber to the west, of evidence of human sacrifice. Here, on an altar now enclosed in a wooden case, were found the remains of a young man with shackled feet and a bronze dagger with which his carotid artery had been cut. Beside him were

The sanctuary

Arkhánes

found a priest in an ecstatic pose and a priestess who had been killed during the sacrifice by the collapse of the building.

In the outer hall were found the remains of a man holding a valuable libation vessel, no doubt about to offer the blood of the sacrificial victim to the image of the god. Presumably the human sacrifice was made, around 1800 B.C., in the hope of warding off earthquakes, but the ceremony was interrupted by the collapse of the building in an earthquake occurring at that moment.

Church of
Asómatos
(Ασόματος)

Of the village of Asómatos, which lay to the south of Arkhánes in the 16th and 17th centuries, there remains only an interesting little church dedicated to the Archangel Michael, with notable frescos of 1315. The church (key from taverna amid trees on platía) is reached by taking a field track (2km/1¼ miles) which goes off on the left beyond the far end of Arkhánes and then keeping left; the church, a simple one-room structure, lies below the track, half concealed.

The paintings, in a festive and sometimes vivid and lively style, are mainly of scenes from the life of Christ and the Archangel Michael.

★Mt Yioúkhtas
(Γιούχτας)

Mt Yioúkhtas (811m/2661ft), to the west of Arkhánes, is a long ridge whose outline can, with sufficient imagination, be seen as resembling a bearded head. It is said to represent the face of Zeus, who according to a Cretan legend is buried in a cave on the hill. This assertion gave Cretans the reputation among mainland Greeks of being liars, since for them Zeus was immortal. No trace of the cave has been found.

A very poor road runs up to the summit of the hill. The ascent is worth it mainly for the magnificent views from the top, extending as far as Iráklion.

On the south peak is the church of Aphéndi Christoú, with a series of four chapels. On the feast of the Transfiguration (August 6th) the church draws worshippers from far and near.

From the last bend before the road reaches the south peak a path runs up to the north peak, on which there is a broadcasting transmitter. Just in front of it is a Minoan peak sanctuary, enclosed by a fence. The sanctuary, which was in use between 2100 and 1700 B.C., is surrounded by a ring wall (diameter 735m/800yd). Within the sanctuary and on the large terrace on which it stood were found numerous idols and votive offerings.

Vathýpetro
(Βαθύπετρο)

3km/2 miles south of Arkhánes, finely situated on a ridge of hill above a beautiful valley, is the Minoan villa of Vathýpetro (open: 9am–2.30pm).

The house was built about 1700 B.C. and abandoned about 1600. It was probably originally planned as a large palace-type residence, the completed part of which was used as a country house.

Going right from the entrance, we come into a court and then, turning right again and crossing another court, to the only three-aisled sanctuary so far found in Crete. On the west side of the court is the principal room of the villa, with a columned porch, to the west of which are a store-room and other subsidiary rooms. Beyond this, at the west end of the villa, is a room containing a recess, interpreted as a treasure-chamber with a cult niche. Adjoining this is a large room (roofed) with two pillars, and beyond this again is another large room with four pillars.

A flight of steps leads to the most interesting complex of rooms (roofed) in the villa, containing a number of *pithoi* and a wine-press. This indicates that wine was made in Minoan times.

Áyios Vasílios
Áyios Ioánnis
Pródromos

To the east of the village of Áyios Vasílios (14km/8½ miles south-east of Arkhánes) is the church of Áyios Ioánnis Pródromos (St John the Baptist), with fine frescos of 1291.

In the apse is a figure of the Panayía (Mother of God), with an Annunciation above it and fathers of the church below it; on the north vaulting are John the Baptist and SS. George and Demetrius on horseback; and on the south vaulting are the burial of John the Baptist and SS Barbara and Cyriace and the Archangel Michael.

Αγία Τριάδα

Nomós: Iráklion
Chief town of nomós: Iráklion

Some 2km/1¼ miles west of the Phaistós excavations, on the northern edge   Situation
of the hill and linked with the palace by a paved road, are the remains of the
Minoan villa of Ayía Triáda (open: Mon.–Sat. 8.30am–3pm, Sun.
9.30am–2.30pm). The road from Phaistós is signposted. The remains are a
short distance below the car park.

For the dating of the Early Minoan (EM I–III), Middle Minoan (MM I–III)
and Late Minoan (LM I–III) periods see the table on p. 34.

Since its ancient name is not known, this large Minoan villa is named after   The ★villa
the 14th century Byzantine church of Ayía Triáda (Holy Trinity), 250m/275yd
south-west, and the former village of that name.

This area was occupied from the 3rd millennium onwards. The villa was
built around 1550 B.C., after the construction of the new palace of Phaistós,
but was destroyed by fire around 1450 B.C. Later, in Late Minoan III or in
Mycenaean times, the area was reoccupied, as is shown by the extensive
building then undertaken. During the Greek classical period Ayía Triáda
was abandoned as a place of residence but remained a cult site, with a
temple dedicated to Zeus Velkhanós.

The site was excavated by Italian archaeologists from 1902 onwards,
bringing to light the remains of the villa and a wealth of material, most of it
now in the Archaeological Museum in Iráklion. The finds included frescos,
fine steatite vases, including the unique Harvester Vase (illustration,
p. 133), and the largest collection of Linear A tablets so far found. The most

Grand staircase in the Ayía Triáda villa

81

Villa of Ayía Triáda

N
↑

30m

Agora

Rampa del mare

19

Áyios Yeóryios

Entrance

1 Minoan street	8 Megaron	15 Principal apartment
2 Shrine	9/10 Store-rooms	16 Court
3 Servants' quarters	11 Corridor	17 Archive room
4 Store-rooms	12 Store-rooms	18 Room with
5/6 Staircase	13 Portico	frescos
7 Living quarters	14 Private room	19 Pillared hall

important item was the famous Ayía Triáda sarcophagus (illustration, p. 138).

Tour of site

To the east of the entrance to the villa, which has an atypical L-shaped plan, is a Late Minoan sanctuary in which frescos with dolphin and octopus motifs were found. To the north are servants' quarters, to the west store-rooms. The south court is believed to have been the scene of cult ceremonies. At its north-east corner is a flight of steps running down to the market square and the residential quarters of the town. To the north of the court another staircase leads up to living quarters on the upper floor, with a number of handsome small rooms lit by light shafts. To the west is a megaron of Late Minoan III, probably one of the earliest princely buildings erected by the Mycenaeans in Crete. Within this structure are store-rooms, still containing *pithoi*. The famous Harvester Vase was found here. The Byzantine chapel of Áyios Yeóryios above the court, which dates from 1302, preserves some frescos.

A few paces west of the chapel is the south end of the villa's west wing, in a corridor in which was found the Chieftain's Cup, one of the masterpieces of Minoan art. Adjoining this are store-rooms. To the north is a two-columned portico giving access to a double light-well. At the east end is a private room (now with a modern roof) with benches on three sides. A door on the north side of this room leads into a smaller chamber, perhaps a bedroom, with a raised slab of gypsum which may have been the base of a bed.

Returning through the light-well and the portico, we come into the principal apartment. On its north side is a door opening into a court, perhaps a terrace, with fine views of the sea and Mount Ida. To the east of the court is the archive room, where large number of Linear A tablets were found. Immediately east is a small room in which the Wild Cat Fresco was discovered. The terrace which the excavators called the Rampa del Mare is reached on a staircase to the north. At its east end is a hall with five pillars. Farther north is a Late Minoan residential district, with the agora (market square).

A gate at the north-east corner of the site gives access to a necropolis containing two tholos tombs and a shaft grave, in which the famous Ayía Triáda sarcophagus, decorated with scenes in the afterlife, was found.

Necropolis

Áyios Nikólaos (Ágios Nikólaos)

D 15

Άγιος Νικόλαος

Chief town of Lassíthi nomós
Population: 8500

In addition to being the chief town of the nomós of Lassíthi, Áyios Nikólaos is one of Greece's leading tourist centres. With excellent beaches in the surrounding area, numerous hotels, some of them of the highest standard, and wide scope for excursions to places of interest in the immediate area and eastern Crete, it attracts great numbers of visitors, many of them spending long holidays here.

General

The particular charm of the picturesque little town of Áyios Nikólaos, on the west side of the very beautiful Gulf of Mirabéllo, lies in its Mediterranean atmosphere. It is a town of lively activity which has inevitably been affected by tourism but has avoided the rowdiness and noise of some tourist resorts. Although the Platía Venizélou is the actual centre of the town its life revolves round the harbour and the beautiful little Lake Voulisméni, where there are many busy restaurants and cafés. The town beaches are shingle or rocks; the nearest sandy one is 2km/1¼ mile away at Almiros.

The ★ town

In antiquity the town was called *Lató pros Kamára*, and from the 3rd century B.C. it was the port of the city of Lató i Etéra. In Byzantine times it remained an important commercial port. Following the fourth Crusade, in the 13th century, the area was hotly contested by the Genoese and Venetians.

History

A fortress built by either the Genoese or the Venetians was called Mirabello because of the beautiful views it enjoyed. The port lost its importance when the Venetians built the more sheltered Porto di San Nicolo north-west of the town, in the Eloúnda area. Around 1870 Sphakiots from western Crete settled here and named the place, then barely inhabited, after the church of Áyios Nikólaos, dedicated to the patron of seafarers, on the promontory flanking the harbour.

Áyios Nikólaos (Ágios Nikólaos)

The picturesque little town of Áyios Nikólaos

Sights in Áyios Nikólaos

★ Lake Voulisméni

Adjoining the harbour is the picturesque Lake Voulisméni, surrounded by rock walls. 64m/210ft deep, it is linked with the harbour by a short canal. Apart from Lake Kournás in the nomós of Chaniá it is the only freshwater lake in Crete. The canal linking it with the sea was cut in the 19th century. Legend has it that the goddess Athene bathed in the lake.

★ Archaeological Museum

Opening times
daily except Mon.
8.30am–3pm

The Archaeological Museum, the most important museum in Crete after the Archaeological Museum in Iráklion, was built in 1970 to house the rich new archaeological finds from eastern Crete, which had previously been held in Iráklion.

With its superb vases, its other remarkable vessels and its strange and mysterious idols, the museum is a must for visitors. The exhibits range in date from the Neolithic to the end of the Greco-Roman period, offering an excellent survey of the development of art in Crete.

For the dating of the Early Minoan (EM I–III), Middle Minoan (MM I–III) and Late Minoan (LM I–III) periods see the table on p. 34.

Tour of
museum

The museum is best seen by going through the rooms in clockwise order. The numbers of the rooms and cases described below correspond to the numbers on the plan.

Room I

Material of the Neolithic and Early Minoan periods (6000–2100 B.C.).

Case 1

Early Minoan material from Phournoú Koriphí (Myrtos): vessels of mottled Vasilikí ware, figures, weights, spindle-whorls and the earliest bronze fish-hooks found in Crete.

The following cases (48, 4, 5 and 46) mainly contain material from the Early Minoan necropolis of Ayía Photiá near Sitía.

Spouted jugs and bronze daggers with a reinforced central rib, including the longest Early Minoan dagger (32cm/1ft). Of particular interest is an excellently preserved dagger with a bent tip which was found beside the dead man. The dagger, like the man, had been "killed" so that it would be able to find its owner in the afterlife.

A rare item is the plain black jug with a large handle and a high spout.

Case 48

Grey burnished ware.

Case 3

Pyxis with incised zigzag pattern; cups and bowls.

Case 4

An hour-glass shaped cup with incised ornament, a fine example of the Pýrgos style; obsidian blades and libation vessels.

Case 5

Bones of the Neolithic period and pottery from a variety of sites.

Case 6

A Neolithic phallus-shaped idol from the Pelekita Cave, Zákros: an unusual item for Crete.

Case 2

An unusual item is a bird-shaped vase with incised decoration. Other interesting vessels are a large *pyxis* with a conical lid and a *kernos* with two *pyxides* on a tall foot. The pear-shaped vase in glossy black ware is the earliest vase type imported from the Cyclades.

Case 46

Early and Middle Minoan periods (2500–1900 B.C.).

Room II

Early Minoan material from Mýrtos: cups, bowls, spouted jugs and Vasilikí and Mýrtos ware. An attractive item is the tripod-footed *pyxis* with a flat lid.

Case 8

Unusual objects from the Early Minoan (II–III) necropolis on the island of Mókhlos: gold jewellery in the form of ribbons, leaves and flowers (e.g. a

Case 9

Archaeological Museum

Áyios Nikólaos

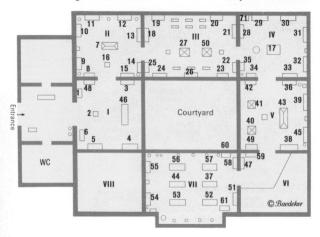

I   Neolithic and Early Minoan
    (600–2100 B.C.)
II Early and Middle Minoan
    (2500–1900 B.C.)
III Middle and Late Minoan
    (1900–1050 B.C.)
IV Late Minoan and Geometric
    (1500–750 B.C.)

V   Geometric and Classi-
    cal
    (800–450 B.C.)
VI Archaic and Classical
    (550–400 B.C.)
VII Hellenistic and Roman
    (4th c. B.C. to
    2nd c. A.D.)

hairpin in the form of a daisy) and a diadem, the finest item of jewellery in the museum, with abstract figures of goats. The jewellery was found in a silver vessel which had been flattened by pressure; vessels of stone or con-glomerate, for example the deli-cately coloured "teapot" vase; mottled Vasilikí ware.

Case 10   Stone vessels from various sites and finds from the Petso-phás/Palaíokhora peak sanctuary.

Case 11   Material from various sites:

The Goddess of Mýrtos

stone vessels; two interesting examples of light-on-dark painting; a conical bowl used as a drinking vessel; a cup with a large handle and rich ornament.

Middle Minoan stone and pottery vessels, e.g. spouted jugs from a tomb at Zákros. — Case 12

Early Minoan material from Mýrtos: vases, seals, figurines and loom weights. Particularly fine is a light-coloured vase with red incised decoration in Mýrtos style (14). — Cases 13 and 14

The "Goddess of Mýrtos", from Phourní, is the museum's principal treasure, a masterpiece of Early Minoan II art. This highly stylised figure has a bell-shaped body, an elongated neck and a tiny head. The breasts are added in relief and the pubic triangle is painted. In one arm the goddess holds a small jug decorated with red lines in the Mýrtos style, the mouth of which is also the mouth of the main vessel. — Case 15

Material of the Middle and Late Minoan periods (1900–1050 B.C.). — **Room III**

Finds from Middle Minoan peak sanctuaries: figures of worshippers, the bare breasts of the women no doubt having a ritual significance in connection with fertility. A unique item is a pair of bull's horns in stucco. There is an interesting example of a bull's head *rhyton*. — Case 18

Finds from the Middle Minoan peak sanctuary of Priniás. Particularly fine is a *rhyton* in the form of a large bull's head (with some restoration). — Case 19

Finds from the Late Minoan villa at Makriyiálos. Particularly fine is an alabastron in the Marine style (21). — Cases 20 and 21

Material from tombs (LM III) at Myrsíni: very beautiful vases. An interesting item is the lid of an incense-burner with horns of consecration. A very elegant three-handled amphora with papyrus decoration. — Case 22

Late Minoan material from Sitía and other sites in eastern Crete: stone vessels, painted pottery in the Floral and Marine styles; loom weights. — Case 23

Material from Makriyiálos, including a conical marble "communion chalice", discoloured in a fire. — Case 26

Material from the Late Minoan necropolis at Mílatos, near Sitía. Notable items are an ivory sphinx, an unusual ivory figure of a crocodile and a pouring bowl with fine incised ornament. — Case 24

Votive offerings from peak sanctuaries: worshippers, animals, human torsos. The male figures are not depicted with phalluses, but wear the typical Minoan loincloth. — Case 25
   In the first case in the centre in a stone vase in the form of a triton shell, with two animal divinities offering a libation.

Material from various sites in eastern Crete. A rare example of a clay bar from Mália, with an inscription in the still undeciphered Linear A script. A fine Late Minoan (I) gold fibula with a blackberry motif and signs in Linear A. — Case 27

Jewellery from various sites, including a small bull's head of the finest gold foil and a miniature octagonal shield of ivory. — Case 50
   In the last case in the middle of the room is a Late Minoan (IIIA) figure of a female worshipper from Myrsíni with a cylindrical lower body and hands folded on her breast in a cult gesture.

Áyios Nikólaos (Ágios Nikólaos)

The sarcophagi in this room come from various sites and date from Late Minoan III. The Minoans buried their dead in short, high sarcophagi, of which there were two forms – the chest type, with feet and a lid, and the bath-tub type. Archaeologists now think that this latter type was used for bathing as each has a plughole at the bottom.

Room IV   Late Minoan and Geometric periods (1500–750 B.C.).

Case 28   Material from the LM IIIB necropolis at Kritsá: chalice-like bowls on tall feet.

Cases 71, 29 and 30   Material from various sites in eastern Crete: two three-handled amphoras with bird motifs and suspended lyres in dark colours on a light ground; a broad-rimmed handled bowl, a masterpiece of Minoan bronze-working (29).

Case 31   Finds from various sites: vessels in the form of ducks, fine masks.

Case 32   Finds from the Sitía area: *pithos* decorated with simple lines and circles, the first signs of geometric decoration.

Case 33   Geometric pottery from the Sitía area: a greyish-brown *hydria* with a painted bee, marking the transition to the Orientalising period.

Cases 34 and 35   Finds from various necropolises (LM III). An unusual item is a tripartite cult vessel (34) with four small birds, their wings spread, symbolising the epiphany (appearance) of the god. Characteristic of this period are the stirrup jugs (particularly fine example, with octopus motif, in case 34). Light-coloured urn (35) with stylised red horns of consecration, one of the earliest evidences of the practice of cremation.

In the centre of the room is an unusual burial of a child in a miniature tholos tomb, transferred to the museum in its original form.

Case 17   Bronze implements and weapons from various tombs. Three large and elegant daggers with ivory hilts.

Room V   Geometric and Classical periods (800–450 B.C.).

Cases 36, 39, 45, 38 and 49   Material from the Sitía area: Daedalic and Archaic pottery statuettes, sometimes only heads, with protruding eyes, with layered coiffures and painted faces; some of them show the "Archaic smile".

Case 40   Daedalic terracottas from the Áyios Nikólaos area. A notable item is a slab with a rare relief figure of a warrior drawing a child behind him (perhaps Achilles and Troilos).

Case 41   Daedalic and Oriental objects from the Anávlokhos peak sanctuary.

Case 42   Terracottas and pottery from Anávlokhos: statuettes with movable heads and inserted eyes. Some of them are rather coarsely made.

In the central case is a finely carved head (originally painted) with the "Archaic smile".

Case 43   Finds from Oloúnda and other sites: miniature animals (lions, pigs, hens, tortoises, etc.), symbols of fertility and marital fidelity.

Room VI   Room VI (still in process of arrangement) displays material of the Archaic and Classical periods (550–400 B.C.).

Cases 59 and 47   Finds from Oloús: terracottas of human beings and animals (a siren); pottery, including bowls, small vases and a large *pyxis* (47).

Room VII   Material of the Greco-Roman period (4th c. B.C. to 2nd c. A.D.), mostly from the Potamós necropolis, Áyios Nikólaos.

Double-handled lidded vessels, bronze vessels, stone reliefs.

Case 51

Terracotta female figures, plain pottery vessels, currycombs.

Case 61

Oil lamps, amphoras, gems, loom weights.

Case 52

Vases, terracottas, oil lamps.
   At the window is an interesting bath-tub. Beside it, against the wall, is a tombstone depicting a husband and wife.

Case 53

Pottery and small objects.
   On the rear wall is a skull with a unique gold circlet of stylised leaves. A silver coin with the head of the Emperor Tiberius was intended to secure the dead man's admission to the world of the dead.

Cases 54–56

Weights, vases, bronze coins.

Case 57

Red-figured vases; oil lamps, including one with 70 openings (58).

Cases 60 and 58

A bronze dish and mirror, bronze currycombs, rings.

Case 37

Perfume bottles, terracottas, a spherical bronze aryballos from the tomb of the man with the gold circlet, a two-handled bronze dish.

Case 44

Other Sights in Áyios Nikólaos

On the ground floor of the harbourmaster's office is the Folk Museum (open: daily except Sat. 10am–1.30pm and 6–9.30pm), with a collection which includes fine woven fabrics, woodcarving, costumes and Byzantine icons.

Folk Museum

Áyios Nikólaos, one of the oldest churches in Crete

Áyios Nikólaos (Ágios Nikólaos)

Church of
Áyios Nikólaos

On the peninsula north-east of the town (within the grounds of the Minos
Palace Hotel, where the key can be obtained) is the 10th century church of
Áyios Nikólaos, one of the oldest churches, still intact, in Crete. This aisleless barrel-vaulted church, a clearly articulated and harmonious structure,
is of particular interest for its remains of frescos. These show the influence
of the period of Iconoclasm (726–843), when figural representation was
banned in churches and the only painting was ornamental. The only example of this ornamental style in Crete can be seen here, though it was
overpainted with figures in the 14th century. In the apse are inscriptions left
by 18th century visitors.

Surroundings of Áyios Nikólaos

Áyii Pántes
(Αγιοι Πάντες)

The offshore island of Áyii Pántes is a reserve for Cretan wild goats.

Psíra
(Ψείρα)

On the island of Psíra ("Louse Island"), at the east end of the Gulf of
Mirabéllo, are the remains of a port settlement of Middle to Late Minoan
times. It can be reached by boat from Áyios Nikólaos or from the village of
Mókhlos. Excavation brought to light frescos and reliefs of high quality,
and the underwater explorer Jacques Cousteau discovered the remains of
a pier and fragments of pottery in the sea.

★★Gulf of
Mirabéllo
(Κόγπος
Μιραμπέλλχυ:
illustration, p. 7)

The beautiful Gulf of Mirabéllo, with its deep blue water, is a delight to the
eye.
    There are fine views of the bay from the road to Eloúnda – the higher the
road, the better the view – and from the very beautiful coast road between
Áyios Nikólaos and Gourniá.

Eloúnda
(Ελούνδα)

11km/7 miles north of Áyios Nikólaos, beautifully situated in a bay sheltered by the peninsula of Spinalónga, is Eloúnda. Well provided with
amenities for visitors and with a small, shallow natural harbour, it is a
popular tourist resort.

Oloús
(Ολούς)

At the near end of the resort (coming from Áyios Nikólaos) a road goes off
on the right to the isthmus which links Spinalónga with the mainland. The
road runs past a number of large ponds, originally constructed by the
Venetians, which until recently were still used as salt pans.
    On the isthmus, now traversed by a small canal, are three disused
windmills. Here the remains of the ancient city of Oloús can be seen, now
partly under the sea. Of particular importance in the classical and Hellenistic periods, it is believed to have been the port of Dréros, lying inland to the
west. The town is said to have possessed a figure of the goddess Britomartis created by Daedalus. Around the beginning of the Christian era it
was notorious as the haunt of pirates. Later, probably in the 4th century,
earthquake shocks caused the isthmus to sink, so that part of the ancient
city was drowned by the sea.

Basilica

Continuing to the right past the windmills, a signpost on the left, just
beyond a bar, points to the site of a three-aisled Early Christian basilica, of
which little remains but fragments of a very beautiful mosaic pavement
with ornamental and marine motifs.

Spinalónga
Island
(Σπιναλόγκα:
illustration, p. 8/9)

At the northern tip of the Spinalónga peninsula is the tiny rocky island of
the same name (Kalydón; area 200 by 300m), which can be reached by boat
from Eloúnda or Áyios Nikólaos. On it is a fortress, one of the strongest in
Crete, which was built by the Venetians in 1579 to protect the port of
Eloúnda. It was regarded as impregnable, and it continued to be held by the
Venetians after the Turkish conquest of Crete (1669), providing a place of
refuge for many Cretans. Finally in 1715 it was ceded to the Turks by treaty
and remained in their hands until 1898.

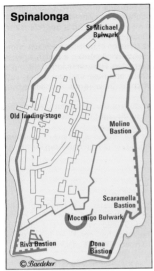

Spinalonga

St Michael Bulwark

Old landing-stage

Molino Bastion

Scaramella Bastion

Mocenigo Bulwark

Riva Bastion

Dona Bastion

© Baedeker

From 1903 to 1957 there was a leper colony on the island. As happened almost everywhere in the world, lepers were excluded from society and compelled to live and die here in isolation. They took over the houses which had been abandoned by Turks, and a kind of community grew up on the island. Some of the lepers even married, and their healthy children were sent to an orphanage on the mainland.

There was no hospital on the island until 1937. Then in 1957 the leper colony was closed down and the last lepers were transferred to a hospital in Athens. The island is now uninhabited.

Leper colony

Visitors land at the south end of the fortress (open: daily 8.30am–3pm). Here, on the left, is the Riva Bastion, under which is a passage leading into the interior; to the right is the Dona Bastion, with the leper colony's cemetery.

Fortress

On the east side of the island was the main defensive line, with the Scaramella and Molino Bastions. In the centre of the island, higher up, is the massive semicircular Mocenigo Bulwark, which houses a battery of cannon (in 1630 there were 35). On a rock in front of the entrance are numerous scratched drawings (sailing ships, coats of arms, etc.), probably the work of lepers.

A second wall runs along the crest of the hill. On the west side are houses and store-rooms and the main gate. At the northern tip is the St Michael Bastion.

The old fishing village of Pláka, 5km/3 miles north of Eloúnda, is now a rising seaside resort, with the usual undesirable side effects such as ruined buildings and over-development. There is good surfing on the beach. Boats take visitors to the island of Spinalónga.

Pláka (Πλάκα)

With its old Venetian mansions and wrought-iron gates and railings, Kastélli (20km/12½ miles north-west of Áyios Nikólaos) is one of the most beautiful villages in the region.

Kastélli (Καστέλλι)

An avenue of tall plane-trees leads from Kastélli to the neighbouring village of Phourní, which has a splendid show of almond-blossom at the end of March.

Phourní (Φουρνή)

8km/5 miles north of Kastélli, high above the sea, lies Moní Aretíou, a once flourishing monastery founded around 1600. Surrounded by tall cypresses and ancient fig-trees, the monastery was long an abandoned ruin but is now being restored. From here there are wide-ranging views.

Moní Aretíou

22km/14 miles north-west of Áyios Nikólaos and 2km/1¼ miles north-east of the village of Neápolis are the scanty remains of ancient Dréros, which was an important city in the Archaic period. A path (10 minutes) leads up to the site, on a hill saddle.

Dréros (Δρήρος)

91

Áyios Nikólaos (Ágios Nikólaos)

On the west side of the site are the remains of buildings laid out on terraces. Excavation has brought to light the massive foundations of a sanctuary of Apollo of the 7th century B.C., one of the most important and best preserved sanctuaries of the Archaic period in Crete.

Within the sanctuary were found the remains of an altar for burnt offerings and a column base, and, in the south-west corner, a bench against which a lower stone cist had been constructed. Here were found the most important items recovered from the site – one male and two female cult figures of beaten bronze on wooden cores (now in the Archaeological Museum in Iráklion).

To the east of the temple is a large cistern of the 3rd century, and to the north is a flight of steps leading down to the agora, on the south side of which can be seen tiers of stone seating.

On the western summit of the saddle is a temple of Athena Polioukhos, and on the eastern summit are fortifications ranging in date from Roman to Venetian times.

★Kritsá (Κριτσά)

The town

The pretty little town of Kritsá, picturesquely situated on the slopes of a hill, lies 11km/7 miles south-west of Áyios Nikólaos. Visitors will find many shops selling the famed local weaving and needlework – not all made in Greece. In spite of this, however, the town has contrived to preserve something of its original character and tranquillity. Its main tourist attraction is the church of the Panayía Kera.

"Greek Passion"

Kritsá was the setting for the film "Greek Passion", based on a novel by Nikos Kazantzákis (see Famous People), shot here by the French director Jules Dassin in 1957, using local actors. The film depicts Christ's Passion, with a mingling of fiction and reality, involving the misuse of power by the leaders of the village, which finally ends in violence.

★★Panayía Kera
(Παναγία Κερα)

One of the finest creations of Byzantine art is the church of the Panayía Kera (open: Tues.–Sun. 8.30am–3pm), which lies on the right of the road from Áyios Nikólaos, 1km/¾ mile before Kritsá. Its picturesque situation in a grove of pines and cypresses gives it a pleasant atmosphere of tranquillity.

The church is famed for its expressive frescos (restored), the finest in Crete.

The Panayía Kera (church of the Mother of God as Mistress) is a handsome three-aisled structure, harmonious in effect in spite of the fact that the three aisles date from different periods. The oldest of the three is the central aisle, built in the mid 13th century, partly destroyed at the end of the century and later rebuilt. It has a shallow dome borne on a drum. The barrel-vaulted and apsed south aisle, dedicated to St Anne, dates from the first half of the 14th century and the north aisle, dedicated to St Anthony, from the middle of that century. The massive buttresses were added later.

Frescos

The frescos are of varying quality. The oldest are in the central aisle, the main apse and the drum (mid 13th c.); the others in these areas date from the end of the 13th century. The south aisle was painted at the time it was built.

The paintings in the central aisle show that from the Middle Byzantine period onwards the various images and scenes were arranged in strict hierarchical order, from the supreme divine power at the highest levels by way of the heavenly hierarchies to the world of men. Particularly fine is the representation of the Ascension. Notable too is the realistic figure of St Anne in the south aisle. The most expressive of the paintings are those in the north aisle. The individual figures and scenes can be identified from the plan and legend on pp. 94/95.

The church of the Panayía Kera, with the finest frescos in Crete ▶

Áyios Nikólaos (Ágios Nikólaos)

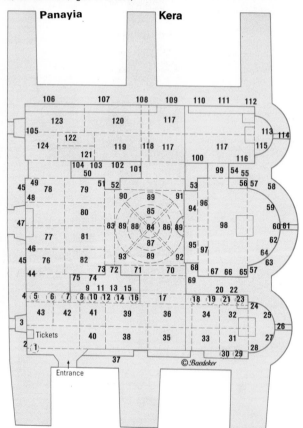

Panayia   Kera

Other Sites in the Surrounding Area

★ **Lató**
(Λατώ)

3km/2 miles north of Kritsá are the remains of the Dorian city of Lató (open: 9am–3pm). It can be reached either on the road which branches off on the right at the near end of Kritsá or on a footpath from the Panayía Kera church which starts beyond the little taverna and joins the road to Lató.

From the site, which lies on a hill, there are superb views of the surrounding hills and the Gulf of Mirabéllo.

History

The city of Lató i Etéra, as it is called in a treaty of the 2nd century B.C., was founded in the 8th or 7th century B.C. It is a typical Dorian town, laid out on a hill with two summits, with its centre on the saddle between them. The remains now visible date from the 5th and 4th centuries. The town's port was Lató pros Kamára, on the site of present-day Áyios Nikólaos. Excavations were begun by French archaeologists around 1900 and have been resumed in recent years.

Tour of site

A tour of Lató should begin at the lower town gate so as to get a general idea of the site as a whole. From there a stepped street runs up to the town centre. On the right are passed two small shops and then a dyer's workshop

ICONOGRAPHY

South aisle

1 St Theophano
2 St Zosimus
3 Donor's inscription
4 St Mary the Egyptian
5 St Justin
6 St John
7 St Martin
8 St Exacustodianus
9 St Irene
10 St Anthony
11 St Cyriace
12 St Maximilian
13 St Barbara
14 St Iamblichus
15 Archangel
16 St Constantine

17 Ornaments
18 St Samonas
19 St Gurias
20 St Leo
21 St Alexius
22 St Romanus
23 Hermit
24 St Peter of Alexandria
25 St Gregory
26 St Anne
27 St Athanasius
28 St Eleutherius
29 St Theodulus
30 St Zoticus
31 Thank-offering
   in Joachim's house

32 Annunciation to
   Joachim
33 St Anne's prayer
34 Meeting of Joachim
   and Anne
35 Birth of the Virgin
36 Mary blessed by
   the priests
37 St Theodore
38 The Caresses
39 Mary Testing the Water
40 Presentation of
   Mary in the Temple
41 Joseph's Dream
42 Journey to Bethlehem
43 Mary with high priest

Central aisle

44 Archangel
45 Torments of Hell
46 St Demetrius
47 Crucifixion
48 St Constantine
49 St Helen
50 St George
51 St Francis
52 St Sergius
53 St Cyricus
54 St Titus
55 St Andrew
56 St Stephen
57 The Annunciation
58 Archangel Gabriel
59 St John Chrysostom
60 Martyr
61 Panayía
62 St Basil

63 Archangel Michael
64 St Gregory
65 St Polycarp
66 St Eleutherius
67 St Romanus
68 St Julitta
69 Christ and the
   Mother of God
70 Pentecost
71 Female martyr
72 St Bacchus
73 St Peter
74 St Anne and Mary
75 St Andrew
76 Paradise
77 Descent into Hades
78 Herod's Feast
79 Mary in the Temple
80 Last Supper

81 Nativity of Christ
82 Massacre of
   the Innocents
83 Mercurius, Nicetas
84 Angel
85 Palm-bearers
86 St Lazarus
87 Baptism of Christ
88 Christ in the Temple
89 The twelve Prophets
90 St Luke
91 St Matthew
92 St Mark
93 St John
94 St Panteleimon
95 St Hermolaus
96 King Solomon
97 King David
98 Ascension of Christ

North aisle

99 St Simon Stylite
100 St Anthony
101 St Eugenius
102 St Mardarius
103 St Orestes
104 St Anempodistus
105 Last Judgment
106 Church Founder
107 St Polychronia
108 St George Diasorites

109 St Anastasia
110 Hosea
111 St John
   Calybite
112 St Theodosius
   the Coenobiarch
113 Glorification
114 Christ Pantocrator
115 St John
   Chrysostom

116 St Macarius
117 Last Judgment
118 Angel
119 Paradise
120 Choir of martyrs
   and holy women
121 Foolish virgins
122 Wise virgins
123 Apocalypse
124 Last Judgment

containing a cistern, a water basin and a trough. Beyond this is a miller's shop, with a stone hand-mill. Opposite this is a watch-tower. Farther up the street are a number of adjoining rooms, the one in the middle containing a cistern, a stone mortar and a large vat.

The street leads to a small square, to the south-west of which a tomb was found; to the north-east are the remains of a flight of steps leading to the upper floor. We now go round a long hall, pass an exedra and reach the central feature of the town, the agora. This served as a meeting-place and also a cult centre, as is shown by a small temple in the centre of the agora. Next to it is a deep cistern. From here a wide and handsome flight of steps

Remains of the Dorian city of Lató

flanked by towers leads up to the *prytaneion*, which has benches round the walls, and beyond this the refectory, also with stone benches. On the south-eastern summit of the hill are the remains of a temple and a theatre.

Church of Áyios Ioánnis

2km/1¼ miles south of Kritsá on the road to Kroustás, on the right, is the church of Áyios Ioánnis, which once belonged to Toploú monastery in eastern Crete. It is three-aisled, with a transverse aisle at the end of the two south aisles. It is notable for its magnificent iconostases.

4km/2½ miles beyond this is Kroustás, and in another 4km/2½ miles a road goes off on the left to another church of Áyios Ioánnis which is famed for its fine frescos of 1347. In the apse is a *deesis*, below this four fathers of the Church and above it an Ascension. In the barrel vaulting are scenes from the life of Christ, and below this, on both sides, friezes of six medallions containing saints. On the west side of the iconostasis is a particularly fine Nativity of Christ.

Katharó plain
(Οποπέδιον Καθαροζύ)

The lonely Katharó plain, lying at an altitude of 1150m/3775ft, is reached on a 17m/11 mile long track from Kritsá. Populated only between May 20th and November 20th, it produces fruit, wine and corn.

Chaniá (Khaniá) B 5

Χανιά

Chief town of the nomós of Chaniá
Population: 62,000

Situation and characteristics

Chaniá, Crete's second largest town, lies on the north coast of the island, in the south-east corner of Chaniá Bay, which opens off the Cretan Sea.

It is a good base from which to explore western Crete, whose attractions lie more in its scenic beauties than in its archaeological sites.

The statesman Elefthérios Venizélos (see Famous People), who was born in the nearby village of Mourniés and is buried on the Akrotíri peninsula, immediately east of the town, is particularly venerated in Chaniá.

The most attractive part of the town is the beautiful Venetian harbour, lined by tavernas and cafés, with the former mosque and the picturesque Topanás quarter with its narrow winding streets. It is an essential part of every visitor's programme to spend some time in the harbour area.

★ The town

This was an important centre in Minoan times. In the Classical period it played a leading role in western Crete, even after its capture by Rome in 69 B.C. In the 13th century it was re-founded by the Venetians under the name of La Canea on the site of ancient Cydonia, and after an interlude of Genoese rule (1267–90) it enjoyed a period of economic prosperity and intellectual flowering, culminating in its heyday around the end of the 16th century. In 1537 the Venetians surrounded the town with walls as a defence against Turkish attack, but in spite of this it was the first Cretan town to be taken by the Turks (1645). Thereafter Chaniá acquired a strongly Turkish character. In 1851 it became the headquarters of the Turkish administration on Crete, and during the various risings against the Turks Turkish inhabitants sought refuge in the town.

History

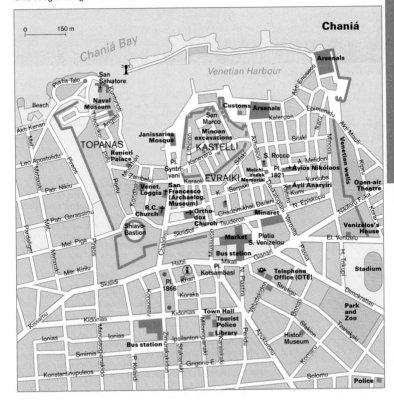

The Venetian Harbour of Chaniá, a must for every visitor

After Crete's liberation from Turkish rule in 1898 Chaniá became capital of the autonomous Cretan state headed by Prince George of Greece as governor-general. The town suffered severely from the events of the Second World War. Until 1971 it was the administrative centre of the whole of Crete.

Sights in Chaniá

★Harbour

On the north side of the town is the picturesque Venetian harbour, the lively hub of the town's life. It was formed in the 14th century by the construction of a mole on which the Venetians and later the Turks carried out executions. Being relatively shallow and insufficiently sheltered from the north winds, the harbour was never of any great importance and was soon supplanted by Soúda Bay. The entrance to the harbour was flanked by minarets, the stumps of which can still be seen. It is now used only by small boats.

Near the east end of the harbour are two groups of Venetian arsenals built in 1497: long stone halls with massive barrel-vaulted roofs, originally covered by lead, which were used for building galleys, housing them during the winter and storing war material. There were originally 23 of them, of which seven survive on the south quay and two on the east quay.

At the end of the mole is a Venetian lighthouse, restored during the period of Egyptian rule in the mid 19th century. From here there are fine views of the harbour, the town and the peaks of the White Mountains.

Janissaries' Mosque

On the east side of the outer harbour is the imposing Janissaries' Mosque, built in 1645, immediately after the Turkish capture of the town. The janissaries were an elite fighting troop formed from Christian boys carried off by the Turks, converted to Islam and subjected to a rigorous military training.

In the picturesque Topanás quarter ▶

Chaniá (Khaniá)

The dome of the mosque forms a striking contrast to the slender external pillars.

Old town

The old town of Chaniá, to the south of the harbour, is surrounded by a 3km/2 mile long circuit of 16th century walls.

★ Topanás

The most picturesque part of Chaniá is the Topanás ("Cannon Court") quarter to the west of the harbour. In its narrow and irregular streets there are still some Venetian and Turkish houses, many of them lovingly restored.

Nowhere else in Crete is there a wider choice of attractive little hotels.

Evraiki

To the east of Topanás is the Evraiki quarter, which in Venetian and Turkish times was the Jewish ghetto. The Jews were frequently exposed to repression by both Christians and Moslems. Most of them were in very modest circumstances; only a few rose to more influential positions, mostly through trade.

In 1944 the German authorities ordered the whole Jewish community to be transported to an extermination camp. The transport ship blew up at sea – whether by intention or as a result of enemy action, as was officially claimed, has never been established.

Kastélli

The oldest part of Chaniá, the Kastélli quarter, lies on the hill to the east of the harbour. In Venetian times the town's official buildings – for example the Rector's palace, the site of which is now occupied by a barracks – stood here. Nothing now remains of its former splendour. Some Minoan remains were found here (see below).

Venetian doorways

At Odós Lithínou 45, in the Kastélli quarter, is the doorway of the Venetian Archives, built in 1624. Adjoining it are a charming courtyard and another fine Venetian doorway.

San Marco

Also in the Kastélli quarter, in Platía Ayiou Titou and Odós Ayiou Markou, which opens off the square, are the remains (mainly a row of round-headed arches) of the Venetian church of San Marco.

Minoan excavations

The Minoan excavations lie between houses in Odós Kanevárou, in the Kastélli quarter. They are not open to the public, but can be seen from the street; they are of no great interest to the ordinary visitor. Remains of Late Minoan and Mycenaean settlement, including a megaron, were found here.

★ Archaeological Museum

24 Odós Khálidon

Opening times
Mon. 11am–5pm, Tues.–Fri. 8am–5pm, Sat., Sun. 8.30am–3pm

Chaniá's Archaeological Museum is housed in the handsome 16th century church of San Francesco (Odós Khálidon). The western annexe was built when the church was converted into a mosque during the Turkish period. There is the base of a minaret at the north-west corner of the building.

This harmoniously proportioned three-aisled basilica makes an impressive setting for the museum's fine collection of antiquities, ranging in date from the Late Neolithic to Roman times.

For the dating of the Early Minoan (EM I–III), Middle Minoan (MM I–III) and Late Minoan (LM I–III) periods see the table on p. 34.

Tour of museum

The case numbers given below correspond to those on the plan and in the museum itself.

Cases 1–4

Material of the Late Neolithic to Late Minoan from the Platyvóla and Skotinó caves: beaked jugs, *pyxides* and vessels with simple incised patterns and spiral motifs and barbotine ware. The tripod-footed *pyxis* in case 4 is the finest of its kind.

Case 5

Neolithic stone vases and implements and Early Minoan pottery and spindles from various sites.

Archaeological Museum
(former church of San Francesco)

Chaniá

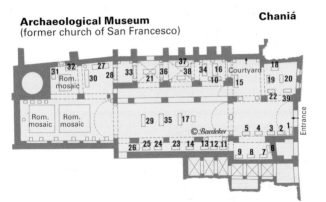

Neolithic to Late Minoan material from the Mameloúkou Trýpa burial cave near Chaniá. The most important item is a fragment of a vase with a Linear B inscription.

Case 6

Middle Minoan material (pottery, weapons and implements) from Vrýses and Nerokoúrou.

Case 7

Late Neolithic to Late Minoan material from Kastélli/Chaniá: pottery, stone vases, small objects, loom weights and clay seals; a magnificent seal (11) depicting a Minoan on a group of buildings in a rocky setting by the sea; a bowl of light-coloured fabric, an import from Cyprus (12).

Cases 8, 9, 11–13

Late Minoan and Geometric material from a necropolis in Chaniá: Late Minoan pottery; models of circular houses; sherd of Geometric pottery with human figures.

Case 14

Geometric material from necropolises at Módi, Kavoúsi and Gavalomoúri: characteristic chequerboard motifs.

Cases 23–26

Late Minoan material: copper articles from tombs in Chaniá, standard lead weights.

Case 29

Coins of the classical, Hellenistic, Roman, Byzantine and Venetian periods.

Case 35

Bronzes (mirrors, daggers) from a Late Minoam tomb in Chaniá.
    Along the sides of the central aisle are a number of pieces of Greco-Roman sculpture: Artemis leaning against a tree, a Roman figure of Heracles, a statue of Hygieia from Áptera, a statue of Pan from Hyrtakína and a large figure of a philosopher from Elýros.
    The Roman mosaics (3rd century A.D.) come from a house in Chaniá.
    Also in the central aisle are two mosaics with the figure of Dionysus. In the south aisle is a mosaic of Poseidon and Amymone.

Case 17

Material of the Classical to Roman periods from various sites: figures, masks, a miniature shield with two warriors, and bas-reliefs of Artemis and Apollo from the Bear Cave on the Akrotíri peninsula.

Case 31

Objects of the classical and Hellenistic periods from various sites: red-figured vases (a lekythos imported from Athens) and idols.

Case 32

Geometric material from the Gavalomoúri necropolis: toys from a child's grave.

Case 27

Chaniá (Khaniá)

Cases 28 and 30	Archaic idols from the Axós necropolis and pottery from a tomb at Kísamos. Particularly fine is a terracotta female figure with her hands covering her breasts and pudenda (30).
Case 33	Classical and Hellenistic material from the Phalásarna necropolis: black-figured vases (fine aryballos from Corinth).
Case 21	Material from the Áptera necropolis: Hellenistic and Roman oil lamps; silver, bronze and bone needles; toy from a child's grave; clay plaques.
Case 36	Archaic and Hellenistic material: a particularly fine urn.
Case 37	Hellenistic grave goods, statuettes, Greco-Roman oil lamps and perfume flasks from Vrýses.
Case 38	Hellenistic material from various shrines. Opposite case 37 is a marble libation table with a Greek inscription from the shrine at Lisós.
Case 34	Greco-Roman jewellery.
Case 16	Late Minoan jewellery and seal-stones.
Case 10	Linear A and Linear B inscriptions from Chaniá.
Case 15	Late Minoan IIIB material from tombs at Chaniá and Soúda: large stirrup-handled jugs and kraters.
Cases 19 and 18	Material from a Late Minoan necropolis in Chaniá: pottery with decoration on a white ground, stirrup-handled jugs and cups.
Case 20	Late Minoan material from various sites: pottery (jugs, bowls) and bronze vessels.
Case 39	Ivories (shields, etc.) and a bronze bowl with a Linear A inscription.

Case 22	Late Minoan pottery with decoration on a white ground and stone vessels from various sites.
	    There are also Late Minoan sarcophagi from various sites with geometric and floral decoration and hunting scenes.
	    In the courtyard of the museum are a Turkish fountain which once stood in a square in the town and a Venetian marble doorway from the Zangarola palace in the Kastélli quarter.

Other Sights in Chaniá

Venetian loggia	At Odós Zambelíou 43–45 is a Venetian loggia in Renaissance style of which only the outer walls remain. Between the windows on the middle floor is a coat of arms with the motto "Nulli parvus est census cui magnus est animus" ("No one is judged of little account who has a great spirit").
Renieri Palace	In Odós Móskhon in the Topanás quarter is the arched gate of the once grand Renieri Palace, with the family's coat of arms and a humorous inscription: "Multa tulit fecitque pater, sudavit, et alsit et studuit, dulces semper requies cenerat" ("The father bore much and did much, sweated and froze and laboured, but sweet repose ever eluded him").
Naval Museum	The Naval Museum (open: May 1st to Oct. 31st daily 10am–4pm, Nov. 1st to Apr. 30th 10am–2pm) is housed in the Venetian Phirkás Tower at the north-west corner of the harbour. The exhibits include ship models (e.g. an Attic trireme), nautical instruments and a collection of shells, depictions of

ancient sea battles, and documents and pictures on the navy of the 19th and 20th centuries (including the battle for Crete in 1941) and on commercial shipping.

On December 1st 1913 King Constantine hoisted the Greek flag on the Phirkás Tower to mark the union of Crete with Greece,

Above the Naval Museum is the little Venetian church of San Salvatore (16th century), which was converted into a mosque during the Turkish period.

San Salvatore

Not much is left of the fortifications of the ancient city. Round the Kastélli hill are remains of a Byzantine and Arab wall which was rebuilt by the Venetians in the 13th and 14th centuries. The more recent fortifications of Chaniá (15th/16th century) were the work of the architect and military engineer Michele Sanmicheli, who also built the walls round Iráklion. The circuit of ramparts, enclosing a rectangular area, had a total length of some 2km/1¼ miles. On the east side of the town a stretch of the walls can be seen. The best preserved of the bastions is the Shiavo Bastion at the south-west corner, from which there are wide views of the town and surrounding area. From here northward the walls are excellently preserved.

Fortifications

In the pretty Platía 1821 in the eastern part of the old town are the churches of Áyios Nikólaos and San Rocco and, under an ancient plane-tree, a memorial to Bishop Melchizedek, who was hanged on this tree by the Turks in 1821 for taking part in a rising.

Áyios Nikólaos, San Rocco

The large church of Áyios Nikólaos was built by the Venetians for a Dominican friary and in Turkish times was converted into a mosque, called the Imperial Mosque in honour of Sultan Ibrahim, the conqueror of Chaniá; the mosque's minaret still survives. The church and its furnishings were remodelled after the First World War.

The little Venetian church of San Rocco (1630), in Renaissance style, is in a rather dilapidated condition. San Rocco (St Roch) was invoked by victims of plague.

San Rocco

To the south is the 16th century church of the Áyii Anáryiri (the "Moneyless Saints", Cosmas and Damian), the town's only Orthodox church during the Venetian and Turkish periods. It has a magnificent carved iconostasis.

Áyii Anáryiri

In Platía 1897 is the decorative Market Hall of 1911, laid out in the form of a cross. The stalls for fish, fruit and mixed goods display all the products of the region.

Market Hall

North-east of the Market Hall, in Odós Khadzimikháli Daliáni, is a small minaret.

Minaret

To the south of the old town, in a handsome villa at Odós Sphakíon 20, is the Historical Museum (open: Mon.–Fri. 9am–1pm), which has a large collection of documents, books and manuscripts, covering both the fight against the Turks and the resistance to the German occupation during the Second World War. Other exhibits include maps and views of the island and a collection of religious art, including woodcarving and manuscripts. There is also a section devoted to Cretan folk traditions, with examples of embroidery, woven fabrics, jewellery, costume and craftmen's tools.

Historical Museum

In the beautiful Municipal Park, a short distance from the Historical Museum, visitors can see Cretan wild goats (kri-kri) living in open enclosures. Popular attractions in the evening are the kafeníon and the open-air cinema.

Municipal Park

1.5km/1 mile east of the town centre is the residential suburb of Khalépa, built around the turn of the century as the government quarter. In this area are various government buildings and consulates.

Khalépa

All kinds of local produce are sold in the market hall

Surroundings of Chaniá

Soúda Bay

4km/2½ miles south-east of the old town is Soúda Bay, the largest and most sheltered natural harbour on the island. It is Chaniá's commercial and ferry port, with daily services to Piraeus, and a naval base.

British war cemetery

On the road from Soúda to the Akrotíri peninsula is a well cared for British war cemetery with the graves of 1527 Commonwealth soldiers who fell in the battle for Crete in 1941.

Kalámi fortress (Καλάμι)

At the mouth of Soúda Bay, just off the expressway which runs along the south side of the bay, is the Turkish fortress of Kalámi, which after the expulsion of the Turks was used as a state prison.

Soúda fortress (Σούδχα το φρούριο)

On the island of Soúda, at the mouth of the bay, is a Venetian fortress, built from 1570 onwards, which served as a base during the war with Turkey. After the Turks took Candia (Iráklion) in 1669 and thus gained control of Crete they sought to intimidate the defenders of the fort by piling up all round it the severed heads of 5000 Christians. But the garrison held out, and the fort remained in Venetian hands until the 18th century.

Akrotíri peninsula

Prophítis Ilías

8km/5 miles north-east of Chaniá, on Mt Prophítis Ilías, is a spaciously laid out memorial area containing the graves of the Cretan statesman Elefthérios Venizélos (see Famous People) and his son Sophoklís. From here there is a magnificent view over the town, extending to the White Mountains.

This is a place of great national significance to the Cretans. Here in 1897 the first Greek flag was hoisted over the island. When the great powers, who were opposed to the union of Crete with Greece, bombarded the hill and destroyed the flagstaff a patriotic Cretan is said to have held the flag aloft himself, whereupon the bombardment was called off. Soon afterwards Crete was granted autonomy.

17km/10½ miles north-east of Chaniá is the monastery of Ayía Triáda (closed 2–5pm), one of the largest and most important in Crete, founded in 1631. It was burned down by the Turks in 1821, but was rebuilt in 1830 and soon recovered its former wealth and prosperity. It is also known as Moní Tzangarólou after its founders, the Venetian Zangarola family.

Ayía Triáda
monastery
(Μονή Αγία
Τριάδα)

The monastery is entered through an imposing gatehouse with four columns, Corinthian capitals and a triangular pediment. The façade of the church is in a plain Renaissance style. A striking feature of the interior is the richly carved iconostasis.

To the left of the entrance is a small icon museum, with 18th and 19th century icons, including some by the painter Emmanuel Skodilis.

Perhaps the finest excursion from Chaniá is to the monastery of Gouvernéto (4km/2½ miles from Ayía Triáda; open: 7.30am–noon and 3–7pm), commandingly situated on a ridge of hill, from which there are superb views.

★Gouvernéto
monastery
(Μονή
Γουβερνέτο)

The rectangular monastery complex, which like many other monasteries is occupied only by a small number of monks, has a fortress-like air. Although it was founded in 1648 it has suffered so much destruction from fires and from the 1821 rising, when most of the monks were murdered by the Turks, that the present buildings are modern.

As at Ayía Triáda, the Renaissance façade of the church, which is crowned by a modern bell-cote and a dome, shows Venetian influence. The furnishings of the interior mostly date from the 19th century.

An icon in the narthex depicts the legend of St John of Gouvernéto or John the Stranger who fled from Asia Minor and, sailing over the sea in his cloak, landed below the present monastery. There he and 98 companions lived as hermits in caves, until he was shot by mistake by a hunter. John's cave can still be seen.

The Renaissance church of the Ayía Triáda

The fortress-like monastery of Gouvernéto

The monastery has a library and a collection of Byzantine religious articles (icons and liturgical utensils).

Bear Cave

From Gouvernéto a broad rocky track runs down to the right and comes to some ruined buildings in front of a large cave, known as the Bear Cave after a stalagmite seen as resembling a bear. It is thought to have been a shrine in the Neolithic and Minoan periods, and in Classical times was dedicated to the cult of Artemis, to whom the bear was sacred. At the mouth of the cave, to the left, is the little 16th century chapel of the Panayía Arkoudió-tissa (the Mother of God of the Bear Cave).

Katholikó monastery (Μονή Καθολικό)

From here a narrow path winds its way down to the magnificently situated but now abandoned Katholikó monastery.

Shortly before the path reaches the monastery numerous caves once occupied by hermits can be seen on the opposite rock face. In front of the entrance to the church, to the left, is the cave occupied by John of Gouvernéto, who lived around 1100. In this cave, which reaches back for some 40m/130ft, are a masonry-built hearth and a water basin.

The narrow gateway leads to a terrace in front of the rock church, which has a Renaissance-style façade showing Venetian influence. A vigil held here on the night before October 7th, the feast of St John of Gouvernéto, draws large numbers of worshippers.

The well preserved monastic buildings date from the 15th and 16th centuries. Later in the 16th century, however, the monastery was abandoned after frequent raids by Arab pirates and the monks withdrew to Gouvernéto.

On the upper floor of the two-storey building to the right was the abbot's lodging. The two holes opening into the gorge on the terrace in front of the monastery are thought to have been lavatories. The gorge is spanned by an imposing bridge 10m/35ft wide, borne on piers which contain store-rooms and a cistern.

There is a pleasant walk down to the sea, where there is an ancient slipway serving the monastery.

In the village of Stavrós, to the west of Gouvernéto, some scenes in the film "Zorba the Greek" were shot; it was on the beach here that Zorba danced the syrtáki. With its heavily polluted beach, however, the village is not to be recommended to visitors. There is a better beach in the village of Khoraphákia to the south of Stavrós – a small sandy beach in a cove sheltered from the wind which slopes down very gently into the sea.

Stavrós
(Σταυρός)

West of Chaniá

9km/5½ miles west of Chaniá on the coast road there is a fine view of the island of Áyii Theodóri, now a reserve for the Cretan wild goat.

Áyii Theodóri
(Άγιοι Θεοδώροι)

On a hill at Máleme, 16km/10 miles west of Chaniá, is a German military cemetery, with the graves of 4465 soldiers, mostly paratroops, who were killed during the German landing in May 1941. The dead were cared for by the monks of Goniás monastery.

Máleme
(Μάλεμε)

Rodopós peninsula (Ροδωπόν)

8km/5 miles west of Máleme a road goes off on the right to the village of Kolymbári, at the head of the Rodopós peninsula. This grandiose and barren finger of land bounds the west side of Chaniá Bay. Only 6km/4 miles across and 16km/10 miles long, it rises to a height of 748m/2454ft above the sea. The summit plateau provides grazing for sheep and goats.

The fortress-like Goniás monastery, also known as the monastery of the Odiyítria (one of the appellations of the Mother of God), has a magnificent situation above the sea to the north of Kolymbári, at the point where Chaniá Bay forms a 90-degree angle (góni = "knee"). The shady monastery courtyard invites visitors to pause and rest.

Goniás monastery
(Μονή Γωνιάς)

Goniás monastery was founded in 1618. This was unfortunately the place where the Turks made their first landing on Crete in 1645, and the monastery was partly destroyed. By 1662, however, it had been rebuilt. During the 19th century it was considerably enlarged. It suffered further destruction, however, during the 19th century risings against the Turks, when it became a hospital for Cretan freedom fighters, and in the Second World War, when it became a military camp. After the Second World War the monks gathered together the remains of the German dead until their burial in the military cemetery – an action all the more admirable in view of what the monastery had suffered during the war.

Opposite the entrance to the monastery is a Venetian fountain under a pointed arch. Notable features of the interior of the church, which shows a mingling of Byzantine and Early Baroque styles, are the richly carved door and the rear and sides of the bishop's throne in the transept. There are 17th century icons on the iconostasis and the walls of the nave.

There is a small museum containing icons, mainly of the 17th and 18th centuries, vestments and ecclesiastical valuables.

A few hundred metres from the monastery is the Oecumenical Academy of the autocephalous Church of Crete, founded by the bishop of Kísamos and Selínos, Irinaíos Galanákos. This progressive churchman committed himself to the improvement of social conditions in his see, promoted the modernisation of agriculture and founded the ANEK shipping line. The Academy is a forum for exchanges within the Orthodox church and between the Eastern and Western churches.

At the north-east end of the Rodopós peninsula, in Meniés Bay near Cape Skála, is the shrine of the nymph Dictynna, which was excavated by German archaeologists during the Second World War. Dictynna was identical

Diktýnnaion
(Δικτύνναιον)

with the Cretan goddess Britomartis and was later equated with Artemis. She was the patroness of fishermen and their nets (*díktyon* = "net"); for when she threw herself into the sea to escape the attentions of King Minos she was rescued by fishermen who caught her in their nets.

The scanty remains of the shrine are most easily reached by boat from Chaniá or Kolymbári. From the landing-stage a path runs up through a little valley in which are the ruins of an abandoned village, and then up the hillside on the left to the excavation site. By land the route runs by way of the village of Rodopoú, from which a poor road runs for 18km/11 miles through a strange rocky landscape. From the end of the road it is a half-hour walk to the site, where there is a pretty little cove with good bathing.

There are the remains of a temple built in the 2nd century A.D. on the site of an earlier building of the 7th century B.C., together with the altar, three cisterns and other structures, including a long building on the steep northern slope of the hill which was probably a hostel for pilgrims.

Other Sights in the Surroundings of Chaniá

25km/15 miles west of Chaniá is the village of Spiliá, named after a cave above the village which was occupied by St John of Gournéto and now contains a small chapel. The village has a church of the Panayía with 14th century frescos of the so-called Cretan school.

Spiliá
(Σπηλιά)

3km/2 miles south of Spiliá, just before the village of Episkopí, is one of the most unusual Byzantine buildings in Crete, the church of the Archangel Michael (second half of 10th century; key from the house above the chapel) with its rotunda enclosed within a square outer structure, which is worth a visit for the sake of its exterior alone. The rotunda is topped by a curious stepped dome consisting of five concentric rings. Its elliptical form points to Eastern influences.

Episkopí
(Επισκοπή)

The remains of a mosaic pavement in the narthex (to left) belonged to an Early Byzantine basilica which occupied the site of the present church. Also in the narthex is a bust of the last bishop, who was executed by the Turks – for, as its name indicates, Episkopí was the see of a bishop from the Middle Byzantine period until 1821. The church preserves only a few fragments of frescos.

9km/5½ miles south of Chaniá, on the road to Omalós, is the village of Ayiá, which has an interesting church of the Panayía, a three-aisled basilica (10th/11th century) with apses. The aisles are separated by two rows of three columns each, two of marble and four of granite.

Ayiá
(Αγιά)

Just beyond Ayiá, at the turn-off for Alikianós, is a monument commemorating 118 partisans who were killed here by German troops. The skulls of the victims are preserved in the substructure of the monument.

Alikianós
(Αλικιανός)

The cross-in-square church of Áyios Kyr Yiánnis, situated amid luxuriant vegetation just north-west of Alikianós, dates from the 14th century. It is named after a hermit known as Kyr Yiánnis who won western Crete back to Christianity after its liberation from the Saracens and built many churches. The dome of this beautifully proportioned church, now in poor condition, was destroyed during the Second World War. The apsidal structure is unusual: a central apse with a pentagonal exterior flanked by two square lateral apses. The frescos, which are badly damaged, mostly date from the 14th century. Outside the church, against the north wall, is a vaulted tomb.

Áyios Kyr Yiánnis
(Άγιος Κυρ
Γιάννης)

20km/12½ miles south of Chaniá, in a valley planted with orange groves, is Mesklá. At the near end of the village, on the left, is the chapel of Sotíros Christoú (Christ the Saviour), a one-room structure with a narthex. It has

Mesklá
(Μεσκλά)

◄ *Entrance to Goniás monastery*

Church of the Archangel Michael, Episkopí

some frescos of 1303, painted by Theódoros Daniel and his nephew Michael Venéris. Particularly notable is a Transfiguration on the south wall.

In the upper part of the village, beside the church of the Panayía, are remains of an Early Christian basilica.

Above Mesklá are remains of an ancient settlement, the name of which is disputed: it may, or may not, be a second Rizenía.

Áptera
(Άπτερα)

14km/8½ miles east of Chaniá on a rocky plateau are the remains of ancient Áptera, whose history goes at least as far back as the Dorian period (from 1000 B.C.). Its heyday was in Hellenistic times.

There are still some well preserved remains of the city's walls of around 300 B.C., which had a total length of 4km/2½ miles. In the centre of the site is a picturesque monastery, to the west of which is a rectangular Roman cistern and to the north a three-aisled Early Byzantine building, probably not a church. To the south-east is another Roman cistern, an impressive tripartite structure. At the south-west corner of the monastery is a small two-room shrine. To the south of the site are the remains of a small Greek theatre, the seating of which can still be distinguished, and of a Byzantine church. To the east of the theatre is a Doric temple, and in the eastern part of the site a temple of the Hellenistic period. At the north-eastern tip of the site is the Turkish fortress of Izzedin (1868–69), from which there are fine views of Soúda Bay and the Akrotíri peninsula.

Stýlos
(Στύλος)

Stýlos, south of Áptera, was the scene of fighting between Cretans and Turks and of the last stage in the battle for Crete in 1941.

North of the village, in an olive grove, is the church of the Panayía, which belonged to the monastery of Áyios Ioánnis Theológos, a dependency of the monastery of St John on the island of Patmos. It is an imposing cross-in-square church of the 11th or Kaly12th century in High Byzantine style, its dome borne on an octagonal drum supported by four square piers. The walls are of dressed and undressed stone with intervening courses of rubble and brick.

To the south of Stýlos is the village of Kyriakosélia, with the church of Áyios Nikólaos (key held by priest), which has frescos of unusual quality. The church itself is a delicately articulated cross-in-square church of the 11th or 12th century, entered through a chapel. The paintings date from 1230–36. In the dome is Christ Pantokrator (Ruler of All); on the drum and pendentives prophets and the Evangelists; on the vaulting the Transfiguration, the Raising of Lazarus, the Ascension and the Descent of the Holy Ghost; in the sanctuary the Mother of God enthroned with two angels, below this apostles and Greek fathers of the Church; on the triumphal arch the Annunciation; and on the walls scenes from the life of St Nicholas.

Kalýves, 18km/11 miles east of Chaniá, is a quiet little coastal town with only a small beach and little accommodation for visitors. In the square is the church of Ayía Paraskeví, which has modern wall paintings in traditional style, with inscriptions naming the local people who contributed to their cost.

The large village of Vrýses, situated on a little river 33km/21 miles southeast of Chaniá, is famed for its tavernas under the shade of plane-trees and its excellent ewes'-milk yoghurt and honey. There is a large memorial to the fight for liberation in 1897.

Near Vrýses is the village of Máza, with the church of Áyios Nikólaos, which has notable frescos of 1325 by the painter Ioánnis Pagoménos.

A few kilometres south of Máza is Alíkambos, with the church of the Panayía, which has particularly fine frescos. The church is on the left of the road just before it bends sharply to the right before reaching the village. The Panayía is a simple barrel-vaulted one-room chapel with a round apse and a decoration of ceramic plates over the entrance. The frescos (1315–16) by Ioánnis Pagoménos show a mingling of folk elements and more refined forms. In the apse is the Panayía, above this the Ascension and below four Greek fathers of the Church; on the entrance wall are the Dormition of the Mother of God and an inscription naming the founder; on the barrel vaulting scenes from the life of Christ; on the south wall Christ enthroned, the Archangel Michael and SS. Constantine and Helen.

Kyriakosélia
(Κυριαχοσέλια)

Kalýves
(Καλύβες)

Vrýses
(Βρύσες)

Máza
(Μάζα)

Alíkambos
(Αλίκαμπος)

Gávdos   F/G 5

Lying in the Libyan Sea some 37km/23 miles off the south-western coast of Crete is the island of Gávdos, Europe's most southerly point. It is reached by boat from Palaiokhóra (55km/34 miles) or Khóra Sphakíon (37km/23 miles).

Situation

This flat wooded island has an area of 35sq.km/13½sq. miles), rising to 345m/1132ft at its highest point. Its four tiny villages have a total population of only 80 in summer and 40 in winter. From Palaiokhóra there is a twice-weekly boat carrying mail and supplies which also takes passengers. In summer there are also day trips from Palaiokhóra and Khóra Sphakíon.

Gávdos has a priest and a teacher, and in summer the government sends a policeman and a doctor to Kástri, the chief place on the island. The inhabitants earn a meagre subsistence from agriculture on the island's barren and waterless soil. In spring and autumn, when many migrant birds rest here, Gávdos is a bird-watcher's paradise.

General

Gávdos is probably the legendary Ogygia (Odyssey VII, 244), the island where Calypso held Odysseus captive for seven years. Undoubtedly, however, it is the island of Clauda on which the Apostle Paul was cast ashore by shipwreck on his voyage from Caesarea to Rome. In 1941 German forces bombed the lighthouse in the north-west of the island, and during the following three years a small detachment of German troops was stationed in the village of Ambelos.

History

Górtys (Gortyn)

Sights   The main tourist attractions of the island are a number of good beaches. It
          is popular with backpackers, who like to camp on Sarakinikó beach. Rooms
          can be rented in private houses only there and in the village of Kástri.
          Other sights are the bombed lighthouse and three sea-caves.

Górtys (Gortyn)   E 10

Γόρτυς

Nomós: Iráklion
Chief town of nomós: Iráklion

Situation   The remains of Górtys, capital of Crete in Roman times, lies 45km/28 miles
             south of Iráklion and just to the west of the village of Áyii Déka, on both
             sides of the main road from Iráklion to Phaistós.

History   In Minoan times (3rd/2nd millennium B.C.) Górtys was overshadowed by
             Phaistós. Its first flowering was during the Dorian period (6th/5th century
             B.C.), when it gradually gained control of the whole of the Mesará plain,

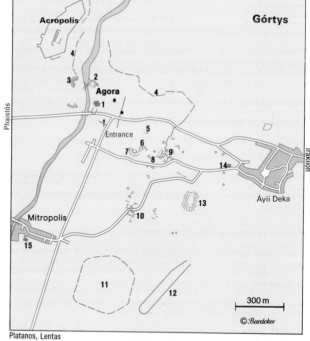

Platanos, Lentas

1 Basilica of St Titus	6 Temple of Apollo Pythios	11 Necropolis
2 Odeon	7 Theatre	12 Circus
3 Theatre	8 Praetorium	13 Amphitheatre
4 Aqueduct	9 Nymphaeum	14 Museum
5 Temple of Isis and Serapis	10 Baths	15 Trilobate church

culminating in the conquest of Phaistós (3rd century B.C.) and its port of Mátala, thus gaining a second port in addition to its own one, Lébena. In subsequent centuries Górtys fought Knossós for dominance in central Crete. Hannibal, fleeing from the Romans, sought refuge here in 189 B.C. Górtys enjoyed a further period of great prosperity after the Roman conquest of Crete in 69 B.C., when it became capital of the island and seat of the praetor of Creta–Cyrenaica. Titus, appointed bishop of Górtys by the Apostle Paul, carried through the Christianisation of the island, and it was probably to him that Paul addressed his Epistle to Titus. In A.D. 330 the town passed into Byzantine hands and continued to exist until the Arab invasion in 826. Excavations of the site of Górtys were carried out by Italian archaeologists from the 1880s onwards.

The remains of Górtys lie scattered to the north and south of the main road. Conducted tours are usually limited to a brief inspection of the most important remains in the northern half of the site; but it is well worth looking round the extensive remains in the olive grove on the south side of the road.

The ★ site
Open daily
(excluding Mon.)
8am–5pm

The tour begins with the northern part of the site. Just beyond the entrance, to the left, is the impressive ruin of the basilica of St Titus (probably 6th century), one of the most important Christian monuments on Crete. The relics of St Titus, now in the church of Áyios Titos in Iráklion, were venerated here. After the destruction of the church by the Arabs in 823 it was rebuilt in 965 and renovated in the 14th century. During the Turkish occupation it fell into ruin and was used by the inhabitants of the surrounding villages as a source of building stone.

Tour of site

The basilica, three-aisled, is in the form of a Latin cross with a dome over the crossing and apses at the ends of the transept. The bema has two lateral apses; the one on the left in the prothesis, with the remains of two bishops' tombs, and the other in the diakonikon.

From here the tour continues by way of the ancient agora to the Roman *odeon*, built in the 1st century B.C. and renovated in the 3rd and 4th centuries A.D. The orchestra is paved with black and white marble slabs, and the *skene* is flanked by two porticoes. In the circular portico surrounding the *odeon* is the famous Code of Górtys, a law code dating from between 500 and 450 B.C. Twelve tables of laws have been preserved out of, probably, an original twenty. The laws are written on 42 stone blocks in *boustrophedon* ("as the ox ploughs") form, i.e. left to right and right to left in alternate lines (illustration, p. 40). This code of civil and penal law for the Dorian city of Górtys is the oldest known European law code. Remarkable features of the code are its mildness (there is no provision for a death penalty) and the privileged position of women in the ownership of property.

To the west of the *odeon*, on the slopes of the hill, are the impressive remains of a Greek theatre, with a *cavea* 120m/395ft in circumference. On the acropolis, above this, are various remains of the Greek and Roman periods, including store-rooms and a temple (7th century B.C.). Lower down the slope is the altar belonging to the temple. Along the side of the acropolis and farther east on the slopes of the hill are aqueducts which brought water from the Zarós area.

To the south of the road, in an olive grove to which there is free access, are extensive Roman remains. The remains of the temple of Isis and Serapis, who were worshipped by the Romans after their conquest of Egypt, include an architrave bearing the names of the two divinities. Outside the south wall of the temple a short flight of steps leads down into a small crypt with two recesses for statues. Farther south is the temple of Apollo Pythios (3rd/2nd century B.C.), the oldest part of which dates from the 6th century. It consists of a *pronaos* with six Doric semi-columns and the main chamber, which is divided into three aisles by two rows of three

The imposing ruins of the basilica of St Titus

columns. In Roman times (2nd century A.D.) a central apse was added. The excavators discovered the temple treasury. In front of the temple is a five-stepped altar. To the south-west is a theatre. Farther east is the *praetorium*, the seat of the Roman governor, built in the 2nd century and renovated in the 4th. It contains a three-apsed hall flanked by porticoes, the so-called basilica, baths and a temple. Public assemblies and court proceedings were held here. Farther along, on the left, is a 2nd century nymphaeum (fountain). To the south are public baths (2nd century), a cemetery area, a circus 374m/409yd long and an amphitheatre, both also dating from the 2nd century. There are also the remains of an Early Christian trilobate church (5th/6th century) on the edge of the village of Mitrópolis. The south conch contains fine mosaics with geometric and figural motifs.

Surroundings of Górtys

Áyii Déka
(Άγιοι Δέκα)

The name of the village of Áyii Déka ("Holy Ten"), immediately east of Górtys, commemorates ten Christians who died by the sword in 250, in the reign of the Emperor Decius, for refusing to take part in the consecration of a pagan temple. The village church, which has some interesting icons, also contains the stone on which they are said to have been executed.

Plátanos
(Πλάτανος)

In the village of Plátanos, 6km/4 miles south of Górtys, are two important Early Minoan circular tombs (*c.* 2500 B.C.). They are reached by leaving the village on the road to Pómbia and then taking a side road to the right. The tomb to the east, with an interior diameter of 13m/43ft, is the largest of its kind in Crete. The paved area in front of the tombs was probably used for cult ceremonies. The tombs, of a type characteristic of the Mesará, have an entrance on the east side. They were probably family or clan tombs which remained in use for several centuries. When room was needed for new

The Odeon, Górtys

burials the remains of older ones would be removed to special chambers (ossuaries) built on to the tombs.

At Léntas, 17km/11 miles south of Górtys, are the remains of the Greco-Roman city of Lebena (from the Phoenician word for "lion"), which took its name from the lion-shaped rock to the west of the town.

Léntas
(Λέντας)

Lebena was a place of importance in the Greco-Roman period as the port of Górtys. It was also famed from the 4th century B.C. for its thermal springs, which were frequented by people from all over Greece seeking a cure for their ailments. The site, above the present village, was excavated by Italian archaeologists.

In the centre of the ancient site is a temple of Asklepios (3rd century B.C.; renovated in 2nd century A.D.). Unusually, the walls have an outer surface of undressed stone and an inner surface of brick. The interior preserves two columns, the base for a cult image, once occupied by statues of Asklepios and Hygieia, and remains of mosaics. In the building immediately to the north is a fine mosaic with a sea-horse and palmettes. In the floor is a 2m/6½ft deep shaft with a round mouth giving access to an underground chamber which housed the temple treasure (robbed in ancient times). There are scanty remains of a monumental marble staircase immediately to the north and a portico on the east side. To the south-east of this complex is the medicinal spring, which is still in use, and to the south are a number of large basins, probably for bathing in. A long house in the village and a large building farther south were probably guest-houses.

The 11th century chapel of Áyios Ioánnis, to the east of the temple, stands in the ruins of a Byzantine basilica built in the 5th/6th century, using stone from ancient buildings. Its frescos date from the 14th/15th centuries.

To the east of Léntas are two Early Minoan circular tombs. Here, on the south coast of Crete, are a number of beautiful beaches; one 3km/2 miles west is popular with naturists.

Gourniá

E 15

Γουρνιά

Nomós: Lassíthi
Chief town of nomós: Áyios Nikólaos

Situation

The partly excavated remains of the Minoan town of Gourniá lie on a hill bordering the coast road some 20km/12½ miles south-east of Áyios Nikólaos.

For the dating of the Early Minoan (EM I–III), Middle Minoan (MM I–III) and Late Minoan (LM I–III) periods see the table on p. 34.

The ★town
(open:
Tues.–Sun.
8.30am–3pm)

This typical Minoan town, with narrow paved streets, small dwelling-houses and a palace and sanctuary on higher ground, gives a vivid impression of the aspect of a city of the Middle Minoan period. It is one of the earliest examples of a European town.

From the site there are fine views over the sea.

History

The town was occupied from 3300 to around 1100 B.C. The remains now visible date from Gourniá's heyday between 1800 and 1500 B.C. The name

Gourniá

Entrance

Shrine

Palace

Market square

Olive-press

© Baedeker

N

30m

Gourniá: one of the earliest examples of European town layout

of the Minoan town is not known; the site was given the name Gourniá ("jugs") in modern times because of the many jugs found here. The area was excavated by American archaeologists in 1901–04.

The town, which was traversed by a kind of "ring road", was occupied by fairly prosperous traders, farmers, craftsmen and fishermen. The small houses, probably of two or three storeys, for the most part abutted on one another, the lower part of the walls being built of undressed stone; they were divided into tiny rooms. Many everyday objects were found by the excavators, and some mortars and stone basins can be seen on the site.

On the highest point of the hill is the market square, on the north side of which is a small palace approached by a short flight of steps. One hall of the palace can still be identified, with store-rooms on its west side. To the north of the palace, at the end of a narrow side street on the right, is a small LM III shrine. Here were found many votive offerings, including female statuettes, figures of animals and votive tablets.

Tour of site

Surroundings of Gourniá

Vasilikí, 5km/3 miles south-east of Gourniá, is famed for its Early Minoan pottery with mottled red and black decoration, known as Vasilikí ware after the find-spot.

Vasilikí
(Βασιλικῄ)

150m/175yd beyond the village, on a low hill, is the site of an important Early Minoan settlement (2700–2200 B.C.), where excavation has revealed a courtyard and a quarter of very small houses. Some stone slabs in the courtyard with small depressions provided bases for votive statues.

Herakleion

See Iráklion

117

Ierápetra

E 15

Ιεράπετρα

Nomós: Lassíthi
Chief town of nomós: Áyios Nikólaos
Population: 11,000

Situation and characteristics

Ierápetra lies on the south coast of Crete, in a rich vegetable- and fruit-growing region with large numbers of hothouses. This most southerly town in Europe already has something of an African air. The life of the inhabitants is centred on agriculture, whose main products are cucumbers and tomatoes. Although at the height of summer it can be unduly hot in Ierápetra, in winter it is the pleasantest place to stay on the island. Even in December and January it is possible to bathe in the Libyan Sea.

The seafront promenade, paved with multicoloured marble and travertine slabs, is lined by busy tavernas and cafés: for holiday visitors this is the hub of the town's life. To the south is the old town, to the north of this the newer part of the town with its market hall, offices and shops. There are good beaches at each end of the seafront promenade.

History

Ierápetra occupies the site of ancient Hierapytna, a strategically important port for trade with Africa. In the 3rd and 4th centuries A.D. it became one of the leading cities in Crete. It was also a place of some consequence in Roman times, when it was equipped with many magnificent buildings, including theatres, temples and baths, though few remains of these have survived. In the 4th century A.D. it was the see of a bishop. In the 9th century it suffered heavy damage from Arab raids. In Venetian and Turkish times it was an important stronghold. Napoleon is said to have spent a night here in 1798 on his way to Egypt. Local legend has it that he came ashore with five sailors to get fresh water and fell into conversation with a lawyer who, not

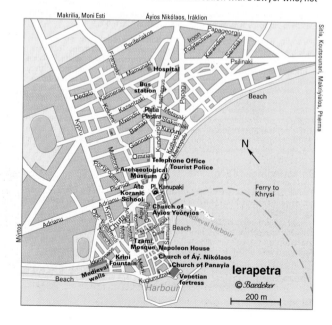

recognising him, invited him to stay in his house. On the following morning, after his guest had gone, the lawyer found on his bed a note signed by Napoleon.

Sights in Ierápetra

On a promontory at the south end of the town is a fortress built by the Venetians in the 13th century to protect the harbour, complete with battlements and four corner towers. Inland from this is the old town, with narrow lanes inherited from the Turkish period. Just north of the fortress is the small two-storey house, the Spíti tou Napoléon, in which Napoleon is said to have spent the night. In the *platía* are a mosque with a restored minaret and a Turkish fountain with niches and capitals.

Old town

Housed in a former Turkish school in Odós Adrianoú is the small Archaeological Museum (open: daily except Mon. 8.30am–3pm), with a large collection of pottery, including mottled Vasilikí ware, stone dishes from Mókhlos and coins. Notable items are a very fine Minoan sarcophagus with scenes of daily life and a magnificent statue of the goddess Demeter (2nd century A.D.).

Archaeological Museum

Surroundings of Ierápetra

7km/4½ miles north of Ierápetra, in Episkopí, is the church of Áyios Yeóryios (12th/13th century), which has some unusual features. It is double-apsed, with elaborately decorated blind arches of brick round the drum bearing the dome. The south aisle has been replaced by a chapel dedicated to Áyios Kharálambos. It has a notable iconostasis with a cross flanked by large figures.

Episkopí (Επισκοπή)

Sea front promenade, Ierápetra

Ierápetra

Anatolí
(Ανατολή)

The road to the hill village of Anatolí (alt. 640m/2100ft), 18km/11 miles north-west of Ierápetra, runs through beautiful mountain scenery. with fantastically shaped pine-covered crags. The almond-trees blossom here in March. From the village there are delightful views.

Khristós
(Χριστός)

The hill village of Khristás, 25km/15 miles north-west of Ierápetra, lies on a steep hillside at an altitude of 700m/2300ft. Just before the village, on higher ground to the right of the road, is the pilgrimage church of Ayía Paraskeví.

Mýrtos
(Μύρτος)

12km/7½ miles west of Ierápetra, on the edge of extensive orange and lemon groves, is the attractive village of Mýrtos, once a favourite haunt of hippies. It has a long sandy beach, and on the road to Tértsa there are lonely coves which also offer good bathing.

Pýrgos
(Πύργος)

Immediately east of the town, on the hill of Pýrgos, archaeologists discovered in 1970 the scanty remains of a Middle Minoan villa of around 1600 B.C. To the south is a paved court with a circular cistern, on the north side of which is a portico giving access to the villa's numerous rooms.
From the hill there are wide views of the coast and the Libyan Sea.

Phoúrnou Koryphí
(Φούρνου Κορυφή)

On the hill of Phoúrnou Koryphí, 2km/1¼ miles east of Mýrtos, an important Early Minoan settlement (2500–2150 B.C.) was discovered in 1968. The excavators recovered a large quantity of mottled Vasilikí ware and Áyios Onoúphrios ware with diagonal linear patterns. The settlement consists of over 100 linked rooms, suggesting that it was the home of a family clan. Two sanctuaries and *kernoi* were also discovered.

Árvi
(Άρβη)

39km/24 miles west of Ierápetra on a road of great scenic beauty is the village of Árvi, set amid plantations of bananas and oranges and fields of vegetables. It is a simple and unglamorous bathing resort with good sand and shingle beaches. Half an hour's walk away is the abandoned monastery of Áyios Antánios.

Áno Viánnos
(Άνω Βιάννος)

36km/22 miles west of Ierápetra, high up in the Dhikti mountains and set amid olive groves, is the large village of Áno Viánnos.
The area was settled in the Early and Middle Minoan periods (3rd/2nd millennium B.C.). This was the site of the Greek city-state of Viennos. In Venetian times Viánnos was a place of some importance.
The main feature of interest in Áno Viánnos is the church of Ayía Pelayía, which has frescos of 1360. Of particular iconographic interest are the scenes from the life of Ayía Pelayía in the naos. On the vaulting can be seen the "Holy Ten", the martyrs of Áyii Déka.

Keratákambos
(Κερατόχαμπος)

The small and scattered village of Keratákambos, 43km/27 miles west of Ierápetra, has a long beach which is very suitable for children.

Khrysí and Kouphonísi
(islands)

Some 18km/11 miles off Ierápetra in the Libyan Sea is the 5km/3 mile long island of Khrysí, and farther east, 5km/3 miles off Cape Goudoúra, is Kouphonísi.
There are daily trips by excursion boats from Ierápetra and Makriyiálos to Khrysí, the "Golden Island", which is also known by the less romantic name of Gaidouronísi ("Asses' Island"). In summer there are three tavernas on the island, which is covered with pines and junipers; at other times it is uninhabited. It offers good bathing on beautiful sandy beaches in crystal-clear water as well as pleasant walking.
The little island of Kouphonísi, which is also uninhabited, has good beaches and remains of the Bronze Age and Roman period. There are occasional excursions to the island from Makriyiálos in summer.

Iráklion (Herakleion · Heraklion)   C 11

Ηράκλειον

Chief town of the nomós of Iráklion
Population: 110,000

Iráklion, situated roughly half way along the northern coast of Crete, is the island's largest town, its administrative and economic centre and its principal commercial port. It is the seat of the Archbishop of Crete and the island's cultural centre, with several faculties of the University of Crete, many schools, a library and several museums, including the important Archaeological Museum.

Situation and characteristics

Although Iráklion has a long history, it has preserved few historic buildings. Many old buildings have been replaced by new ones, with the result that the modern aspect of the town is not particularly attractive.

The town

Iráklion's main features of interest almost all lie within the town's ring of Venetian walls, most of which is well preserved. The atmosphere of this bustling town can best be felt in Platía Venizélou, with the Morosini Fountain in the centre and numerous restaurants, tavernas and cafés all around. From this central point radiate the town's main arteries: Leophoros Dikaiosínis, its principal street, lined with shops, court buildings, offices and cafés; Odós 15 Avgoústou, which runs down to the harbour, with its banks, travel agencies and car rental firms; Odós Daidalou, a pedestrian lane with

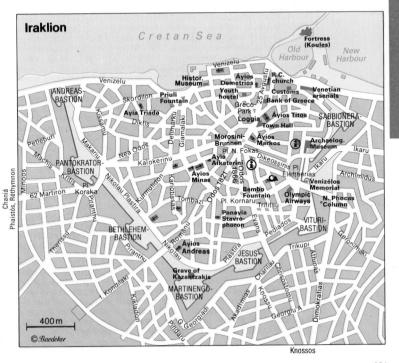

souvenir shops, travel agencies and restaurants; Odós 1866, the town's
market street with its foodshops; and Odós Kalokairinoú, the towns-
people's main shopping street. The town's second focal point is the
spacious Platía Eleftherías, always busy with traffic, with the magnificent
Archaeological Museum and a number of large cafés.

History

In Minoan times Iráklion was the port of Knossós. Tradition has it that the
town was called Heraclea in antiquity after Heracles, who carried off the
Cretan Bull as his seventh labour. Little is known of its history in Roman and
Early Byzantine times. In A.D. 824 it was captured by the Arabs, renamed
Rhabd El Khandak ("Castle of the Ditch") and developed into a military
base. The Byzantine general Nicephorus Phocas recovered the town in 961,
sacked it and destroyed the Arab fortress. The town's name was now
abbreviated to Chandax. Seeking to secure his position, Nicephorus Phocas founded a new town 19km/12 miles south of the old one, with the
fortress of Témenos. The local people, however, preferred Chandax, and
the older town was then rebuilt.

After Crete came into the hands of the Venetians in 1204 and had been
wrested from the Genoese the town became the seat of the governor of the
island, and both the town and the island were renamed Candia (which in
English usage became Candy). The town now gained importance as a base
for Venetian trade in the Levant, and thereafter acquired many handsome
buildings, since all the leading Venetian and Greek families had to have a
house here. There were a number of revolts against foreign rule, notably in
1274–77, when the Duke of Crete and many Venetian nobles were killed,
and in 1458–60. From 1538 onwards the Italian architect and military engineer Michele Sanmicheli surrounded the town with a massive circuit of
walls and fortifications.

After the Turks captured Crete in 1648 they laid siege to Candia. The town
put up a stubborn defence, in which French and German troops also took
part. The siege lasted 21 years, costing the lives of 31,000 defenders and
119,000 Turks, and finally ending in 1669 with the surrender of the fortress
to the Turks. The town was destroyed, and almost all its Christian inhabitants left it. The Cretans gave Candia the name of Megalo Kastro ("Great
Fortress"), and it is referred to under that name in Kazantzákis's novel
"Zorba the Greek".

The town now became the seat of a pasha but lost all its economic
importance. In the 16th and 17th centuries there was an important school of
painters here, one member of which was the celebrated painter El Greco
(see Famous People). Iráklion recovered its economic importance only
after the union of Crete with Greece in 1898. During the Second World War
half the town was destroyed. In 1971 Iráklion became capital of Crete.

Sights in Iráklion

★Morosini
Fountain

The handsome Morosini Fountain, the central feature of the town, was
erected in 1628 by the Venetian governor Francesco Morosini, incorporating four figures of lions which probably date from the 14th century. It
consists of eight almost circular basins arranged in a circle round a central
basin borne on lions. The outside walls are decorated with reliefs on
themes from Greek mythology, including Europa on the bull and various
fabulous creatures.

Áyios Márkos

Opposite the Morosini Fountain is the church of Áyios Márkos (San Marco),
dedicated to Venice's patron saint. Built by the Venetians in 1239, during
the Venetian period it was the seat of the Latin Archbishop of Crete and the
court and burial church of the Dukes of Crete. It was badly damaged by
earthquakes in 1303 and again in 1508. During the period of Turkish rule it
became the Defterda Mosque, which remained in use from 1669 to 1915.
Restored in 1960, it is now a hall for exhibitions and other events.

The handsome Venetian Loggia ▶

The Morosini Fountain, at the hub of the town's life

The campanile which once stood to the right of the church was replaced during the Turkish period by a minaret, the foundations of which can still be seen. The two lateral aisles of the basilica are linked with the nave by six arcades, each with five columns of green marble. On the north side is a handsome doorway with pointed arches. The church's main attraction is a collection of copies of frescos from well-known Cretan churches, including the Panayía Kera at Kritsá.

Venetian Loggia Armoury

A little way north is the Loggia, one of the handsomest and most harmonious Venetian monuments in Crete. Like the Morosini Fountain, it was built by Francesco Morosini between 1626 and 1628. Originally designed as a meeting-place for high officials and Creto-Venetian nobles, it was used by the Turks to house government offices. It was rebuilt after suffering damage during the Second World War.

A two-storey building with a balustrade round the roof, it has seven arcades along the front and two at each end, with Doric columns on the ground floor and Ionic columns on the upper floor. On the metopes between the two floors are military trophies and the lion of St Mark.

Adjoining the Loggia on the east is the large Venetian Armoury (Armería), built in the 17th century. It is now the Town Hall (Dimarkhíon).

Sagredo Fountain

To the north of the Loggia and the Armoury is the little Sagredo Fountain, erected by Duca Sagredo in 1602. It has been altered in the course of time, but the female figure (badly damaged), flanked by Ionic pilasters (also partly destroyed), and the slab with the inscription "Cura Sagredi profluit ista ducis" ("This fountain flows thanks to Duke Sagredo") are original.

Áyios Títos

Farther north is the church of Áyios Títos (10th/11th century; open: daily 7am–noon and 5–8pm), which is dedicated to St Titus, first bishop of Crete. The church was several times destroyed by earthquake and fire and repeatedly rebuilt and altered. In 1862 it was converted into a mosque, which after a further earthquake was renovated in 1872, with a decorative Islamic exterior. After the Turkish withdrawal from Crete the church was altered to revert to its earlier use as an Orthodox church. Three apses were added to the Islamic structure with its central dome and four subsidiary domes over the corners. Two Islamic prayer niches have been preserved in the outer wall and in the narthex.

The interior is modern, but it is of great interest for its woodcarving. In the little chapel of St Titus, entered from the narthex, is the skull of St Titus, housed in a gold reliquary. Carried off to Venice in 1669, after the Turkish conquest of Crete, it was returned to Iráklion in 1966.

At the far end of Odós 25 Avgoústou is the old Venetian harbour with its imposing fortress, known in Turkish times as the Koúles (open: Tues.–Sun. 8.30am–3pm). On the outer walls of the fortress, built between 1523 and 1540, are high reliefs of the lion of St Mark. At the north-east corner is the stump of a minaret. A ramp, up which cannon could be transported, runs up to the upper level, which is edged by battlements. The fortress contains numerous store-rooms, living quarters and casemates.

Venetian fortress (Koúles) (illustration, p. 59)

On the harbour are a number of Venetian arsenals with barrel-vaulted roofs in which galleys were built and repaired.

Arsenals

★★ Archaeological Museum (plans on pp. 144/145)

In the eastern part of the old town is the Archaeological Museum, Iráklion's principal tourist attraction and one of the most important in Crete. Here can be seen the treasures recovered by archaeologists from the palaces and houses of Knossós, Phaistós, Ayía Triáda and other sites on the island, giving a vivid impression of the flourishing pre-Greek cultures of Crete.

This magnificent collection is a must for all visitors to Crete.

For the dating of the Early Minoan (EM I–III), Middle Minoan (MM I–III) and Late Minoan (LM I–III) periods see the table on p. 34.

Opening times
Mon. 11–5pm,
Tues.–Fri.
8am–5pm
Sat., Sun. and
holidays
8.30am–3pm

The tour, starting on the ground floor, follows the numbering of the rooms and cases shown in the plans on pp. 128/129, which follows the numbering used in the museum. The arrangement of the cases is not final and there may be changes.

Tour of museum

Material of the Neolithic and Minoan (Prepalatial) periods (5000–2100 B.C.).

Room I

Pottery with simple incised patterns from Knossós, votive figures of animals, female idols and cult vessels; axes, clubs and bone implements from various sites.

Case 1

Vases and the figure of a worshipper from Knossós; strainer from Phaistós.

Case 2

Conical cups in Pýrgos style and vessels with simple linear ornament in the Áyios Onoúphrios style.

Case 3

Finds from the circular tombs at Lebena (Léntas): pottery, jewellery, stone vessels and bronze spearheads.

Cases 4 and 5

Vasilikí ware with mottled decoration and the characteristic spouts.

Case 6

Fine stone vases from the island of Mákhlos; magnificently worked *pyxis* lid with a handle in the form of a recumbent dog (illustration, p. 126).

Case 7

Vasilikí ware and pottery from Mákhlos with white and red patterns on a black ground; particularly fine are the model of a sacred ship and the figure of a bare-breasted goddess.

Case 8

Barbotine ware with pinched relief decoration; a very beautiful spouted jug.

Case 9

125

The superbly decorated lid of a pyxis

Case 10	Cups, jugs, fruit dishes, etc., from the Minoan settlement at Palaíkastro. Particularly fine is a votive dish with a relief of shepherds and a flock of sheep.
Case 11	Stone and ivory seals, some of them in the form of animals, from tombs in the Mesará and at Phourní. Note particularly a cylinder seal of the Babylonian king Hammurabi, a fourteen-sided ivory seal, one of the earliest evidences of Minoan script, and a seal in the form of a fly.
Case 12	Cult vessels and vases from various sites. Interesting items are an offering vessel in the form of a bull with three acrobats (a representation of the ritual bull-leaping game) and a very beautiful spouted jug with red incised decoration.
Case 13	Obsidian blades, Cycladic idols and stone vessels from various sites.
Case 14	Blades – the oldest examples of copper-working on Crete – and silver spearheads from various sites.
Case 15	Objects from tombs in the Mesará: offering vessels, pottery figures of animals, including a bull with an acrobat.
Cases 16 and 17	Rock-crystal, cornelian and gold jewellery (e.g. a tiny frog) from various sites.
Case 18	Seals, including some of ivory and steatite and some with hieroglyphic signs.
Case 18A	Jewellery from the Phourní necropolis. A Cycladic idol is evidence of Crete's extensive trading contacts.

Mainly material from Knossós, Mália and peak sanctuaries of the Proto-palatial period (2050–1800 B.C.).	**Room II**
Beautiful examples of Vasilikí ware; cult vessel with the figure of a goddess.	Case 19
Bell-shaped cult utensils with horns and painted faces.	Case 20
Figures of male and female worshippers, animal figures and sacrificial utensils.	Case 21
Bronze double axes, miniature animal idols and stone utensils with Egyptian hieroglyphs.	Case 21A
Fine Kamáres-style pottery with white and red patterns on a black ground.	Case 22
Thin-walled "eggshell" ware and small vessels of faience and gold.	Case 23
Figures of male and female worshippers; tri-columnar shrines with doves, symbolising the apparition of the divinity; altars with horns of consecration; a miniature palanquin.	Case 24
Faience plaques depicting house-fronts, probably parts of a decorative feature or perhaps a toy; a fine gold-hilted dagger.	Case 25
Pottery decorated with animal and plant motifs in relief, gold pendants and seals.	Cases 26 and 26A
Kamáres-style and barbotine pottery.	Case 27
A variety of delicately worked seals with figural and ornamental designs.	Case 28
Storage jars in Kamáres style; a handsome pithos decorated with palms.	Case 29
Material of the Protopalatial period (2050–1800 B.C.) from Phaistós.	**Room III**
Kamáres-style and barbotine ware, some with octopus motifs. Particularly notable are a fruit-press (30); a hanging vessel with a large opening in the side, perhaps a lamp (31); a beautiful vase with applied shell ornament (32); and fruit-stands with white painted decoration (32A).	Cases 30–32 and 32A
Pottery and stone vessels, fine Kamáres ware, a *kernos* with twelve cavities for offerings, a vase with a representation of two worshippers, a *rhyton* with a spout in the form of a lily.	Case 33
A unique stand, perhaps for a vase, with relief ornament depicting the bottom of the sea, with dolphins.	Case 33A
Fine Kamáres-style pottery, including eggshell ware (cups, dishes). Two particularly fine examples are a thin-walled handled cup and a spouted jug with white double spirals (34). Another interesting item is a grater (35).	Cases 34–36
Fragmentary seals, some with hieroglyphic signs.	Case 37
Kamáres ware: cups, amphoras, *pithoi*; *rhytons*, some in the form of bulls' heads.	Case 38
Storage jars in barbotine style with relief decoration. Note particularly a magnificent amphora and an elegant jug with white spiral patterns.	Case 39
Seal-stones with fine ornamental and figural decoration, including figures of animals.	Case 40

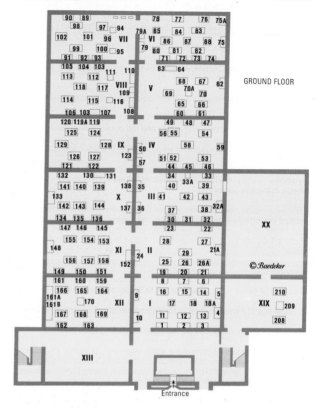

GROUND FLOOR

I   Neolithic and Prepalatial
(5000–2100 B.C.)

II   Protopalatial: Knossos, Mália
(2100–1800 B.C.)

III Protopalatial: Phaistós
(2050–1800 B.C.)

IV Neopalatial: Knossos, Phaistós, Mália
(1800–1410 B.C.)

V   Late Neopalatial: Knossos
(1450–1410 B.C.)

VI Neopalatial, Postpalatial:
Knossos, Phaistós, Arkhánes
(1600–1300 B.C.)

VII Neopalatial, Postpalatial:
Central Crete
(1800–1300 B.C.)

VIII Neopalatial: Kato Zakros
(1800–1410 B.C.)

IX Neopalatial: Eastern Crete
(1800–1410 B.C.)

X   Postpalatial: Central and Eastern Crete
(1410–1050 B.C.)

XI Sub-Minoan (1050–990 B.C.)
Early Geometric (990–810 B.C.)

XII Mature Geometric (810–710 B.C.)
Orientalising (710–620 B.C.)

XIII Minoan sarcophagi

XIX Archaic and Daedalic monumental art
(620–480 B.C.)

XX Sculpture of the early Greek,
Hellenistic and Roman periods
(5th c. B.C. to 4th c. A.D.)

Case 41   The famous Phaistós Disc (illustration, p. 35) – one of the museum's greatest treasures – with hieroglyphs running in a spiral from the outside to the centre: the earliest example of printed script.

Case 42   Cult objects: pottery offering dishes, including one with a representation of two doves, symbolising the apparition of the divinity.

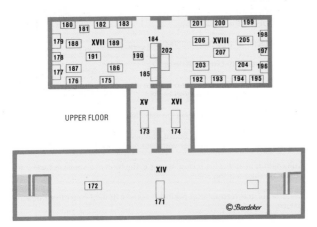

XIV, XV, XVI	XVII
Neopalatial period:	Giamalakis Collection
frescos from central	XVIII
and eastern Crete	Pottery, bronzes, coins
(1800–1410 B.C.)	(7th c. B.C. to 4th c. A.D.)

Magnificent examples of Kamáres ware, notable a large fruit-stand with a lace-like rim and spiral patterns and a large krater with white flowers in relief.	Case 43
In Room IV are displayed the museum's finest pieces of the Neopalatial period (1800–1410 B.C.) from the palaces at Knossós, Phaistós and Mália, including the bull's head *rhyton* (case 51) and the snake goddess (case 50) and collections of weapons and tools.	**Room IV**
Pottery. Note particularly an amphora and two bowls, both with Linear A characters; "lily vases".	Cases 44 and 45
Vessels for the snake cult: clay tubes attached to bowls; vessels with the sacred symbols of the double axe and the knot.	Case 46
Bronze utensils. Particularly fine is the hilt of a cult axe, perhaps a sceptre, in the form of a panther.	Case 47
Lamps, offering table and various vessels, including a fine jug in Marine style (with representations of sea creatures).	Case 48
Pottery and other vessels with Linear A inscriptions; a fine spouted jug with delicate reed decoration – a masterpiece of Minoan art (illustration, p. 7).	Case 49
Cult objects from the underground treasure chambers in the central sanctuary at Knossós, including the three famous snake goddesses with snakes as cult attributes (illustration, p. 38). Among other remarkable items are the flying fish and the rock-crystal rosettes.	Case 50
The steatite bull's head *rhyton* (with some restoration; illustration, p. 1) is one of the great masterpieces of Minoan art. The eyes are of rock crystal and jasper.	Case 51
Swords with ivory and rock-crystal hilts (on one gold hilt the figure of an acrobat); stone vessels with engraved ornament; an interesting scene	Case 52

129

depicting a sacrifice in front of a cave shrine, with cult symbols such as the sacral knot and the double axe.

Case 53	Metal objects: a large two-handled saw; jug, bowls.
Case 54	Pottery: vases with birds and discs.
Case 55	Cult objects: a marble cross, two faience plaques depicting a cow suckling her calf and a wild goat suckling her kid.
Case 56	An ivory figure of a bull-leaper in the act of leaping – a very important piece.
Case 57	A magnificent royal gaming board of ivory with gold, silver, rock-crystal and lapis lazuli inlays, together with four pieces, also of ivory.
Cases 58 and 59	Cult *rhytons* of alabaster, including one in the form of a lioness's head (59), and of marble; a triton shell.
Room V	Material of the Neopalatial period (1800–1410 B.C.) from the Knossós palace.
Case 60	A variety of vessels, including some in the Floral style.
	To the right of the case is an alabaster *pithos* with incised and applied spiral patterns.
Case 61	Stone friezes with split and whole rosettes in relief; a very rare bronze statuette of a god wearing a pointed cap.
Case 62	Porphyry oil lamps; a large stone weight (29kg/64lb), also of porphyry, with octopus decoration; an interesting hair-style in black stone; imported objects from the East and from Egypt (including an alabaster *pyxis* lid with a hieroglyphic cartouche giving the name of a pharaoh of the Hyksos dynasty.
	Beside case 62 is a model of the royal villa at Knossós.
Cases 63 and 64	Pottery: cups, bowls; a tripod-footed offering table.
Case 65	Seals made from semi-precious stones from various sites.
Case 66	Alabaster libation vessels with spiral ornament, probably used for cult ceremonies shortly before the destruction of the palace.

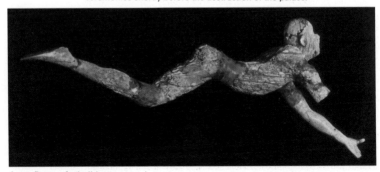

Ivory figure of a bull-leaper

Large vessels and sherds in the Floral, Marine and Palace styles (this last found only at Knossós); lid with representation of three birds (68).	Cases 67 and 68
Clay tablets in Linear A and Linear B script (Linear A has not been deciphered; Linear B has been identified as archaic Greek).	Case 69
Small items and jewellery; interesting model of a Minoan house (70A).	Cases 70 and 70A
Material of the Neopalatial and Postpalatial periods (1600–1300 B.C.) from necropolises at Knossós, Phaistós and Arkhánes.	**Room VI**
Terracotta objects depicting cult ceremonies: four figures, probably the deified dead, in a rectangular room, with two other figures depositing offerings in front of them; four figures dancing a sacred round dance; a figure observing a cult ceremony (not now identifiable).	Case 71
Very fine stone and pottery vases.	Case 72
Pottery: jug with nipples (74); fine terracotta statuette of a kourotrophos, probably a goddess with a new-born divine child.	Cases 73 and 74
Bronze, pottery and stone vessels.	Case 75
Skeleton of a horse, as found heaped up for ritual burial.	Case 75A
Three-handled amphora with boar's-tusk helmets; beautiful jug with birds and fishes.	Case 76
On the wall is a reconstruction drawing of a tomb.	
Weapons; gold cup with spiral patterns.	Case 77
Boar's-tusk helmet, unique in Crete.	Case 78
Stone and pottery vessels with bird and fish patterns; *rhyton* fashioned from a triton shell.	Case 79
Cylindrical ivory *pyxis* with representation of a bull hunt.	Case 79A
A well preserved libation jug with spiked decoration (probably an imitation of a metal model): one of the most important items of this period.	Case 80
Jewellery: necklaces of heart-shaped ivy leaves (the earliest of their kind), rings, diadems; toilet articles, small cube-shaped weights for weighing souls in the kingdom of the dead; ivory models of ships.	Case 81
Various vessels: a beautiful alabaster vase with the cartouche of Pharaoh Tuthmosis III; large amphoras (83).	Cases 82 and 83
Weapons: gold-hilted sword, with a representation of a lion hunting a wild goat.	Case 84
Bronze helmet with cheek-pieces: the only Minoan metal helmet.	Case 85
Beautiful jewellery and other grave goods: ring with four dancing women and another figure, probably a goddess, hovering above, a masterpiece from Isópata (87); fine ivory plaque representing a wild goat (88).	Cases 86–88
Material from villas, palaces and sacred caves of the Neopalatial and Postpalatial periods (1600–1300 B.C.).	**Room VII**
Immediately on the right are the largest known double axes and horns of consecration; to the left are three large bronze cauldrons.	

Iráklion (Herakleion · Heraklion)

Cases 89–91	Stone lamps, vases and small objects (e.g. the expressive little figures of worshippers: 89); pottery; a handsome obsidian *rhyton*.
Case 92	Figures of worshippers, double axes, votive figures of animals.
Case 93	Amphoras, a jug with double axes and a sacral knot; charred remains of food (corn, pulses).
Case 94	The steatite Harvesters' Vase, one of the museum's principal treasures, with a lively representation of men returning, singing, from the corn harvest.
Case 95	The steatite Chieftain's Cup, with fine relief decoration showing a young man bearing a sceptre, in front of him a dignitary with a sword over his shoulder and behind him three men carrying animal skins.
Case 96	A conical steatite *rhyton* with representations of boxing, wrestling and bull-leaping.
Cases 97 and 98	Bronze swords; figures of worshippers; double axes, one of them with hieroglyphs (98); various small objects.
Case 99	Bronze bars used as currency, each weighing one talent (29kg/64lb).
Case 100	Bronze tools; two potter's wheels; small objects.
Case 101	Gold jewellery: the famous bee pendant from Mália (illustration, p. 53); a gold ring with the only representation of a ship, perhaps with a goddess in front of a tree shrine; double axes, bulls' heads.
Case 102	Figures of worshippers; bronze figures of animals (e.g. the oldest representation of horses; goats); triton shell in obsidian.
Room VIII	Material of the Neopalatial period (1800–1410 B.C.) from the Káto Zákros palace.
Case 104	Cult vessels with figure-of-eight handles.
Case 105	Stone, pottery and bronze vessels, including an incense-burner decorated with ivy leaves.
	To the left of case 105 are three large *pithoi*; the middle one has an inscription in Linear A. Above them, on the wall, is a frieze from the dining-room of the palace with relief spiral patterns.
Cases 103–107	Numerous *rhytons* and other vessels, including pots and jugs in Floral and Marine style.
Case 108	Pottery and stone vessels; stone capital with *abacus*.
Case 109	Another masterpiece: a *rhyton* of rock crystal, with a handle of crystal beads and a circlet of gilded beads round the neck (illustration, p. 53).
Case 110	*Rhyton* in Marine style with starfishes and triton shells; a small head of a wild goat.
Case 111	An important *rhyton* of greyish-green stone in the form of a peak sanctuary (see drawing on wall), decorated with horns of consecration, spiral patterns and wild goats.
Case 112	Swords, bronze axes and everyday objects.
Case 113	Fragmentary elephants' tusks, copper bars, vases in Marine style.

The steatite Harvester Vase   *Goddess in a swing*

Stone vessels: *rhytons*, chalices, cups.	Case 114
Bronze tools, including two-handled saws.	Case 115
Steatite rhyton of similar quality to the one in case 51.	Case 116
Small objects: axes, ivory butterfly, cat's head, faience shell.	Case 117
Cult vessels: stone rhyton with clover-leaf foot, amphora veined in grey and white. Against the west wall are six large pithoi, some of which have inscriptions in Linear A.	Case 118
Material from eastern Crete, also of the Neopalatial period (1800–1410 B.C.).	**Room IX**
Pottery with Floral and Marine decoration, stone and bronze vessels, small pottery figures, *kernos*, bottle with octopus motif (120).	Cases 119, 119A, 120, 121
Fine *rhytons*, including one in the form of a bull with delicate reticulate decoration; vessel in the form of a handled basket with double axes.	Case 122
Terracotta figures of worshippers, pottery beetles.	Case 123
Seal impressions with a variety of cult motifs; ivories, including unique figures of a seated and a standing child and plaques with sacral knots and double axes.	Case 124
Pottery, some in Marine style; stone objects; bronze tools and weapons (127).	Cases 125–127
Fine seal-stones of semi-precious stones with representations of animals, cult scenes and portraits, including one of a bearded man.	Case 128

Iráklion (Herakleion · Heraklion)

Case 129	At present empty.
Room X	Material of the Postpalatial period (1410–1050 B.C.) from central and eastern Crete, mainly from chamber tombs.
Cases 130 and 131	A variety of vessels (vases, cups, bowls, cult utensils).
Case 132	Incense-burners with bird patterns; priestesses dancing to the music of a lyre.
Case 133	Female idols with raised hands and caps bearing sacred attributes such as poppy-heads, double horns and birds.
Case 134	Pottery; stone *kernos* with five dishes for offerings.
Case 135	Female divinities with cult attributes (snakes, diadem); beautiful votive statuettes; clay pipes, probably used in the snake cult.
Cases 136–138	Handsome jug with spiral patterns (136); *pyxis*, in which jewellery was found (137); figures of animals and children's urns (138).
Cases 139–141	Moulds for cult objects such as double axes and horns (139); model of a shrine (140); *kraters*, including one with the representation of a horseman (138).
Cases 142 and 143	Clay pipes (142); collection of idols, including the unique figure of a goddess in a swing, with two birds (143; illustration, p. 133).
Case 144	Bronze objects: weapons, implements and the oldest fibula found in Crete.
Room XI	Materials of the Subminoan and Geometric periods (1050–710 B.C.) from various sites.
Cases 145 and 146	Vases; circular *kernos* with with small *pithoi* and human figures (145); pottery; bronze tripod (146).
Cases 147 and 148	Bronze statuettes (147); goddesses with raised hands; *rhyton* in the form of an ox-cart (148).
Case 149	Votive objects from the Cave of Eileithyia, goddess of fertility and birth.
Cases 150 and 151	Vases and other objects (idols of divinities, jewellery, bronze objects).
Case 152	At present empty.
Case 153	The earliest iron objects found in Crete: weapons, tools, jewellery.
Cases 154 and 155	Cult objects and vases; clay model with horns of consecration (154); amphoras (155).
Case 156	Large vases and jugs, a huge *krater* with representations of worshippers and horses.
Case 157	Amphoras and urns with meander, rosette and spiral patterns.
Case 158	Cult objects: jewellery, bronze votive offerings and scarabs.
Room XII	Material of the Geometric and Orientalising periods (810–620 B.C.) from central Crete.
Cases 159–161	Pottery; clay and bronze statuettes; stone vessels; Hellenistic figures and votive objects (161).

Bronze sheets from the sanctuary of Hermes Dendrites at Sými, with hunting scenes. — Case 161A

Vases and small sculpture: unique representation of a pair of lovers, probably Theseus and Ariadne, on the neck of a jug; urn with mourning scene (both 163). — Cases 162 and 163

Magnificent bronze belt with figures of two women and a man, accompanied by archers defending them against attacking chariots. — Case 164

Ash-urns; grave goods, including a cauldron-like mixing vessel with sculptured griffins' heads (168). — Cases 165–168

Bronze objects. Note particularly the fragmentary stand for a cauldron with the representation of a couple, perhaps Theseus and Ariadne, on a ship (169). Gold jewellery (170). — Cases 169 and 170

Room XIII displays Minoan sarcophagi. There are two types – rectangular and oval – in which the dead were buried in a crouching position. The sarcophagi are mainly decorated with floral and animal motifs. — **Room XIII**

Room XIX is devoted to Daedalic and Archaic monumental art (620–480 B.C.). The finest pieces in this room come from the temples of Rizenía. — **Room XIX**

West wall: frieze of horsemen from Temple A in Rizenía, showing Oriental influence; sculpture from a temple in Górtys; limestone birds from the sanctuary of Zeus Thenatas in Amnisós; fragmentary limestone figure of a seated goddess, also from a temple in Górtys; head from Axós; stele from Dréros; reliefs of goddesses.
    North wall: torso from Eleftherna; terracotta waterspout from the temple of Zeus at Palaíkastro.
    South wall: Hymn to Zeus from the Palaíkastro temple; column capital in the form of a flower and lion's head from Phaistós; torso of seated goddess from Máles; upper part of the body of a seated figure from Astrítsi.

Votive shields and tympana (hand drums) from the Idaean Cave. — Cases 208 and 209

Three statuettes of Apollo, Artemis and Leto in hammered bronze. — Case 210

In the passage leading to Room XX is sculptural decoration from the entrance to Temple A at Rizenía: two symmetrically arranged goddesses, below these two reliefs of panthers and grazing deer, and on the underside a relief of the goddesses.

Room XX contains sculpture of the Classical, Hellenistic and Roman periods (480 B.C.–A.D. 337). — **Room XX**
    South wall: fragmentary metope from a temple at Knossós depicting Heracles killing the Erymanthian Boar; monumental funerary stele from Iráklion with a scene of farewell; fragmentary funerary stele from Ayía Pelayía depicting an archer.
    West wall: sarcophagus from Iráklion; mosaic from Knossós depicting Poseidon; fragmentary doorway with traces of colouring.
    North wall: copies of sculpture from Górtys: Athena Parthenos, after Phidias; Polycletes' famous Spearbearer; kneeling figure of Aphrodite.
    East wall: marble sarcophagus from Mália inscribed "Polybios"; Leda with the swan; various fragmentary sarcophagi with reliefs.
    Centre: colossal statue of Apollo from his temple in Górtys.

In Room XIV are displayed the celebrated frescos of the Neopalatial period (1800–1410 B.C.) from central and eastern Crete. Although these masterpieces have been extensively restored they give an excellent impression of the refinement of Minoan culture. — **Room XIV** (upper floor)

North wall (from right to left): three fragments of processional frescos showing priestesses leading sacrificial animals; cats stalking birds; a goddess seated in front of a shrine; a woman in prayer amid flowers; a griffin; several fragments of the great frieze from the processional corridor at Knossós, depicting offering-bearers and musicians; fragmentary bull's foot.

South wall (from right to left): very beautiful and finely painted red and white lilies; a bull-leaper somersaulting from the bull's horns over its back (illustration, p. 26); lively and colourful paintings of partridges; spiral patterns; dolphins from the Queen's Megaron at Knossós; three elegant ladies of the court, painted in blue; a fine bas-relief of a bull's head; the well-known Prince of the Lilies (illustration, p. 54), with a crown of lilies; octagonal shield.

Case 171 Ayía Triáda sarcophagus	The famous Ayía Triáda sarcophagus (*c.* 1400 B.C.), the only Minoan stone sarcophagus, probably contained the body of a king. The excellently preserved frescos on the sarcophagus depict cult ceremonies, in which the women are distinguished by white and the men by red skin. A priestess deposits an offering on an altar which stands in front of a cult building decorated with double horns; the bird on the double axe symbolises the presence of the divinity. Another priestess is sacrificing a bull, accompanied by a flute-player. Two goddesses come in from the right in a chariot drawn by two griffins. On the other side of the sarcophagus, forming part of the same scene, two priestesses accompanied by a lyre-player pour the liquids for a libation into a mixing jug. The second part of this side shows a different scene: a dead man (recognisable as such by the fact that he has no arms) stands in front of a tomb, while three men bring him two animals and (probably) a boat for the dead and two women and other bearers of gifts come in from the right.

Room XIV

Contains a model of the Knossós palace.

Case 172

Fragments of frescos: flowers, a lady of the court; fragments of a female figure.

Room XV

Room XV contains frescos of the Neopalatial period (1800–1410 B.C.) from Knossós and Týlissos.

West wall: ceremonial dance by priestesses in a sacred grove; tripartite shrine with a great crowd of spectators; the "Parisienne", a priestess with the sacral knot over her neck (illustration, p. 137); scene of sacrifice with a male and a female divinity.

North wall: blue-painted stucco ceiling with spiral pattern and rosettes.

East wall: athletes taking part in bull sports; two griffins tied to a column tail to tail.

Case 173

Fragments of frescos: labyrinth; finger holding a necklace with pendants in the form of human heads; sphinxes.

Room XVI

The frescos in Room XVI also date from the Neopalatial period.

West wall: the Saffron Gatherer, formerly thought to be a man but now seen to be a monkey, as the painting with the original fragments shows; the "Captain of the Blacks"; a tri-columnar shrine.

East wall: a blue bird; monkeys; a goddess seated on a rock.

South wall: sacral knot.

Case 174

Fragments of frescos: the "Palanquin Fresco"; bull's head and bull-leaping; court scene.

The elegant "Parisienne" ▶

The Ayía Triáda sarcophagus, the only Minoan stone sarcophagus

Room XVII
Giamalákis
Collection

In Room XVII is displayed the collection assembled by Dr Stylianos Giama-lákis, which was acquired by the State in 1962. In addition to masterpieces of Minoan art it contains material dating from the Geometric, Archaic, Greek, Roman and Byzantine periods.

Room XVIII

Continuing from Room XII on the ground floor, Room XVIII displays material of the Archaic, Greek and Roman periods (7th century B.C. to 4th century A.D.)

Other Sights in Iráklion

Bembo Fountain

At the end of Odós 1966, south-west of the Archaeological Museum, is the Bembo Fountain, erected by Zuane Bembo in 1588, using fragments of ancient architecture and sculpture. On an ancient base decorated with acanthus leaves a headless Roman statue stands between pilasters and columns, and the fountain basin is an ancient sarcophagus. Next to the pilasters are the coats of arms of Venetian families, surmounted by a lion's head and a winged lion of St Mark.

Beside the fountain is a polygonal Turkish pump-house, now occupied by a café.

Santa Maria
dei Crocioferi/
Panayía
Stavropháron

Farther south-west is the monastic church of Santa Maria dei Crocioferi (Our Lady of the Crusaders), known in Greek as Panayía Stavropháron, a handsome three-aisled basilica which dates from the 14th century.

Áyios Minás

In Platía Aikaterínis is the large metropolitan church of Áyios Minás, the town's principal church, built in the second half of the 19th century in Neo-Byzantine style. The ground-plan of this five-aisled church with a dome over the crossing is in the form of a Latin cross. The interior is sumptuous but of no great artistic interest.

The Bembo Fountain, incorporating fragments from ancient buildings

To the west is the small original church of Áyios Minás, the oldest part of which is thought to date from the 15th/16th century. Its principal treasures are the richly carved iconostases, the work of the Gastrophylákos brothers between 1740 and 1760.

To the north-east is the church of Ayía Aikateríni (1555), which in the 16th and 17th centuries housed a college belonging to St Catherine's monastery in Sinai. Among its students were the painters Michael Damaskinás and El Greco and the writers Vitzéntzos Kornáros and Yeáryios Khortátzis (for all of these see Famous People). The college was an important centre for interchange between Orthodox and Latin cultures. During the Turkish period the church became a mosque; thereafter it was used as a library and a public hall; and it finally became a museum of icons and other religious art.

★Icon Museum (former church of Ayía Aikateríni)

The most important items in the Icon Museum (closed at present 1996) are six icons by Michael Damaskinás, painted between 1580 and 1591 for Vrondísi monastery. On the north wall of the nave are the Adoration of the Kings, the Last Supper and the Mother of God of the Burning Bush (signed below, left); on the south wall are the Divine Liturgy, the Oecumenical Council of Nicaea and the Noli Me Tangere.

Another masterpiece in the collection is the expressive icon of Áyios Phanoúrios (also on the north wall). Beside it is another icon (15th century) of high quality with two finely painted scenes: Christ appearing to Mary Magdalene and the miracle of St Phanurius.

In the cases are displayed church books, an *epitáphios* (funeral cloth) and liturgical vestments. There are also important fragments of frescos in the north transept and the adjoining church of the Áyii Déka.

Near Platía Neárkhou, on Koum Kapi Bay, is the Renaissance-style Priuli or Delimarkos Fountain, erected in 1666 by the Venetian governor, Antonio Priuli. It was the last structure built by the Venetians, after the Turks destroyed the aqueduct between Mt Yioúkhtas and the town.

Priuli Fountain

Icons – Sacred Images

Icons are portable images of saints and Biblical scenes which down the centuries have played an important part in Orthodox worship and belief.

Icons are found not only in churches but also in many private houses and in vehicles. They are carried on journeys and are the object of pilgrimages. They may be decorated with precious metals and precious stones, screens, rings and watches. Icons bring the saints close to men and are therefore the subject of great veneration. This veneration is addressed not to the icon but to the saint with whom it is equated. In churches the icons are arranged in a particular order on the iconostasis, a high wooden screen which separates the sanctuary from the body of the church. On a stand in the centre, the icon of the saint or the festival of the particular day is displayed.

Icon painting is regarded as a liturgical act, which originally could be performed only by a priest. The composition, colouring and materials to be used in the painting of an icon are precisely regulated, so that the painter is left with little freedom in the shaping of his picture and cannot develop any individual style. He may not give an icon any personal expression, and he remains nameless. His task is to maintain the established tradition. As a result icons tend to be very similar to one another, no matter in what century they are painted. Venetian influence relaxed the Byzantine forms in some respects, but the content of the icons remained the same.

A characteristic feature of icons is that the natural and architectural settings, treated abstractly, are played down, so as to emphasise the timeless divinity or holiness of the figures. The flat, two-dimensional

"Last Supper" by the famous icon-painter Michael Damaskinós

effect of the icons results from the lack of shadow, in line with the conception that the divine light permeates everything. Icons appeal to the spectator with their richness of colour, achieved through a complicated process of preparation. They are usually painted on wood with mineral colours and then covered with a coat of boiled linseed oil. This ensures the extraordinary durability of icons, which are not only contemplated but kissed and touched.

There are numerous stories of wonderworking icons. An icon of the Mother of God, for example, was stolen from the Kardiátissa monastery and taken to Constantinople, where it was chained to a column; but both the icon and the column were miraculously transported back to the monastery, where they may still be seen today.

The church of Ayía Aikateríni, now housing the Icon Museum

In a Neo-Classical building in the north-west of the town is the Historical Museum (open: Mon.–Sat. 9am–2pm), which was opened in 1953. Its collection ranges in date from late antiquity to the present day.

★**Historical Museum**

Room 1: Early Christian architectural elements (ambo, choir screen, capitals) from the church of St Titus in Górtys; relief panels from a fountain in a house in Iráklion.

Basement

Room 2: metopes from the Venetian Loggia in Iráklion; a stone slab from the entrance to the San Demetrio Bastion with the lion of St Mark and an inscription "Regnum Cretae protego" ("I protect the kingdom of Crete"); tombstones of Venetian nobles, including that of Ioánnis Pashaligos, with an inscription of 1605.

Room 2A: round window and relief of an angel from the destroyed church of San Francesco in Iráklion; Gothic head of Christ, the only one of its kind in Crete; torso of St Onuphrius.

Room 3: tombstones and inscriptions from various places; Turkish wall paintings depicting the siege of Iráklion.

Room 4: Turkish tombstones, some with turban-like tops, and Jewish stones.

Room 5: bronze objects, particularly liturgical utensils, from the church of St Titus in Górtys (6th century); throne and lectern from Valsamánero monastery; icons of the 15th–18th centuries from churches in Crete; an important icon of the Panayía Zoodákhos Piyí (the Mother of God as the Fountain of Life; 1655) from Savvathianá nunnery.

Ground floor

Room 6: a collection of icons from the former monastery of the Panayía Gouverniótissa; pottery (16th/17th century); liturgical vestments and utensils from the Asómatos monastery; jewellery and seals; coins of the Byzantine, Arab and Venetian periods.

Room 7: material of the Venetian and Turkish periods and the years of Cretan independence (1898–1908): weapons; a lithograph depicting the blowing-up of Arkádi monastery; robes and desk which belonged to Prince George of Greece.

Mezzanine

Landing: documentary photographs of the battle for Crete in 1941.

Room to right: the study of the Greek prime minister Emanouíl Tsoudéros; collection of postage stamps; historic maps and views; a utopian map of Greater Greece (1797) by the Greek poet Rígas.

Room to left: the library and study of Nikos Kazantzákis (see Famous People).

Upper floor

Landing: Cretan costumes: male costume with high boots, breeches (*vrákes*) and fringed head-scarf (*saríki* or *mandíli*); female costume with self-coloured skirt (*phoústa*),embroidered apron, bolero (*zipáni*) and jacket (*sákkos*).

Rooms 8–10: woven fabrics and needlework (17th–19th centuries); jewellery; musical instruments; wedding bread; chests; domestic equipment.

Room 11: a Cretan peasant house, with hearth, box beds and loom.

San Pietro

A little way north-east of the Historical Museum are the ruins of the Venetian monastic church of San Pietro, which dates from the first half of the 14th century. During the Turkish occupation it became a mosque, as the stump of a minaret shows.

Town walls

The fortifications of the town, which were in existence at least as early as Byzantine times, were extended and strengthened by the Venetians in the 16th century to the plans of the Veronese architect Michele Sanmicheli. The circuit of walls, some 3km/2 miles in length, consists of five bastions and two half-bastions with casemates on several levels. On some of the bastions are "cavaliers", raised platforms for cannon. Outside the walls there was a dry moat between 20 and 60m (65 and 200ft) in width, still visible in places, and beyond this a ring of polygonal outer bastions, since demolished. The various parts of the fortifications were linked with one another by a system of tunnels between 15 and 20m (50 and 65ft) underground. Most of the town's eight gates survive.

Martinengo Bastion

From the Martinengo Bastion (still preserving its cavalier), on the south side of the circuit of walls, there are good views over the town. On this bastion is the grave of the great Cretan writer Nikos Kazantzákis (see Famous People), a freethinker, who was buried here because the church refused to let him be buried in consecrated ground. The grave is marked by a plain slab of stone and a simple cross, with the inscription "I hope for nothing, I fear nothing: I am free".

Surroundings of Iráklion

Amnisós

Amnisós, 7km/4½ miles east of Iráklion, was probably a port for Knossós in Minoan times. Later there was a shrine here associated with the Cave of Eileithyia, a cult site. The village was abandoned in Turkish times.

There are only scanty remains of the ancient town (harbour installations, houses and a massive fountain-house). Under the west side of the hill, facing the sea, are the remains of the celebrated altar of Zeus Thenátas of the Archaic period. A Minoan villa known as the Harbour Commander's House was also found here. Nearby are the remains of another two-storey Minoan villa of around 1800 B.C. (destroyed by fire around 1650 B.C.), known as the House of the Lilies after its very beautiful frescos (now in the Archaeological Museum in Iráklion). It has a paved terrace from which there is a view of the sea and a large hall entered by a polythyron.

Cave of Eileithyia
(Ειλειθυια
Σπηλια)

The Cave of Eileithyia (an early Cretan goddess of birth) lies 1km/¾ mile south of Amnisós, a few yards below the road at a fig-tree. The site is enclosed and can be seen only with special permission from the Archaeological Museum in Iráklion.

In Neolithic times the cave was occupied as a dwelling-place, and from the 3rd century B.C. to the 6th century A.D. it was a cult site for a number of different cultures and religions, as is evidenced by the quantity of pottery and the number of idols found on the site. The cave, 63m/207ft long and 19m/62ft wide, contains stalagmites which bear traces of cult practices, for example a conical stalagmite with an indentation, known as the Navel, which was thought to look like the belly of a pregnant woman. In ancient times women used to rub their belly against it, believing that this would ensure an easy delivery. Another stalagmite in the form of a phallus is surrounded by walls. Recesses in the wall are flanked by stalactites and basins containing what was believed to be healing water. In the rear part of the cave is a narrow hole giving access to an underground cult area with four connected chambers.

At Nírou Kháni, 15km/9 miles east of Iráklion on the coast road, are the remains of a very well preserved Late Minoan villa (1700 B.C.; open: daily except Mon. 8.30am–3pm) which was excavated by Sir Arthur Evans in 1919. Many cult objects were found here – bowls, altars and the largest known double axes (now in the Archaeological Museum, Iráklion).

Nírou Kháni
(Νίρου Χάνι)

The entrance leads into a court paved with slate slabs and beyond this an anteroom with two columns, beyond which is the main room in the house, paved with stone slabs. The west doorway of this room opens into a passage which ends in a light-well. This gives admission to the shrine, the Room of the Four Double Axes. At the end of the passage is a staircase leading to the upper floor. To the left of the main room a passage formerly decorated with frescos leads to a room lined with benches, a reception room or banqueting room. To the east is a dark room, once lit only by lamps, and to the south are two other rooms known as the Altar Store because of the large number of cult vessels and tripod-footed offering tables found here. To the north of the residential apartments are numerous store-rooms in which many *pithoi* were discovered.

23km/14 miles west of Iráklion and 1.5km/1 mile south of the village of Skotinó is the cave of that name, which was a sacred shrine from Middle Minoan to Roman times and was visited by the Venetians, who took it for the Labyrinth, as a tourist sight. Here too there are a church and the remains of an earlier one. The cave, which is one of the largest on Crete (100m/330ft long and 40m/130ft wide), contains stalagmites.

Skotinó Cave
(Σκοτεινό Σπήλια)

13km/8 miles west of Iráklion is Arolíthos, a village established in 1987 as a tourist attraction designed to preserve old Cretan traditions, but nevertheless an idyllic place in its own right. Here a variety of craftsmen, most of them wearing traditional dress, can be seen at work, using traditional methods – weavers, potters, bakers, etc.

Arolíthos

On the outskirts of the village of Týlissos, 2km/1¼ miles south of Arolíthos, are the very interesting remains of three Late Minoan villas of different types (17th/16th century B.C.; open: Tues.–Sun. 8.30am–3pm), built in the heyday of a little town which was rapidly reoccupied after its destruction around 1500 B.C. Thereafter it continued to exist into Byzantine times.

★Týlissos
(Τύλισσος)

A notable feature of the villas is the handsome outer walls, carefully constructed of large blocks of dressed stone and stabilised by vertical wooden beams. The inside walls were plastered and painted, and the windows opened inward into light-wells. The houses had flat roofs.

To the right of the entrance is House B, the smallest of the buildings. It is regularly planned but poorly preserved.

House B

House A, the largest of the villas, is divided into a southern part, with the residential apartments, and a northern part with store-rooms and subsidiary rooms. The entrance, on the east side, is flanked by two pillars and leads into an anteroom, on the far side of which was a staircase to the upper

House A

143

A Late Minoan villa at Týlissos

floor. A doorway on the left opens into a passage, on the right of which is a store-room with a central pillar. At the far end of the passage is a large room with a light-well. Adjoining this is another room, and in the chamber beyond this, massive bronze cauldrons (now in the Archaeological Museum, Iráklion) were found. In the northern part of the villa are two large store-rooms with massive pillars, in which many *pithoi* were found, and a series of smaller rooms.

House C   The finest of the three villas is House C. Here too the entrance is on the east side, leading into an anteroom on the right of which is the porter's room. The anteroom opens into a passage, on the right of which are rooms which have preserved their floors. On the left of the passage a staircase led to the upper floor. To the left of the staircase is a room which probably served some cult function. At the end of the passage, on the right, is a doorway giving access to a number of store-rooms, in one of which is a column base. Opposite the staircase is another passage, on the left of which is another staircase, and on the right a small room with well preserved walls. From here still another passage runs east, ending at another staircase. To the north is another room, and to the north-west of this still another, opening into a light-well through three doorways flanked by pillars and an anteroom with two columns.

At the north-east corner of the complex is a cistern, from which a system of clay pipes carried water into the houses. To the north of House C a *megaron*, of which there remain the substructures under the columns in the antechamber, the wall of the cella and a massive threshold, was built in Mycenaean times. Adjoining this, in a paved court, is the altar of a classical temple.

Sklavókambos   At Sklavókambos, 9km/5½ miles west of Týlissos, on the left of the road, are (Σκλαβόκαμπος)   the scanty remains of a Late Minoan villa dating from around 1500 B.C.

144

which was excavated in the 1930s. It was badly damaged by road works during the Second World War.

The main entrance, on the east side, leads through a doorway with two intermediate pillars into a living room, on the west side of which is another room, interpreted as a shrine. Under a staircase farther to the west was found a stone slab pierced by a hole and provided with a drainage channel, probably a lavatory. On the north-west side of the building is a veranda with two pillars. In the centre of the house is a light-well.

The large village of Anóyia, situated 20km/12½ miles west of Iráklion at an altitude of 700m/2300ft, was totally destroyed by German troops in 1944 in retaliation for the kidnapping of General Kreipe, and all the male inhabitants were shot. The event is commemorated by a tablet on the modern town hall. A few old houses still survive in the lowest part of the village round the pretty *platía*. Here a signpost points to the Grílios Museum, which is devoted to the work of the naïve painter and wood-carver Alkivíades Skoulás Grílios. The village, once a centre of hand-weaving, is famed for its festival and during the season is often overcrowded with visitors. It is a good base for walks and climbs in the Mount Ida range.

Anóyia
(Ανώγια)

The main attractions of Axós, a hill village 5km/3 miles north-west of Anóyia which was the site of a Minoan settlement, are its Byzantine churches. The church of Ayía Iríni is a charming combination of an older one-room chapel and a cross-in-square church which adjoins it and serves as a narthex. The drum supporting the dome has elegant blind arcading.

The simple one-room chapel of Áyios Ioánnis, set in a churchyard, is built on the foundations of an Early Christian basilica, fragments of whose mosaic pavement survive. It contains fine frescos of the 14th and 15th centuries. There are only scanty remains of ancient Axos on the hill above the church. From the site there are wide views.

Axós
(Αξός)

The road from Rogdiá to the nunnery of Savvathianá, 18km/11 miles west of Iráklion, runs through vineyards, with superb views of Iráklion Bay. Well maintained and picturesque, the nunnery lies at the head of a valley and is surrounded by tall trees. It has two churches with icons of the 17th and 18th centuries, notably an icon (1741) of St Anthony with scenes from his life.

Savvathianá nunnery
(Μονή Σαββαθιανών)

The pretty village of Phódele, set amid orange and olive groves 29km/18 miles west of Iráklion, is traversed by a tree-lined stream, on the banks of which, opposite the centre of the village, is a shady picnic place. The area is particularly beautiful when the orange-trees are in blossom and the whole valley is filled with their fragrance.

The great painter El Greco (see Famous People) is said to have been born in Phódele. In the centre of the village, under an ancient plane-tree, is a memorial tablet presented by the Spanish university of Valladolid, and in the church is a book with reproductions of his most famous pictures. To the north of the village centre, reached by way of a bridge over the stream (to left), is the church of the Panayía, a finely proportioned 13th century cross-in-square church built on the site of a three-aisled pillared basilica of the 8th century. It contains frescos of excellent quality, mostly of the 13th century. From the church a path to the left runs up to the house in which El Greco is said to have been born.

Phódele
(Φόδελε)

On a green hill above the village of Krousónas, 25km/15 miles south-west of Iráklion, is the nunnery of Ayía Iríni, built since the last war. The 24 nuns lovingly care for the flowers in the courtyard of the nunnery and live by selling their needlework.

Nunnery of Ayía Iríni
(Μονή Αγίας Ειρήνης)

The village of Ayía Varvára lies at a height of 600m/2000ft 30km/19 miles south of Iráklion. At the northern entrance to the village is a white-washed crag known as the Navel of Crete, the geographical centre of the island, on which stands the church of Prophítis Ilías.

Ayía Varvára
(Αγία Βαρβάρα)

Iráklion (Herakleion · Heraklion)

Priniás
(Πρινιάς)

5km/3 miles north of Ayía Varvára is the village of Priniás. Here, on Mt Patéla (680m/2230ft), are the scanty remains of ancient Rizenía. The site is reached by taking a road which runs north from the village and in 2km/1¼ miles, at a rock formation, climbing a hill on the right; then, 200m/220yd before the chapel of Áyios Panteléimon, the site, enclosed by a fence, is seen on the right. From here there are spectacular views of the sea and the surrounding area.

The site, which was occupied from Late Minoan times, was fortified in the late Classical and Hellenistic periods by the building of town walls and a fortress.

Excavation brought to light the foundation walls of two temples dating from the 7th and 6th centuries B.C., the oldest surviving temples of the Archaic period in Crete. The northern temple (Temple A), dedicated to Rhea, consists of a pronaos and a naos with a bench along the south side. Temple B, which is narrower and slightly out of alignment, has an episthodomos in addition to the naos and pronaos. Both temples had unusual rectangular sacrificial altars consisting of heaps of stones enclosed by stone slabs and covered with clay. Temple A is noted for its unique sculptural decoration, a frieze of horsemen and a figure of the goddess Britomartis on the door-frame of the naos (now in the Archaeological Museum, Iráklion).

To the east of the temples, in the northern part of the site, are the remains of a settlement of the Geometric period. To the west are the foundations of a square fortress of the 4th century B.C. with four projecting corner towers.

Zarós
(Ζαρός)

The large village of Zarós (alt. 340m/1115ft), 47km/29 miles south-west of Iráklion, is reached from the Ayía Varvára–Kamáres road. On the road, just before the village of Yéryeri, is a memorial to 25 hostages shot by the Germans in 1944. Zarós is famed for its trout farm and for the good walking in the area. Excellent trout are to be had in the Votomos taverna.

500m/550yd beyond the village a road (2km/1¼ miles) runs up to the two-aisled monastic church of Áyios Nikólaos, which has 15th century frescos. Higher up (a 40 minute walk) is a cave with the chapel of Áyios Efthímios. From here there are wide views over the southern foothills of the Mount Ida range and the Mesará. The few surviving 14th century frescos in the chapel include a representation of Christ as the Man of Sorrows, of considerable artistic quality. Legend has it that Áyios Efthímios (Euthymius) lived in the cave, One day, being in great need, he stole some fruit but was caught in the act and shot. He is now regarded as the patron saint of those who steal because they are in need.

Vrondísi monastery
(Μονή Βροντίσι)

From the Vrondísi monastery, 4km/2½ miles west of Zarós, there are wide views into the valley. Under a mighty plane-tree outside the entrance to the monastery, on the left, is a handsome Venetian fountain (15th century) with figures of Adam and Eve. There are four spouts in the form of heads, personifying the four rivers of Paradise. It is not known when the monastery was founded. The present buildings date from 1630–39, but in the older part of the church there are the remains of 14th century frescos. The church of Áyios Antónios, a jewel of Byzantine art, has two aisles of different heights, the north aisle being the older, and a separate bell-tower, a Venetian-style campanile which is one of the oldest in Crete. There are frescos of excellent quality in the south aisle. Uniquely placed in the vaulting of the apse is a representation of the Last Supper, and on the vaulting of the naos, unusually, are numerous saints. On the vaulting of the sanctuary are angels bearing Christ's winding-sheet. Notable among the icons on the iconostasis are an angel with the symbol of the vine, the Panayía Odiyítria and St Anthony.

★Valsamónero monastery
(Μονή Βαλσαμόνερο)

The monastery of Valsamónero ("balsam water") is 2km/1¼ miles from the village of Vorízia and 8km/5 miles from Zarós. It can be seen only with the keeper of the key, who lives in Vorízia. It is reached on a poor road which runs down on the left just beyond the village. It is beautifully situated, with marvellous views of the Mount Ida range.

The church of Vrondísi monastery, with its old bell-tower

The church of Valsamónero monastery, which has magnificent frescos

There are only a few remnants of the monastery itself, but the church of Áyios Phanoúrios with its famous frescos is excellently preserved. On the south front, in Gothic/Venetian style, is a handsome belfry. The oldest part of the church, which contains work of different periods, is the wider north aisle, dedicated to the Panayía, which was built around 1330. The narrower south aisle, dedicated to John the Baptist, dates from 1400. The transept was added in 1426. The narthex (15th/16th century) has a decorated pointed doorway and above this a circular window.

The iconostases are finely carved with vine-leaves and shells but have lost their icons.

The frescos (14th/15th century) are of high quality and great artistic interest. In the south aisle, above the entrance, is the Massacre of the Innocents; to the left and above the arches opposite, scenes from the life of John the Baptist; on the north wall the Crucifixion and the Entombment; in the apse John the Baptist; and on the south wall the Betrayal. In the north aisle, on the south wall St Jerome with the lion; on the vaulting mostly scenes from the life of Christ; on the north wall, from left to right, Christ, St John of Damascus, the Birth of the Virgin, St Jerome with the lion and Christ between two angels; and in the apse the Annunciation. In the transept: in the conch of the apse Christ Pantokrator, above this the Trinity, and below the Divine Liturgy. In the narthex is the Tree of Jesse.

Myrtiá
(Μυρτιά)

In the wine-growing village of Myrtiá, 17km/10½ miles south of Iráklion, is the Kazantzákis Museum (opened in 1983), with numerous mementoes (personal effects, books, oil paintings, drawings) of Crete's greatest writer, Nikos Kazantzákis (see Famous People). For those interested in Kazantzákis's works a visit to this museum is a must, though some of the exhibits tend to over-stress the "pagan" aspects of his thought. There is a slide show on his life, with commentaries in many languages.

Angarathós monastery
(Μονή Αγχαραθού)

23km/14 miles south of Iráklion is the Angarathós monastery, which is believed to have been founded in 960 and dates in its present form from the Venetian period. In this flower-decked monastery live 18 monks, most of them elderly. The church, rebuilt in 1941, contains an unusual icon of the Mother of God suckling the Child.

Émbaros
(Έμπαρος)

At Émbaros, 46km/29 miles south-east of Iráklion, is the simple one-room chapel of Áyios Yeóryios, with magnificent and well preserved frescos of 1436–37, the earliest works of Manuel Phokás.

Thrapsanó
(Θραψανό)

In the village of Thrapsanó, 31km/19 miles south-east of Iráklion, the main street is lined with potters' workshops (where the potters can be seen at work). The village, with its winding lanes and old Turkish houses, has hardly changed for centuries.

Asími
(Ασήμι)

In the village of Asími, 50km/31 miles south of Iráklion, there is a large peasant market every Thursday morning.

Tsoútsouros
(Τσούτσουρος)

Tsoútsouros, situated 76km/47 miles from Iráklion in a wide bay on the beautiful south coast, has good beaches. Above the beach is a cave dedicated to the Cretan fertility goddess Eileithyia in which much material of the Geometric period was found.

Kastéli Kisámou   B 2

Καστέλι Κισάμου

Nomós: Chaniá
Chief town of nomós: Chaniá
Population: 3000

Kastéli Kisámou, Crete's most westerly town, situated on the south side of Kísamos Bay, a wide, deep inlet between two peninsulas, is the centre of an intensive wine-growing area.

The particular charm of the town, which is gradually succumbing to tourism, lies in its situation at the head of the bay against a background of green hills.

In antiquity Kastéli, under the name of Kísamos, was the port of Polyrinía (Polyrrhenia), a few kilometres south, and it continued in that function under the Romans, the Byzantines and the Venetians, who fortified the town. In Roman times, thanks to the increasing fame of the nearby sanctuary of Dictynna, it was able to break away from Polyrinía and develop independently. During the Venetian period Kastéli was the see of a Roman Catholic bishop.

Only fragments of the town walls of that period survive, since after the First World War the walls and the town's mosques were pulled down and used in the extension of the harbour. A small folklore museum displays locally found domestic items.

Surroundings of Kastéli Kisámou

A half-hour walk above the village of Polyrinía (6km/4 miles south of Kastéli Kisámou), on an open hill, are the remains of the city of Polyrrhenia, founded by Dorians in the 8th century B.C. During the Greek period it was the most important town in western Crete after Phalásarna. From that period there remain only a few foundations on the acropolis on the northern slope of the hill; from the Byzantine period there is a church incorporating many architectural fragments from ancient buildings; from the Venetian period there are the massive fortress walls.

From the site there are fine views of Kísamos Bay.

The road to Kefáli, 29km/18 miles south of Kastéli Kisámou, runs through chestnut forests and olive groves, past hillsides covered with holm oaks and tall plane-trees. The village itself nestles on the hillside below the road. In its narrow winding streets can be seen beautiful inner courtyards, vegetable gardens, orchards and some ruins of Venetian mansions.

In the churchyard is the little one-room chapel of Sotirás Christoú, with two bays roofed with barrel-vaulting. It is richly decorated with frescos of 1320 in two different styles.

The village of Váthi, 1km/¾ mile south of Kefáli, has two small churches with frescos. In the village itself is the one-room chapel of Áyios Yeóryios, with fragmentary paintings dating, according to the founder's inscription, from 1284. To the south of the village is the church of the Archangel Michael, which has well preserved 14th century frescos.

The little whitewashed Khrysoskalítissa monastery (17th century), 10km/6 miles from Váthi, is conspicuously situated on a low crag above the sea. The monastery, which now has a rather modern aspect, was frequently abandoned in the course of its eventful history, and in 1944 the Germans destroyed many of its buildings. It is now occupied only by one monk and one nun.

6km/4 miles south of Khrysoskalítissa monastery, off a beach which has something of the atmosphere of the South Seas, is the little island of Elaphonísi. In summer it is linked with the mainland by a sandbank, and the sea then shimmers in varied tones of blue and green. The beach, with many little inlets, is shaded by tamarisks and slopes down very gently, making it suitable for children. The sand is given a pink tinge by tiny shell fragments. Unfortunately this idyllic retreat is spoiled by the refuse left by bathers and

Kastéli Kisámou

The commandingly situated Khrysoskalítissa monastery

by lumps of tar which are not always immediately visible. In summer there are boat trips to the beach from Palaiokhóra.

Phalásarna
(Φαλάσαρνα)

The town of Phalásarna, 19km/12 miles west of Kastéli Kisámou, was founded in the 5th/4th century B.C. and was probably abandoned in the 4th or 6th century A.D. when as a result of tectonic movements the coast was raised by almost 7m/23ft, leaving the harbour high and dry.

On the excavation site visitors come first to the necropolis of the ancient city and then, on the left, to a "throne", the function of which still puzzles archaeologists. Of particular interest are the harbour installations, with a watch-tower which still stands 5m/16ft high and a channel leading to the sea. The excavators also found remains of a town wall, built of regular blocks of dressed stone, running round the slopes of the hill with the foundations of towers projecting from the wall.

By following the walls to the bay north of the cape it can be seen how high the water once reached. On the saddle of the hill, from which there are fine views, can be seen the remains of a building and a flight of steps.

To the south of Cape Koútri there is a beautiful long sandy beach, ideal for bathing.

Tigáni
(Τηγάνι)

The beach of white sand at Tigáni, on the west coast of the Gramvoúsa peninsula, can be reached only by a 3-hour walk from Kalyvianí. There are also occasional boat trips from Kastéli Kisámou.

Gramvoúsa Islands
(Γραμβούσα)

To the west of the northern tip of the Gramvoúsa peninsula are the islands of Gramvoúsa and Ágria Gramvoúsa, which can be reached only by boat from Kastéli Kisámou.

Above the steep west coast of Gramvoúsa island, at a height of 445ft, is a fortress which continued to be held by the Venetians after the conquest of

Crete by the Turks in 1669. The little Roman Catholic church with a Renaissance façade is also Venetian.

Around 1800 Gramvoúsa was dreaded as a pirates' lair: in the two years between 1825 and 1827 alone 155 ships were taken by pirates. Thereupon a British and French punitive expedition destroyed the place, which then had a population of some 8000, and freed many prisoners who were languishing in caves. The caves can still be seen.

Káto Zákros   E 18

Κάτω Ζάκρος

Nomós: Lassíthi
Chief town of nomós: Áyios Nikólaos

46km/29 miles south-east of Sitía, in Káto Zákros Bay, is the Minoan site of Káto Zákros. The road is at first of poor quality, but the final stretch is a magnificent panoramic highway running high above the sea.

Situation

Just beyond the end of the little town of Zákros, on the right, are the remains of a Late Minoan villa.

Minoan villa

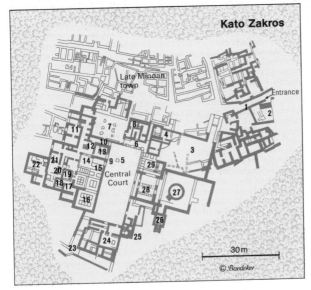

Kato Zakros

1 Road from harbour	11 Store-rooms	21 Archive room
2 Metal foundry	12 Room with tiled floor	22 Workshop
3 North-East Court	13 Antechamber	23 South entrance
4 Lustral basin	14 Light-well	24 Workshops and store-rooms
5 Square base	15 Large columned hall	25 Round well
6 Portico	16 Banqueting hall	26 Square basin
7 Kitchen and dining room	17 Workshop	27 Large circular basin
8 Room with kitchen equipment	18 Treasury	28 King's Megaron
9 Entrance to west wing	19 Lustral basin	29 Queen's Megaron
10 Corridor	20 Shrine	

Khóra Sphakíon

Valley of the Dead

Beyond Zákros the road to the site runs through the Valley of the Dead, so called because of the Minoan burials found here. The rock caves in which the dead were buried can be seen.

For the dating of the Early Minoan (EM I–III), Middle Minoan (MM I–III) and Late Minoan (LM I–III) periods see the table on p. 34.

History

The area was inhabited from Early Minoan times (2700–2250 B.C.). The palace and the port were in existence from 1600 to 1410 B.C., enjoying their period of greatest prosperity thanks to trade with Egypt and the East. After the destruction of the town by the Mycenaeans it continued to be occupied for more than a century, but the palace was neither rebuilt nor plundered.

The excavation of the site, which yielded rich finds, was begun by the British archaeologist David Hogarth in 1901 and continued by Nikólaos Pláton the Cretan, from 1962 until his death in 1992.

The ★ Palace
(open: Tues.–Sun. 8.30am–3pm)

Visitors enter the site from the east by way of the road from the harbour, along which are the remains of houses, shops and workshops (including a metal smelting works). The road, bearing left, leads to a stepped street and into the North-East Court, at the north corner of which is a lustral basin. From the west side of the court a narrow passage leads into the Central Court (30m/100ft by 12m/40ft). At the north-west corner is a square stone, perhaps the base of an altar. A portico at the north-east corner of the court leads into a hall (9m/30ft by 12m/40ft) with six pillars, probably a kitchen and dining-room, for much kitchen equipment was found in a small adjoining room. Here too there is a staircase leading to the upper floor.

On the north side of the central court a narrow passage leads to a square room with a tiled floor, from which store-rooms (to the north) and an antechamber and the main staircase (to the south-east) can be reached.

To the south-west is a light-well lined by columns, adjoining which is a columned hall which was used for royal ceremonial occasions. On the south side of this is the Banqueting Hall, in which numerous drinking vessels were found. The room to the west is thought to be a workshop, since large quantities of different kinds of stone were discovered here.

Also on the west side of the complex is the Treasury, with stone chests in which fine pottery, stone vessels and objects with inlays of precious materials such as ivory and rock crystal (now in the Archaeological Museum, Iráklion) were found. A short flight of steps leads down from here into a lustral basin.

To the west is the Central Shrine, in which religious rites and ceremonies were held. Adjoining this is the Archive Room, in which clay tablets with Linear A inscriptions were found. The workshop (with lavatory) which adjoins it on the south-west has a separate entrance to the south.

In the south-west corner of the Central Court is the south entrance of the palace, with a long passage leading to the southern districts of the town. In the south wing were workshops and store-rooms.

In the east wing are a circular well, to the north-east a square basin with steps leading down to it, and adjoining this a large circular basin, probably a cistern, which also has steps leading down to it. The two rooms on the west side of the cistern room have been identified as the Queen's Megaron (to the north) and the King's Megaron (to the south). On their west side, opening on to the Central Court, is a veranda. On the north side of the palace complex are the residential quarters of the town.

Khóra Sphakíon

D 5

Χώρα Σφακίων

Nomós: Chaniá
Chief town of nomós: Chaniá
Population: 350

Khóra Sphakíon (the chief place, *khóra,* of Sphakiá), a little town of white-washed houses and narrow lanes picturesquely situated in a bay on the south coast of Crete, has developed in recent years into the tourist centre of this region, with plenty of accommodation for visitors and numerous tavernas. It is a gathering-point for walkers down the Samariá Gorge, who come here from Ayía Roúmeli by boat to catch a bus back to Chaniá. As a result there tend to be large numbers of visitors round the harbour on summer afternoons. During the summer there are also boat trips to Loutró, Palaiokhóra and the island of Gávdos.

There is a very attractive beach at Glykánera, where freshwater and seawater mingle.

In earlier centuries Khóra Sphakíon was an important trading centre, and the Venetians built a small fortress here, the remains of which can be seen above the town. It was the centre of many risings against Turkish rule.

History

This was the home of the freedom fighter Ioánnis Vlákhos, known as Daskaloyánnis (the Teacher), the most important leader of the 1770 rebellion. He went to Iráklion under a safe conduct for negotiations with the Turks but was taken prisoner and skinned alive in 1771. To the Cretans he is a national hero.

After the battle for Crete in 1941 Khóra Sphakíon became the main base for the evacuation of British and Commonwealth troops, an event commemorated by a tablet on the quay wall.

Surroundings of Khóra Sphakíon

The Sphakiá Plain, to the north of Khóra Sphakíon, ranks with Lassíthi as the most densely populated plain on the island. Its inhabitants hold fast to their traditions and have the reputation of being proud and aggressive. Until the middle of the 20th century the blood feud was still part of their way of life. The Sphakiotes have repeatedly fought against foreign rule, whether by Arabs, Venetians, Turks or Germans. This inaccessible region was never really brought under Turkish control, a fact of which modern Sphakiotes are still proud. Visitors are struck by the numbers of old people, still hale and hearty, whom they see here. The region's main sources of income are stock farming and the cultivation of potatoes, wine, fruit and walnuts. A local speciality is *sphakianés pites* (pancakes filled with goats'-milk cheese and spread with honey).

Sphakiá Plain

To the north of Khóra Sphakíon is the wild and beautiful Imbros Gorge, still little known to visitors. Just under 7km/4½ miles long, it is even steeper and narrower than the Samariá Gorge, closing in to only 2m/6½ft at its narrowest point. From Imbros, a village on the Sphakiá plain which is inhabited only in summer, it is a 3-hour walk through the gorge to the village of Komitádes.

★ Imbros Gorge

To the south of Komitádes, at the mouth of the Imbros Gorge, is the church of Áyios Yeóryios, which has the oldest surviving frescos (1314) by Ioánnis Pagoménos, mainly scenes from the life of Christ, SS George and Demetrius and the Archangel Michael. Outside the church is a dilapidated altar of a later period.

Komitádes
(Κομιτάδες)

The village of Loutró, picturesquely situated in a bay 3km/2 miles west of Khóra Sphakíon, is best reached from there by boat; the alternative is a walk of over 2½ hours. Bathing is possible mainly from rocks and in small coves.

Loutró
(Λουτρό)

Loutró, the ancient Phoenix, was an important port in antiquity and a haven offering safe shelter in winter (cf. Acts 27,12). Until the early 19th century it was still a port of some consequence.

On the headland to the west of the village, in a beautiful setting, are some Roman and Byzantine remains (cisterns, terrace walls, foundations of houses and tombs). Here too is the church of Sotíros Christoú (Christ the Saviour), in the older part of which are 14th and 15th century frescos.

Anópolis
(Ανώπολη)

Above Khóra Sphakíon, to the west, is the straggling village of Anópolis. From the church of Ayía Aikateríni, on a hill (20–30 minutes' climb) to the south of the village, are magnificent views of the White Mountains, with Mt Pakhnes (2453m/8048ft) as the highest peak, to the north and of the coast to the south. From Anópolis it is an hour's walk to Loutró.

In the large square in the western part of the village is a monument to the freedom fighter Daskaloyánnis (see above).

Arádena
(Αράδενα)

The village of Arádena, to the west of Anópolis, occupies the site of ancient Araden, of which some remains can be seen in the surrounding area. It has the interesting church of the Archangel Michael, built in the 14th century with stone from ancient buildings: a cross-in-square church with a dome borne on a drum, with frescos. In rocks in the surrounding area are caves which were occupied as dwellings in prehistoric times.

Frangokastéllo
(Φραγκοκαστέλο)

10km/6 miles east of Khóra Sphakíon is Frangokastéllo, whose sandy beaches and beautiful backdrop of hills have made it a holiday resort which is particularly popular with young people.

Venetian fort

Just above the shore is a a massive Venetian fort, built in 1371 and thus one of the oldest Venetian strongholds in Crete. It was originally named after the neighbouring church of Áyios Nikítas but became known to the Cretans as Frangokastéllo, the "Frankish castle". Commandingly situated on the sea, against its background of hills, it is a striking sight.

The rectangular circuit of battlemented walls is reinforced at the corners with massive towers. Above the main entrance, on the seaward side, is the lion of St Mark. Little of the interior has survived.

The mighty Venetian fort of Frangokastéllo

The monument at the north-east corner of the fort commemorates Khat-zimikháli Daliánis, who with 700 Sphakiotes held the fort against the Turks in in 1828 but lost the battle and was killed. It is said that every year on the day of the battle (May 17th) armed black figures – the souls of the fallen – march past the fort. Since this happens in the early dawn they are known as the "men of the dew". Scientists explain this phenomenon as a mirage.

To the east of the fort, on the left of the road, is the little church of Áyios Nikítas, built on the site of an Early Christian basilica, from which there survive fragments of a fine mosaic pavement in a geometric design.

Áyios Nikítas

Farther north the road to Chaniá runs over the Askýphou plain (alt. 800m/2625ft), on which potatoes, wine, fruit and nuts are grown, mostly with the help of irrigation. Down the centuries this area has seen much fighting between various conquerors and the Sphakiotes.

Askýphou plain
(Ασκύφου)

Knossós

D 11

Κνωσός

Nomós: Iráklion
Chief town of nomós: Iráklion

5km/3 miles south-east of Iráklion (regular bus services; 15 minutes), near the village of Makrytíkhos, are the excavated remains of the large Minoan palace of Knossós, the island's earliest capital. Open: Mon.–Fri. 8am–5pm, Sat., Sun. 8.30am–3pm.

Situation

Nowhere else in Crete can visitors get such a comprehensive and vivid impression of Minoan palace architecture as at Knossós, thanks largely to extensive reconstruction. Stretches of wall and columns and sometimes whole rooms have been rebuilt in coloured concrete on the basis of the archaeological evidence revealed by excavation. The remains of the frescos which are now in the Archaeological Museum in Iráklion have been replaced by copies, so that – in spite of some criticisms that have been levelled at the reconstructions – visitors can get a three-dimensional view of one of the largest of the Minoan palaces, which covers an area of some 20,000sq.m/24,000sq.yd and has something like 800 rooms. In its heyday, between 1600 and 1400 B.C., the palace was probably much bigger still and may have had four storeys. It is believed by archaeologists that 10,000 people may have lived within the palace complex and its immediate surroundings.

The ★★Palace

Although alternative theories have been put forward – Hans-Georg Wunderlich, for example, believes that the palace was the cult centre of a necropolis like the mortuary temples of Egypt, while P. Faure sees it as a shrine – most scholars now agree that the palace was the residence of a powerful ruler and the administrative, economic and religious centre of a wide area.

The beginnings of settlement at Knossós date back to the Neolithic period: the remains of a Neolithic timber house have been assigned a date between 6500 and 6100 B.C. Altogether archaeologists have identified ten settlement levels in the area of the palace's West Court. The first palace, dating from around 2000 B.C., was built in terraces on a low and gently sloping hill above the Kératos valley on top of a 6.5m/21ft thick accumulation of occupation debris. It set the pattern for the Minoan palaces with its central courts and complex layout, with state and private apartments, cult chambers, workshops and store-rooms linked by a network of passages and staircases. Then around 1700 B.C. the Protopalatial or Old Palace period came to an end when the palace was destroyed in an earthquake.

History

Around 1600 B.C. a new and still more splendid palace of several storeys with a lavishly decorated interior was built, the impressive remains of which are still to be seen. When, around 1400 B.C., the Mycenaeans seized power in Crete, palace building came to a halt at Knossós, as it did elsewhere on the island; parts of the palaces were destroyed and never rebuilt. The conquerors continued to use the palace at Knossós but altered it to suit their own requirements. It may have been at this time that a new territorial unit came into existence, ruled by a powerful king who is named in Egyptian sources as Menus or Minus. It is not impossible that this was the origin of the name of the legendary King Minos.

Around 1375 B.C. much of the palace was destroyed by fire, whether as a result of a rebellion or a natural catastrophe is not known. Little of the older Minoan architecture survived the subsequent renovation and rebuilding. Then about 1200 B.C. the palace was completely destroyed by foreign intruders. In the course of the 10th century B.C. the Dorians thrust into the territory of Knossós, though this did not lead to the establishment of any new system of government.

In the 8th and 7th centuries Knossós was under the influence of the Greek world and achieved a modest prosperity and cultural flowering. During this period the myths and legends about King Minos, Ariadne and Theseus were developed. The Greeks believed that the palace of Knossós, with its complicated layout, was Minos's Labyrinth; for the word "labyrinth" is derived from the Lydian word *labrys* for a double axe and thus means the "house of the double axe" – and the double axe was a central cult symbol in Minoan culture. From the 6th century onwards, evidently under the confusing impression of the extensive ruins of the palace, gold coins depicting the Labyrinth (illustration, p. 24) and the Minotaur were minted at Knossós. There were also three temples dedicated to Zeus, Hera and Demeter.

In the 4th century B.C. Knossós recovered a certain predominance, but later was perpetually involved with other city-states on the island in a struggle for dominance. In 67 B.C. the Romans occupied Crete, and Knossós, under the name of Colonia Julia Nobilis, became along with Górtys, a centre of Roman rule. When the Byzantines gained control of the island in the 4th century A.D. Knossós was still inhabited, but thereafter it was lost in the darkness of later centuries and the ruins of the palace disappeared from the scene.

The palace was not rediscovered until 1878, when a local amateur archaeologist, Minos Kalokairinós, excavated two store-rooms in the west wing. After Crete gained independence, the British archaeologist Arthur Evans (see Famous People) acquired the site of the palace and in the spring of 1900 began systematic excavation. By 1903, with anything up to 200 men working on the site, he had brought to light a considerable proportion of the palace, and until his death in 1941, he continued his investigation and study of the site. Since then excavations have been carried on by the British School of Archaeology in Athens and are now concentrated on the area round the palace.

Evans not only established the first comprehensive chronology of the Minoan palace culture but also gave the various rooms in the Knossós Palace the names by which they are now known – the Queen's Bathroom, the Throne Room, the Hall of the Double Axes and so on – although these designations have not been supported by any finds of archaeological material. To make it easier for visitors to find their way about the site, however, Evans's names have remained in use.

The palace is now entered by way of the large paved West Court, at the south-west corner of which is a bronze bust of Evans (1935). Raised walks run across the court to the West Entrance and the Theatral Area. In front of the monumental West Façade, which fronts a range of store-rooms, are two altar bases, suggesting that the West Court had some cult function, perhaps for the assembling of processions which would then make their way

Tour of site
West Court

◄ *Knossós: the largest and most splendid of the Minoan palaces*

to the Theatral Area or by way of the Corridor of the Procession Fresco to the Central Court. The circular pits, 5m/16ft deep, in the centre of the court, in which the excavators found cult utensils and animal bones, served for the reception of sacred offerings; they date from the Protopalatial period but were later filled in when the court was replanned.

West Entrance

The later palace is entered through four main entrances facing north, south, east and west. In the West Entrance and Porch can be seen the stone base of a wooden column which divided the doorway into two and supported the roof. A vestibule, which originally had a bull-leaping fresco on the wall, leads into a square room for porters or guards.

South Wing

In Minoan times visitors then passed through a door into the Corridor of the Procession Fresco, named after a long fresco of some 500 life-size male and female offering-bearers advancing towards a female figure (a queen or goddess). The corridor at first runs south and then turns east, giving access to the south wing of the palace with its intricate system of corridors leading to the South Entrance, from which a stepped way lined by columns continued out of the palace. Nearby is the South House, with a kind of pillared crypt in which cult objects were found, suggesting that this may have been the dwelling of a priest.

Following the Corridor of the Procession Fresco eastward and then turning north, we come to the part of the corridor in which the fresco of the Prince of the Lilies (illustration, p. 54) was found. From here we pass through the South Propylaea, a hall with columns and frescos (copies: young offering-bearers), to reach a monumental staircase leading to the upper storey, the Piano Nobile. In the centre of this upper floor there were cult rooms, including the tri-columnar shrine depicted in frescos which was presumably the goal of the solemn processions. From the Upper Long Corridor running north–south on the upper floor visitors can look down into the western range of store-rooms containing large clay storage jars.

The Throne Room with its alabaster throne and copies of frescos

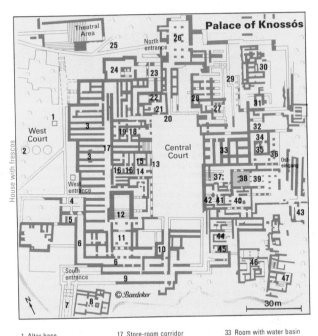

Palace of Knossós

1 Altar base
2 Circular pits
3 Store-rooms
4 West Propylaea
5 Guard-room
6 Processional corridor
7 Columned staircase
8 South House
9 South corridor
10 Corridor
11 South Propylaea
12 Staircase
13 Shrine
14 Antechamber
15 Central shrine
16 Pillar crypt

17 Store-room corridor
18 Throne Room
19 Cult chamber
20 North ramp
21 Prison
22 Cult chamber
23 North-West Propylaea
24 Cult area
25 Royal Road
26 Custom House
27 North-East Hall
28 North-east store-rooms
29 Potters' workshops (?)
30 Potters' workshops
31 Store-room
32 Loght-well

33 Room with water basin
34 Potters' workshop
35 Stone-cutter's workshop
36 East veranda
37 Staircase
38 Hall of Double Axes
39 King's Megaron
40 Queen's Megaron
41 Queen's Bathroom
42 Queen's Dressing Room
43 Eastern bastions
44 Shrine of Double Axes
45 Lustral basin
46 House of the
   Chancel Screen
47 South-East House

One room, reconstructed, contains copies of frescos from different parts of the palace.

From here a small spiral staircase descends to the antechamber of the Throne Room on the ground floor of the west wing. It is a good idea, however, to take a longer way round by way of the Central Court, from which you can get a better idea of the wings of the palace with their show façades and their system of staircases, column-lined corridors and verandas, with stylised bulls' horns as decoration on the various parts of the façade and the staircases.

From the Central Court, in which cult ceremonies and court festivals took place, there is a good view of the west wing, with a staircase and to the left of this the Tripartite Shrine, in which presumably secret mysteries were performed. Behind this are rooms with column bases and a bench which lead to the central shrine with its underground treasure chamber.

West Wing

159

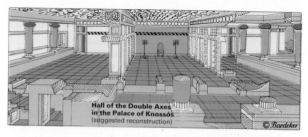

Hall of the Double Axes
in the Palace of Knossós
(suggested reconstruction)

© Baedeker

In the so-called Pillar Crypts, once lit only by torches, earth and fertility goddesses were probably worshipped; the double axe symbol marks these as sacred chambers. To the right of the columned staircase is the ante-chamber, containing a porphyry basin, which leads into the Throne Room with its inner shrine. Against the north wall, decorated with a fresco of griffins (copy), of the Throne Room is the alabaster throne, flanked by benches. On the west side are steps leading into a cult chamber with no natural light, and on the south side are steps leading down to the cave shrine of a mother goddess.

North Wing

From the Central Court a ramp leads to the north wing of the palace, with a group of rooms at the north-west corner which Evans interpreted as prison cells. The rooms beyond and above this evidently served cult purposes and were decorated with beautiful wall paintings, including a monkey in the palace garden, a sacred grove and the façade of a tripartite shrine. The north ramp, which was flanked for part of the way by high columned passages or verandas with stucco reliefs of bulls, also leads to the northern columned hall, which Evans called the Custom House, assuming that visitors coming from the port to the palace would have their gifts recorded here. More probably, however, it was used for cult ceremonies and court festivals.

Nearby are the North-West Propylaea and a so-called initiation area consisting of a hall with a sunk lustral basin, presumably used for ritual purification. To the west of the north entrance is the Royal Road, a processional way leading to the Theatral Area, with two wide flights of steps set at right angles to one another. From these steps the inhabitants may have watched the bull-leaping games or the reception of important guests or cult or court ceremonies. Farther west along the Royal Road is the House of the Frescos, perhaps the residence of a palace official, in which the Bluebird and other frescos were found.

East Wing

In the north-eastern part of the palace complex the first feature encountered is a staircase, turning several times at right angles, with parallel drainage channels and settling tanks for rainwater, which was collected in cistern-like basins near the East Bastion. Part of the elaborate water supply system can be seen in a light-well, and in another room is a stone water-basin associated with the workshops in this area of the palace.

The North-East Hall originally had four massive columns, the bases of which survive. The adjoining store-rooms were probably used for storing pottery, since they are near the potters' workshops (though these have also been identified as stables). There were other workshops and store-rooms with huge storage jars in this area.

The north-east range of the palace was evidently the "services" area, with another potter's workshop and a stone-cutter's workshop. Along this wing ran an open columned veranda with views of the east entrance to the palace and the Kératos valley. It has also been suggested that the bull-leaping games in the valley were watched from here. The retaining walls on the hillside belonged to the older palace (before 1700 B.C.).

In the south-eastern part of the palace is a grand staircase running down to three lower floors, with numerous fragments of the original structure. This leads to the Hall of the Royal Guard and then the Hall of the Double Axes, which was decorated with incised double axes on the west wall, which opened into a light-well. One of the royal apartments, it was probably used for official receptions. Along with the King's Megaron (containing a reconstruction of a wooden throne) and the Queen's Megaron, Bathroom and Dressing Room, it gives an impressive idea of the amenities of Minoan life. The king's and queen's apartments were decorated with frescos on a variety of motifs (rosettes, running spirals, dolphins, dances, etc.). The rooms were articulated by pillars and columns and the walls were broken up by several doorways, giving an overall impression of colour, lightness and openness.

Also in the south-eastern part of the palace are another, smaller lustral basin and a small shrine of the double axe, so called because of the steatite double axe, a symbol of divine power, which was found here.

At the south-east corner of the palace complex are the South-East House and the House of the Chancel Screen, which contains a paved room with a raised platform flanked by columns, probably for the display of a cult image.

In the immediate surroundings of the palace there are other Minoan excavations. They are fenced in and can be seen only with special permission.

Surroundings of Knossós

The so-called Royal Villa to the north-east of the palace, situated among still unexcavated remains of the Minoan city, is probably not a dependency of the palace, as Evans supposed, but a private house dating from 1500–1450 B.C., originally of three storeys. An unusual type of staircase gives access to the various floors. On the ground floor are an entrance hall with a lavatory and a bathroom, beyond which are an inner hall, a columned hall, a light-well and a kind of pillar crypt used for cult purposes.

Royal Villa

On the road from Iráklion to Knossós, just before the village, is a group of buildings dating from 1600–1500 B.C., with handsome state apartments and cult rooms. Here too, as in the main palace, are megarons, pillar crypts and lustral basins. An architectural innovation is the enlargement of the light-well into a peristyle hall. In the so-called Fetish Shrine were found stone idols dating from around 1300 B.C.

Little Palace

South-east of the main palace, near the road to Arkhánes, is a building (1600–1500 B.C.) known as the Caravanserai or Guesthouse. The partial reconstruction includes two rooms in which a painted frieze of partridges (now replaced by a copy) was found, along with other frescos. Numerous fountain basins and a fountain-house containing bath-tubs supplied guests with fresh spring water.

Caravanserai

To the south of Knossós, also on the road to Arkhánes, is the burial-place of some great personage (1600–1500 B.C.), which was excavated by Evans in 1931. It consists of the "temple", a cult building, and a tomb chamber hewn from the rock. An unpretentious entrance leads into an antechamber with two columns and beyond this a paved court, in which presumably the mourners assembled, facing a monumental façade in a style reminiscent of palace architecture. The funeral ceremonies were held on the veranda-like upper storey, which was reached by an internal staircase. On the lower floor a doorway led into an inner hall and then through a pillared shrine to the cave-like tomb chamber, which was faced with gypsum and painted.

Temple tomb

Lassíthi Plain

D/E 13/14

Λασίθι

Nomós: Lassíthi
Chief town of nomós: Áyios Nikólaos

The plain of Lassíthi

Entrance to the Dictaean Cave, birthplace of Zeus

Some 50km/30 miles south-east of Iráklion and 30–40km/20–25 miles west of Áyios Nikólaos, lying at an altitude of around 820m/2700ft in the Dikti range, is the fertile karstic plateau of Lassíthi, some 8km/5 miles by 5km/3 miles in extent. The roads to Lassíthi from both Iráklion and Áyios Nikólaos runs through country of great beauty.

Situation

The Lassíthi plain itself, within its frame of hills, is an area of great scenic beauty, known as the "Valley of Windmills" from the windmills with white cloth sails which spangle the fields. The windmills, which are used between mid June and mid September to supply water to the irrigation system, are now increasingly giving place to motor pumps.

★Scenery

They feed water into collecting basins and from there into a network of channels laid out in a chequerboard pattern, fostering a luxuriant growth of vegetation. The main products are potatoes, apples and wheat.

The villages all lie on the edge of the plain, at the foot of the hills.

The Lassíthi plain was occupied by man from Neolithic times. Throughout history it provided a place of refuge for the people of Crete, for example in post-Minoan times when the Dorians settled on the coasts and, in a later period, when the island was conquered by Venice. In 1263 the Venetians expelled all the inhabitants of Lassíthi and the surrounding hills and banned any settlement or farming in the plain. The ban remained in force for 200 years, until shortage of food on the island led the Venetian authorities to allow people to occupy and cultivate the plain. In later times, too, Lassíthi was a safe retreat for the rural population of eastern Crete and a base for rebels against Turkish rule. The Turks responded by devastating the plain in 1867.

History

Sights on the Lassíthi Plain

In the village of Áyios Yeóryios, on the southern edge of the plain, is a Folk Museum run by a local society (open: 10am–4pm). It occupies the only house on Lassíthi which has preserved its original form, dating from around 1800. For greater security, the house has no windows. In the main room are a stove with cooking utensils and the loom which was an essential item of domestic equipment. Below the bed in a smaller room is a wine-press. The pottery jars in the store-room are very similar to their Minoan predecessors. Agricultural implements are displayed in the stable, and in another room are the tools used by various craftsmen (smiths, carpenters, cobblers). In a modern annexe are displayed embroidery and contemporary painting.

Áyios Yeóryios
(Άγιος Γεόργιος)

On the south-western edge of the plain, above the village of Psykhró, is the much visited Diktaíon Antron, the Dictaean Cave (open: 10.30am–5pm). This legendary stalactitic cave is reached on a steep path from the village (15 minutes); donkeys can be hired to take you up. The cave has no electric light, but guides with gas lamps are very ready to offer their services. It is advisable to have a pocket torch and to wear a pullover or jacket, for it is damp and cold inside the cave.

★Dictaean Cave
(Διχταίον
Άντρον)

According to legend Zeus was born in the cave because his mother Rhea was afraid that the child's father, Cronus (Kronos), would devour his son as he had devoured his other children, fearing that they would dethrone him. The cave was a cult site from at least the Middle Minoan period.

From the imposing entrance (14m/46ft by 8m/26ft) visitors enter the upper cave, in which was found, at the far right-hand side, a sacred precinct with pottery, altars and idols. The adjoining lower cave has a striking display of stalactites and stalagmites. On the floor of the cave, in winter and spring, is a small pool in which Zeus is said to have bathed. A stalactite to the right is known as Zeus's Cloak. To the left is a small chamber, with a recess in which Zeus is said to have been born. Numerous votive offerings (knives, implements, double axes, etc.) were found in the lower cave.

Mália

Karphí
(Καρφί)

A visit to the post-Minoan site (1050–990 B.C.) on Mt Karphí (1100m/3600ft), on the northern edge of the plain, is worth while not so much for its archaeological interest, since there are only scanty remains to be seen, as for the beauty of the scenery.

The excavations, 2km/1¼ mile above the village of Kerá, can be reached either by an hour's climb from the village or from Tzermiádon by way of the Nísimos plateau. The latter route runs past a number of small tholos tombs. This was a large settlement, built on the remains of a Middle Minoan site, with a population of around 3500. Some 100 rooms or houses with a common façade, paved streets and squares were found by the excavators. Building types were already Mycenaean. The most notable features of the site are the Great House in the main square, the residence of the town's principal citizen, and, on the north side of the site, a temple, the north wall of which has collapsed, containing a masonry bench and an altar.

The most important finds from the site were large female pottery idols (now in the Archaeological Museum, Iráklion).

Mália (town)

Μάλια

Nomós: Iráklion. Chief town of nomós: Iráklion

Situation and
characteristics

The bathing resort of Mália, an increasingly popular tourist centre, lies on the north coast of Crete 34km/21 miles east of Iráklion in an intensively cultivated agricultural area (oranges, melons, Cretan bananas). It has beautiful long sandy beaches with dunes and facilities for all kinds of water sports. In the older part of the little town there is still something of a Cretan atmosphere, but Mália is not the place to go to for a quiet holiday, with its ubiquitous mopeds and music. The part of town offering a little peace and quiet is round the old harbour at the east end of the long sandy beach.

Surroundings of Mália

Limín
Chersonísou/
Hersonissó
(Λιμήν
Χερσονίσου)

Chersónisos (11km/7 miles north-west of Mália), one of Crete's largest tourist centres, consists of the old village of Chersónisos, with its pretty village square, situated amid olive groves a little way inland, and the seaside resort of Limín Chersonísou, with dozens of hotels, discothèques, cafés and tavernas. The sand and shingle beaches are too small for the increasing numbers of visitors.

In Limín Chersonísou are the remains of two Early Christian three-aisled basilicas with mosaic pavements: one on the rocky headland above the boating harbour at the west end of the town and the other in the grounds of the Nora Hotel at the east end. On the waterfront is a Roman fountain of the 2nd/3rd century A.D. with mosaics – an indication of the importance of the town at that period..

In the Lykhnostatis open-air museum (open: daily 9.30am–2pm), by the sea, visitors can see a typical Cretan village, complete with a chapel, a windmill, a weaving shop and a dyer's workshop, as well as a garden in which herbs and flowers are grown.

Mílatos Cave
(Μίλατος)

3km/2 miles east of Mílatos (13km/8 miles east of Mália) is the intricately ramified stalactitic cave of that name; the access road is signposted. Here in 1823 2700 women and children and 150 men who had hidden in the cave were besieged by the Turks. When they were finally forced to surrender many of them were killed and both men and women were sold into slavery. This atrocity is commemorated by a chapel and a small ossuary containing the remains of some of the victims.

One of the oldest plane-trees in Crete, in the village of Krási ▶

Mália

Potamiés
(Ποταμιές)

11km/7 miles south-east of Mália on the road to the Lassíthi plain is the village of Potamiés. Some 200m/220yd before the village a road goes off on the left to the abandoned Gouverniótissa monastery, probably founded around the year 1000, the most notable feature in which is the little cross-in-square church (key in the kafeníon in Potamiés). On the way there is the chapel of Sotíros Christoú (Christ the Saviour), with expressive frescos dating from the first half of the 14th century. The church of the Panayía Gouverniótissa has a high drum decorated with blind arcading. It contains lively frescos of the second half of the 14th century, many of them in a poor state of preservation.

Avdoú
(Αβδού)

The village of Avdoú, 6km/4 miles south-east of Potamiés, has several Byzantine churches. The best known is the one-room chapel of Áyios Antónios, reached on a road which goes off opposite the first kafeníon in the village (coming from Potamiés). It has very expressive frescos of the early 14th century, predominantly in brown tones. On the northern part of the barrel vaulting are the Crucifixion, the Last Supper and the Washing of the Feet; on the southern part are the Transfiguration, the Descent into Hades, the Nativity and the Baptism of Christ. A road which goes off on the right just before the village leads in 1km/¾ mile to the little one-room chapel of Áyios Konstantínos, which has poorly preserved frescos by the brothers Manuel and Ioánnis Phokás (1445). At the far end of the village is the church of the Panayía, a cross-in-square church, probably of the 16th century, with Venetian Gothic features.

Mokhós
(Μοχός)

The large hill village of Mokhós, situated at an altitude of 400m/1300ft, is an authentic Cretan village, in sharp contrast to Mália, 12km/7½ miles away. Here, in the pretty village square with its tavernas shaded by mulberry-trees and planes, visitors can rest from their exertions.

Krási
(Κράσι)

7km/4½ miles east of Avdoú on the road to the Lassíthi plain is the village of Krási, where travellers can rest in the shade of one of the oldest and mightiest plane-trees in Crete. A few yards away is a Venetian fountain-house.

Kardiótissa/Kerá monastery
(Μονή Καρδιότισσα)

Just below the village of Kerá (alt. 560m/1840ft), 1km/¾ mile south of Krási, is the little Kardiótissa or Kerá monastery (closed: 1–3.30pm). Surrounded by cypresses, with its atmospheric little courtyard and flower-filled garden, it is a picturesque sight.

Like other Cretan monasteries, this was a spiritual and educational centre for the Orthodox population during the period of Turkish rule. Outside the south front, enclosed by railings, is a small pillar to which a legend is attached. It is said that the wonderworking icon of the Mother of God on the iconostasis of the church was stolen and carried off to Constantinople, where it was chained to a column: whereupon it miraculously returned to the monastery along with the column.

Built of undressed stone, the church dates from the 14th century. It is three-aisled, though only the central and north aisles have apses. The narthex at the west end is decorated with brick blind arcading.

The church has very beautiful wall paintings. In the south aisle are scenes from the Last Judgment, Christ between the Mother of God and John the Baptist, angels, and Christ with the wise and foolish virgins; in the central aisle are scenes from the life of Christ, including the Nativity, the Descent into Hades and the Descent of the Holy Ghost; in the north aisle are fragments depicting various saints; on the barrel vaulting a grandiose Ascension and scenes from the life of the Mother of God, including the annunciation to Joachim, the birth of the Virgin and her presentation in the Temple; and in the apse the Panayía with the infant Christ.

The picturesque monastery of Kardiótissa/Kera ▶

Mál`i`a

Piyí
(Πηγή)

27km/17 miles south-west of Málía is Piyí, with the interesting church of Áyios Panteléimon, which stands to the south of the village under tall oaks by a spring which was once a much visited shrine. From this spring (*piyí*) the village takes its name.

The church, three-aisled, with pointed barrel vaulting (12th/13th century), is partly built of stone from Roman and Byzantine buildings: for example there are marble blocks with Greek inscriptions built into the masonry, a makeshift column in the interior is constructed from four Corinthian capitals, and on the south wall are Roman funerary stelae. The south front of the church is richly decorated with blind arcading, and the three apses have arched windows. The church has frescos of the 13th and 14th centuries; the apse is dominated by a figure of Mary with the infant Christ, flanked by two angels, with the Last Supper below this and fathers of the Church below this again.

Lilianó
(Λιλιανό)

In the village of Lilianó, 8km/5 miles south of Piyí, is the basilica of Áyios Ioánnis, which probably dates from the 11th–13th centuries. The church consists of a narthex and three barrel-vaulted aisles ending in apses. Fragments from ancient buildings – e.g. gravestones on the outside wall and columns with Corinthian capitals – are incorporated in the structure. Against the south wall of the church is a broken column which probably supported a pulpit with steps leading up to it. Relics of more recent date are the remains of inscriptions by German airmen, who used the church as a command post during the Second World War.

Sklaverokhórion
(Σκλαβεροχώριον)

Just before the road from Piyí reaches Sklaverokhórion (4km/2½ miles), to the left, is the one-room chapel of the Isódia tis Theotókou (Presentation of the Virgin; 13th/14th century), which has notable frescos of the 15th century. On the north wall is a rare representation of St Francis.

Málía (palace ruins)   D 14

Μάλια

Nomós: Iráklion. Chief town of nomós: Iráklion

Situation

Set in a fertile depression irrigated by windmills 34km/21 miles west of Áyios Nikólaos, near the holiday resort of Málía (from which it is an hour's walk along the beach), are the remains of the Middle Minoan palace of Málía, the most important of the Cretan palaces after Knossós and Phaistós.

For the dating of the Early Minoan (EM I–III), Middle Minoan (MM I–III) and Late Minoan (LM I–III) periods see the table on p. 34.

History

Legend has it that King Sarpedon, Minos's brother, was the owner of this palace. There is evidence of settlement here reaching back to Early Minoan II. The palace itself was built in Middle Mlnoan II (1900–1800 B.C.), rebuilt in Middle Minoan III (1800–1700 B.C.) and destroyed by the Mycenaeans around 1420. Thanks to its situation on the main route between central and eastern Crete Málía soon developed into one of the most important cities on the island.

Excavation was begun by Khatzidákis and continued by the French School of Archaeology in Athens, which is still working on the site. Since the Minoan name of the site is not known, it was named after the nearby village of Málía.

The ★Palace

The remains visible today are mainly of the New Palace; little is left of the earlier complex. The style of the building is more archaic and less refined than at Knossós. Opening times: Tues.–Sun. 8.30am–3pm.

Palace, Mália

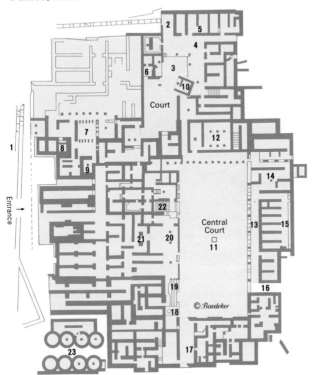

Court

Central
Court

© Baedeker

Entrance →

1 West Court	9 Archive room	17 South entrance
2 North entrance	10 Shrine (?)	18 Kernos
3 Forecourt	11 Altar	19 Grand staircase
4 Portico	12 Pillared hall	20 Antechamber
5 Store-rooms	13 Hall	21 Pillar crypt
6 Workshops	14 Kitchen	22 "Loggia"
7 Polythyron	15 East store-rooms	23 Circular
8 Bath	16 South-east entrance	structures

The tour begins in the West Court, from which a raised way leads to the   Tour of site
North Entrance. Inside the entrance is a forecourt enclosed on two sides by
a portico, behind which are store-rooms (to north and east) and workshops
(to west). Beyond this is the North Court, with a forecourt on the west
leading to the royal private apartments, in which are a polythyron and, to
the south-west, a bath. To the south of these rooms was an archive room. In
front of the corridor leading from the North Court to the Central Court is
a later building at an oblique alignment, probably a shrine. At the north
end of the Central Court, in the centre of which is an altar, is an antechamber with a single pillar giving access to a pillared hall, identified by the
excavators as a dining room. On the east side of the court is another
hall with alternating pillars and columns. To the north of this is the kitchen
and to the east store-rooms, with channels in the floor for draining away
any leaking liquids. To the south is the South-East Entrance to the

Mália

Remains of the palace of Mália, the most important in Crete after Knossós and Phaistós

palace and at the south-west corner of the court the South Entrance. At this corner, too, is Mália's most celebrated find, a round *kernos* or libation table with small hollows for offerings, possibly harvest offerings of the first fruits, to the right of this is a grand staircase. Farther north is an antechamber with two columns and adjoining this a pillar crypt. Beyond this again are a staircase leading to the upper floor and the "Loggia", a once magnificent room. At the north-west corner of the palace complex are eight circular pits, either store-rooms or cisterns.

Surroundings of the palace

House E

Within the extensive area of the Minoan town which surrounded the palace are the remains of a large house (House E) whose function has not been determined. It lies 100m/110yd along the access road to the palace from the main road, on the right.

Delta quarter

To the west of the palace is the Delta quarter, in which a good example of a Minoan house can be seen. A paved entrance hall leads into a passage which runs north to a bath and lavatory and ends in the main room of the house, on the north side of which is a light-well. To the south are storerooms and domestic offices. A staircase led up to the family's living quarters on the upper floor.

Hypostyle Crypt

The so-called Hypostyle Crypt, to the north-west of the palace, lies below ground level and is approached by a flight of steps, It consists of two inter-connected halls and a series of store-rooms. It was probably a place of assembly for secular purposes.

Shrine

South-west of the local museum the excavators found the remains of a shrine, identified as such by the bulls' horns found in it.

Khrysólakkos necropolis

Farther north, beyond the Alpha quarter, is the necropolis of Khrysólakkos ("Pit of Gold"), the city's burial ground, which was in use from Early Minoan III onwards. An enclosure measuring 30m/100ft by 39m/130ft surrounded by walls of large blocks, it contains a cult room with an altar and numerous burial chambers. On the east side is a pillared hall. Here was found the famous bee pendant (in Archaeological Museum, Iráklion; illustration, p. 53).

Mount Ida · Psilorítis D/E 9/10

Nomós: Réthymnon
Chief town of nomós: Réthymnon

The myth-encrusted Mount Ida ("wooded hill") is the highest and most impressive range of mountains in Crete, with its principal peak, Mt Psilorítis, rising to a height of 2456m/8058ft above sea level. Legend has it that Zeus, father of the gods, grew up in the Idaean Cave.

★Topography

The ascent of Mt Psilorítis is a very rewarding climb, either from the village of Kamáres to the Kamáres Cave and from there to the summit or from the Nida plain, which can be reached on a gravel road by way of Anóyia. The climb is possible only from June to September, and should be undertaken only with a guide. Essential requirements are fitness, warm and weatherproof clothing, stout shoes with treaded soles, adequate supplies of food and water and, for the Kamáres route, a sleeping-bag.

Ascent

The ascent from Kamáres (alt. 600m/1970ft) is to be recommended mainly for those who want to see the Kamáres Cave. On this route it is necessary to spend the night either in the cave, on the alpine pastures of Kólita or on Mt Psilorítis itself. The best starting-point is at a snack bar on the main road. Following the route marked by red splashes of paint, it takes about 3 hours to reach the cave, below the prominent double peak of Mt Márvi (1981m/6500ft).

From Kamáres

The myth-encrusted Mount Ida range

Kamáres Cave
(Σπήλαιο
Καμαρών)

The Kamáres Cave (alt. 1525m/5005ft), which in Middle Minoan times was a shrine venerated all over the Mesará plain, was excavated in 1913. The excavators found numerous polychrome vases of the Middle Minoan period in what became known as the Kamáres style (now in the Archaeological Museum, Iráklion). They are made of the finest clay – the so-called "eggshell" ware being particularly thin – and are decorated with white, yellow and red plant and spiral patterns on a dark ground.

From the cave it takes another 3½ hours to reach the alpine pastures of Kólita. Soon after this the Kamáres route is joined by the road from the Nida plain: for the continuation of the route from this point, see below. Altogether the ascent, depending on the climber's fitness and the rests taken, takes between 6 and 7½ hours.

Nida plain

The Nida plain, reached from Anóyia on a 21km/13 mile long track, is mainly grazing for sheep and goats. The road runs through a wild and romantic mountain landscape, passing areas of alpine pasture, and comes in 13km/8 miles to a pass (1500m/4900ft) from which there is a beautiful view of the plain.

The landlord of the state-owned taverna, the only permanent building on the plain, will point out the way to the Idaean Cave. From the church of the Análipsis (Ascension) the track winds its way up to the cave, situated on the northern flank of Mount Ida at an altitude of 1540m/5055ft.

Idaean Cave
(Ιδαίον Άντρον)

The Idaean Cave is the most celebrated cave in Crete after the Dictaean Cave on the Lassíthi plain.

Here, according to the myth, Zeus was brought up by nymphs on the milk of the goat Amaltheia and on honey. His mother Rhea had brought him here to protect him from his father Cronus (Kronos), who had devoured all his children because of a prophecy that he would be deprived of power by one of his sons. Earlier she had told the Curetes, her priests, to clash their bronze shields together so that Cronus should not hear the child crying.

The cave was a cult centre from Minoan to Roman times.

To the left of the entrance is a projecting rock which was converted into an altar. The cave, which was investigated from 1884 onwards, consists of a large main chamber and three subsidiary chambers, the middle one of which, the innermost shrine, lies at a height of 8m/26ft and can be reached only with a ladder. Here were found important bronze articles, including the famous shields of the Curetes (now in the Archaeological Museum, Iráklion), as well as pottery, gold and silver objects and Roman oil lamps.

Ascent from
Nida plain

The ascent of Mt Psilorítis from the Nida plain and the return descent take a whole day. The starting-point is again the Análipsis church. The route, for at least part of the way, is marked by red spots and signs on stones. On the summit are a church, a mountain hut and a cistern containing melt-water. From here there are magnificent panoramic views, extending in the south-west to the island of Gávdos, in the west to the White Mountains, in the north to Iráklion, in the east to the hills round the Lassíthi plain and in the south over the Mesará to the Asteroúsia Hills.

Palaiokhóra   D 2

Παλαιοχώρα

Nomós: Chaniá
Chief town of nomós: Chaniá
Population: 1400

Situation and
characteristics

Palaiokhóra lies 77km/48 miles south-west of Chaniá on a promontory on the south coast of Crete. The "bride of the Libyan Sea", as the inhabitants liked to call their town, formerly very isolated, is now a popular seaside resort with long beaches of sand and shingle, including the very busy Pákhia Beach in the bay to the west of the town.

The centre of the village is chock-a-block with tavernas, but accommodation for visitors is limited to small guesthouses and apartment houses. Palaiokhóra loses all its individual character in summer, when holiday visitors considerably outnumber the local inhabitants.

In 1282 the Venetians built the fortress of Selínou, from which there is a view of the island of Gávdos.

Surroundings of Palaiokhóra

It is a pleasant walk to the hill village of Anýdri, lying at a height of 180m/590ft above the coast, 5km/3 miles north-east of Palaiokhóra. In the centre of the village is the church of Áyios Yeóryios (enquire in kafeníon for key). Originally a one-room chapel, it has been joined to another chapel built on its south side in the 20th century. It has wall paintings (1323) by Ioánnis Pagoménos, some of which are well preserved, notably the figures of the church's patron, St George.

2km/1¼ miles below the village is Anýdri Beach, with three small coves which can be reached only on foot or by boat.

Anýdri
(Ανύδροι)

Above the village of Prodrómi, 5km/3 miles north-east of Anýdri, is the picturesque church of the Panayía tis Skaphidianís, which has an apse with decorative brickwork. It contains interesting frescos of 1347; particularly fine is the painting of the horses of SS George and Demetrius on the south wall.

Prodrómi
(Προδρόμι)

18km/11 miles north of Palaiokhóra is the large village of Kándanos, which was destroyed by the Germans in 1941 in retaliation for an attack on a German paratroop unit. There are Greek and German memorial tablets commemorating the dead on both sides. Almost the whole village was rebuilt after the war.

Kándanos
(Κάντανος)

The village of Anisaráki, 2km/1¼ miles west of Kándanos, has four modest one-room Byzantine chapels. The church of Ayía Ánna has frescos of 1462 and a stone iconostasis, a rare feature on Crete. In the churchyard is the church of Ayía Paraskeví, which has frescos, mostly rather faded, dating from the first half of the 14th century. The church of Áyios Yeóryios, with decorative brickwork on the outside wall of the apse, has frescos of around 1400. The walls of the church of the Panayía are covered with frescos, some of them in very poor condition.

Anisaráki
(Ανισαράκι)

In Teménia, 11km/7 miles south of Kándanos, is the church of the Sotír (Saviour; 13th/14th century), which is notable for its unusual architectural form. The church, on a hill 1km/⅔ mile south of the village, on the right of the road, consists of an older one-room chapel to the east, with simple barrel vaulting and an apse, and a later small cross-in-square church to the west, which architecturally is more interesting than the earlier church. It has a low dome, barely 3m/10ft high, and the arms of the transept are given greater width by shallow recesses. It has frescos, including a Descent of the Holy Ghost of notable artistic quality; the scenes featuring Pilate, which are rarely depicted, are of particular iconographic interest.

Teménia
(Τεμένια)

In Moní, 8km/5 miles east of Teménia, is the church of Áyios Nikólaos, in a setting of great scenic beauty. At a fountain on the outskirts of the village (when coming from the north) is a house where the key can be obtained, and from here a path on the left runs down to the church. It is a simple aisleless structure with thick walls and solid pillars and a later barrel-vaulted narthex (second half of 14th century?). It has an unusual free-standing bell-tower with a spiral staircase.

The frescos, now partly destroyed, were painted by Ioánnis Pagoménos in 1316. Among them is a very fine over-lifesize figure of St Nicholas, the church's patron.

Moní
(Μονή)

173

Church of the Saviour, Teménia

Soúyia
(Σούγια)

Soúyia, 6km/4 miles south of Moní on the south coast, has two good shingle beaches which are very busy in summer. At some points there are caves, which offer pleasant shady retreats from the heat of the day. The village church occupies the site of an Early Christian basilica, from which there survives a fine 6th century mosaic pavement, consisting mainly of geometric patterns but with some figures of birds and the Christian symbol of a fish.

Lissós
(Λισσός)

From Soúyia, which can be reached either by road or by boat from Palaiokhóra, there is a path over the hills to the west to the neighbouring bay of Áyios Kyrikós. It can also be reached from Soúyia by boat, but the walk (1½ hours) is well worth it for the beauty of the scenery. In the bay is the site of ancient Lissos, which, particularly in Roman times, was famed for its healing springs.

The main feature of interest on the site is a temple of Asclepius of the Hellenistic period, of which there survive the walls of the cella, a mosaic pavement, a base for cult images and a pit for libations. Water from the sacred spring runs under the floor to a fountain at the north-west corner of the temple. On the north of the site are late Roman houses, and on the western slope of the hill tombs of the Hellenistic and Roman periods.

Near the shore is a chapel of Áyios Kyrikós, and to the west of the temple a chapel of the Panayía, both built over the remains of Early Christian basilicas.

Sklavopoúla
(Σκλαβοπούλα)

The frescos in the church of Áyios Yeóryios in Sklavopoúla, 20km/12½ miles north of Palaiokhóra, are among the oldest in Crete, dating from around 1300, but they are only partly preserved. Particularly notable are the figures of SS. George and Theodore and the Archangel Michael.

In an olive-grove outside the village are two other chapels, the Panayía and the Sotíros Christoú (Christ the Saviour), which both have poorly preserved 15th century frescos.

Phaistós

Φαιστός

Nomós: Iráklion
Chief town of nomós: Iráklion

The remains of Phaistós (63km/39 miles south-west of Iráklion) are magnificently situated on a hill in the beautiful Mesará plain.

Situation and characteristics

In size and importance the Minoan palace of Phaistós, with an area of 8500sq.m/91,500sq.ft, takes second place among the Cretan palaces after Knossós. Less restoration has been done here than at Knossós, but the view of the palace, lying lower down, from the entrance to the site is still highly impressive.

For the dating of the Early Minoan (EM I–III), Middle Minoan (MM I–III) and Late Minoan (LM I–III) periods see the table on p. 34.

Legend has it that the city of Phaistós, named after a nephew of Heracles, was founded by King Minos. The site was already occupied in Neolithic times, but the oldest material found here dates from the Early Minoan period (c. 3000 B.C.).

History

The heyday of the town began with the building of the Old Palace around 1900 B.C., when Phaistós was at least as important as Knossós. The palace was several times destroyed by earthquake and fire, most recently around 1700 B.C. The New Palace, comparable with the Knossós palace, was built after 1700, but was destroyed by a catastrophic fire around 1450 B.C. The site was still occupied, however, in the post-Minoan, Geometric and Classical periods, but was finally conquered and destroyed by Górtys in the 2nd century B.C.

The prophet and priest Epimenides (see Famous People) was a native of Phaistós.

The excavation of the site was begun by Italian archaeologists in 1900 and is still continuing.

Most of the surviving structures belong to the New Palace. Of the original palace complex, laid out round a central court, only the ruins of the west and north wings have been preserved; the south and east wings collapsed in an earthquake. On the west and north sides of the remaining parts of the New Palace can be seen some remains of the older one.

The ★Palace
Opening times
Mon.–Fri.
8am–5pm; Sat.,
Sun. and holidays
8.30am–3pm

There are also some later buildings which were not demolished, as others were to permit excavation of the Minoan settlement levels. Round the palace, on the slopes of the hill, are Minoan, Geometric and Hellenistic buildings erected after the destruction of the palace.

Visitors enter the site on the west side and come first into the North Court, which is traversed from north to south by a Minoan paved way and bordered by buildings of the Hellenistic period. A narrow flight of steps leads into the West Court, which belonged to the Old Palace. Traces of the fire which destroyed it can be seen on the lowest courses of stones. On the north side of the court is a broad staircase, and a processional way runs diagonally across it. A narrower branch of this way runs west to a circular structure resembling a cistern, where a road coming up from the town enters the West Court. At the end of the processional way is the main entrance to the Old Palace, with a central column, from which a passage runs to the Central Court. To the north of this passage are store-rooms, in which *pithoi* can be seen in their original place. At the north-east corner of the West Court is a three-roomed shrine with a round cavity in the rock for libations. Farther east a grand staircase 14m/46ft wide leads to the *propylon* of the New Palace, which has a column 1.3m/4ft 3in. in diameter

Tour of site

Grand staircase in the palace of Phaistós

between *antae*. From here, passing through three rooms, we come into a light-well with three columns. From here a staircase leads down into a hall with two central columns, opening on the west side into a broad passage flanked on both sides by store-rooms. Farther south is a corridor to the Central Court, with a guard-room on the left. Beyond this are two rooms with alabaster benches, perhaps used for sacrificial ceremonies. Still farther south is a room with two pillars, perhaps a pillar crypt.

At the south-west corner of the palace is a Greek temple.

The large Central Court (43m/141ft by 23m/75ft), the south-east corner of which was destroyed in an earthquake, was probably surrounded by colonnades. At its north-east corner is a complex of rooms consisting of a main chamber, a pillared room and a light-well. At the end of this complex a flight of steps leads to a lustral basin. In the north-west corner of the Central Court is a stepped structure, probably an altar. A double doorway flanked by two half-columns and two recesses for guards or cult objects (perhaps double axes) gives access, along the north side of the court, to the north wing, which contains the royal apartments. A flight of steps on the left of the corridor leads to a peristyle. The corridor ends in a small court, to the east of which is the East Court of the palace, with a metal-worker's foundry.

To the north of the small court are the queen's apartments. The gypsum-paved Queen's Megaron has a light-well with four columns. The King's Megaron, adjoining it on the north, has polythyra and on the east side a light-well with two columns. From the open veranda with three columns on the north side of the megaron there is a superb view of the Mesará plain with its framing of hills.

To the west, reached by a flight of steps, is a lustral basin. In a separate complex of buildings to the north-east, in which the famous Phaistós Disc (now in the Archaeological Museum, Iráklion) was found, the most notable feature is the peristyle. To the east are potters' workshops.

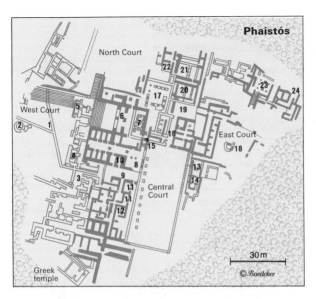

1 Processional way
2 Circular structure
3 Main entrance
4 Store-rooms
5 Shrine
6 Propylon
7 Light-well
8 Hall with columns
9 Entrance to store-rooms
10 Guard-room
11 Rooms with
   alabaster benches
12/13 Pillared room
14 Lustral basin
15 Altar
16 Corridor
17 Peristyle
18 Foundry
19 Small court
20 Queen's Megaron
21 King's Megaron
22 Lustral basin
23 Peristyle
24 Potters' workshops

Surroundings of Phaistós

5km/3 miles north of Phaistós is the village of Vóri, which has the finest and most interesting folk museum in Crete (Museum of Cretan Ethnology, open: daily 10am–6pm). This excellently arranged and labelled collection of material from the last three to five centuries covers a wide range – fishing, agriculture, forestry, stock farming, crafts (metalworking, shoemaking), weaving, basketwork, pottery, etc. – and also includes domestic equipment, religious objects, musical instruments and weapons.

★Vóri
(Βώροι)

In the village of Áyios Ioánnis, immediately south of Phaistós, is the church of Áyios Pávlos, a building of great architectural interest standing in a churchyard at the far end of the village. It is made up of three separate parts, the oldest of which is the square domed structure at the east end, probably a baptistery of the 4th/5th century. The middle section, on a central plan with a dome borne on a high drum, dates from 1303, and the open narthex in Venetian style was added in the 15th/16th century. There are remains of frescos of 1303–04. Against the east wall of the churchyard is a small charnel-house.

Áyios Ioánnis
(Άγιος Ιωάννης)

The fortress-like Odiyítria monastery, in a lonely setting in the western Asteroúsia Hills 12km/7½ miles south of Phaistós, dates from the Venetian period. Now occupied only by a very few monks, it is dedicated to the Panayía Odiyítria (Mother of God "Shower of the Way"). Here in 1829

Odiyítria
monastery
(Μονή Οδηγήτρια)

Phaistós

The beautiful beach of Mátala with its limestone cliffs and caves

the freedom fighter Xopatéras ("Ex-priest"), with his family and a few monks, held out against the Turks for days before being killed.

Features of interest in the church are valuable icons by the painter called Angelos, liturgical vestments and utensils, and some frescos in the south aisle.

Kalí Liménes
(Καλοί Λιμένες)

The tiny hamlet of Kalí Liménes lies 30km/19 miles south of Phaistós in a sheltered bay. There are beautiful beaches to east and west of the village.

This was the Fair Havens where Paul landed on his voyage to Rome (Acts 27,8). The church to the west of the village is dedicated to him.

Pitsídia
(Πιτσίδια)

For individual travellers the charming village of Pitsídia, 5km/3 miles south-west of Áyios Ioánnis, is a good alternative to the overcrowded resort of Mátala. The hub of village life is the *platía*, with the old-established kafeníon of Kóstas. In the Fábrika ouzeria Cretan musicians frequently play.

Kommós
(Κομμός)

Kommós, 3km/2 miles west of Pitsídia, was settled from Middle Minoan times (from 2100 B.C.) and was one of the ports of Phaistós. The place was abandoned in the 1st century B.C. The site has been under excavation by Canadian archaeologists since 1976.

In the northern and central parts of the site can be seen the ground-plans of several Middle and Late Minoan houses, including one with seven rooms, and a street. To the south was found a well preserved sanctuary of the Classical and Hellenistic periods, which was founded in the 8th/7th century B.C. and destroyed in 150 A.D. but continued in use until A.D. 125. There are two buildings with benches round the sides, two central columns and a sacrificial altar. To the east of the temple is a circular structure of unknown function.

Mátala
(Μάταλα)

5km/3 miles south-west of Pitsídia, on the coast, is Mátala, which was probably a port for Phaistós in the Minoan period and for Górtys in Roman times. In the rocks round the shallow harbour inlet are caves which were used for burial in Early Christian times. The Arabs landed here in 826. According to the Greek myth Zeus also landed here in the form of a bull with the Phoenician princess Europa whom he had carried off. In the 1960s Mátala became a favourite haunt of hippies, who lived in the caves above the beach. Later it became a settlement of dropouts and backpackers, who were eventually expelled on hygienic grounds. The caves are now closed by grilles. Mátala is still, however, a favourite bathing resort, particularly for young people, and large numbers of day-trippers are brought in by buses. There is a beautiful sandy beach against an attractive backdrop of limestone cliffs. Mátala is now well equipped to cater for visitors, with numerous tavernas and souvenir shops.

Psilorítis

See Mount Ida

Réthymnon (Rethimnon)   C 7

Ρέθυμνον

Chief town of Réthymnon nomós
Population: 20,000

Réthymnon, Crete's third largest town and the administrative centre of Réthymnon nomós, lies on a small peninsula on the north coast. It features an attractive mingling of cultures, bearing the marks of both Venetian and Turkish rule. The town is a considerable intellectual and cultural centre, with the faculty of philosophy of the University of Crete, a theatre and a Philharmonic Society. In summer performances are given by visiting musical ensembles and dramatic companies, both Greek and foreign.
    The writer Pantélis Prevelákis (see Famous People) described his home town, Réthymnon, in his book "Chronicle of a Town".
    Réthymnon has a sandy beach 12km/7½ miles long extending west from the harbour mole, lined by numbers of hotels, guest houses and apartment blocks. On the landward side, beyond the line of the old town walls, now followed for much of the way by a major traffic artery, is the extensive area of the modern town.

Situation and characteristics

Little is known of the history of Réthymnon. The peninsula on which it stands may have been settled only since Late Minoan times. In antiquity it was a prosperous town, under the name of Rithymna, which minted its own coins. In the Venetian period it was Crete's most important town after Iráklion and Chaniá. In 1303 it was devastated by an earthquake. After the Turkish conquest of Constantinople and the Peloponnese in 1460 many refugees from these areas settled in the town. In the 16th century, after a series of raids by pirates, the Venetians surrounded the town with walls and built the Fortezza. In 1646 the Turks took Réthymnon and made it their administrative centre.

History

Sights in Réthymnon

The picturesque old town, with its charming narrow lanes, numerous remains of the Venetian period, Turkish houses with their roofed and latticed balconies, mosques and minarets, is full of atmosphere.

★Old town

At the south end of Odós Antistaséos, a street of bustling and colourful activity, is one of the old Venetian town gates, the Megáli Pórta (16th century).

Megáli Pórta

179

Réthymnon (Rethimnon)

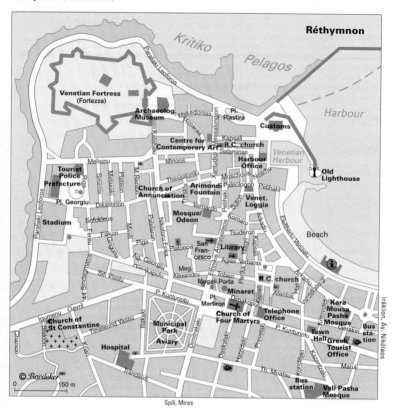

Réthymnon

Kritiko Pelagos

Harbour

Venetian Fortress (Fortezza)

Archaeolog. Museum

Pl. Plastira

Customs

Centre for Contemporary Art

R.C. church

Harbour Office

Venetian Harbour

Old Lighthouse

Tourist Police Prefecture

Church of Annunciation

Arimóndi Fountain

Venet. Loggia

Pl. Georgiu

Mosque/ Odeon

Stadium

Beach

San Fran-cesco

Library

R.C. church

Megali Porta

Minaret

Kara Mousa Pasha Mosque

Bus sta-tion

Municipal Park Aviary

Pl. Martiron

Church of Four Martyrs

Telephone Office

Town Hall

Greek Tourist Office

Church of St Constantine

Hospital

Bus station

Veli Pasha Mosque

© Baedeker

0   150 m

Iráklion, Áy. Nikólaos

Spili, Mires

San Francesco	In a short cul-de-sac off Odós Antistaséos is the aisleless church of San Francesco (16th/17th century; open: 3–7pm), now used for exhibitions and a variety of functions. On the north side is a handsome Renaissance door-way with Corinthian pilasters and half-columns. Beside the church is another Venetian doorway flanked by reliefs of the lion of St Mark, which leads into the spacious courtyard of a school. A smaller doorway decorated with crescents was inserted during the Turkish period.
Nerandzes Mosque	A striking feature of the town is the Nerandzes Mosque in Odós Vernardo, with three domes and a minaret which can be climbed (open: 11am–7pm). It now houses a music school and concert hall. (At present (1996) closed because of danger of collapse.)
Venetian houses	Also in Odós Vernardo are a number of Venetian houses with wooden balconies added in the Turkish period (e.g. Nos. 16, 30 and 36).
★Arimóndi Fountain	In Platía Títou Petikháki, in the heart of the taverna quarter, is the very beautiful Arimóndi Fountain (1623), with three lion's-head water-spouts between slender half-columns with Corinthian capitals. On the architrave is a fragmentary inscription. During the Turkish period the fountain was given a projecting domed roof, of which remains can still be seen.

The charming Arimóndi Fountain in the centre of Réthymnon

The 17th century Venetian Loggia in Odós Arkadíou, with three arched embrasures, was the meeting-place of the Venetian nobility and is now being turned into a library.

Venetian Loggia

On the east side of the old town is the romantic Venetian Harbour with its mole and lighthouse. Unchanged for centuries, it has always had the problem of silting up. It is now used by pleasure craft and fishing boats. With its many cafés, tavernas and fish restaurants, it is particularly busy in the evening.

★ Venetian Harbour (illustration on front cover)

In the Centre for Contemporary Art and the Kanakakis Gallery – Centre for Modern Art (Odós Mesolongíou; open: daily 10am–1pm and 6–10pm) there are frequent exhibitions.

Centre for Contemporary Art

★ Archaeological Museum

The Archaeological Museum, installed in new premises in the former Venetian prison in 1990, is a model of arrangement and presentation.
The cases are not numbered. The tour suggested here goes in a clockwise direction within the museum.

Opening times
daily except Mon.
8.30am–3pm

For the dating of the Early Minoan (EM I–III), Middle Minoan (MM I–III) and Late Minoan (LM I–III) periods see the table on p. 34.

Neolithic material (5700–2800 B.C.) from various caves: pottery, stone implements, fertility idols.

Cases 1 and 2

MM II pottery from Monastiráki and Apodoúlou: clay model of a shrine.

Cases 3 and 4

MM II shrine at Vrýsini: terracottas, bronzes, fertility idols. In the corner of the room is a serpentine oil lamp from the villa at Mixórrouma, near Spilí.

Case 5

Réthymnon (Rethimnon)

Pyxis *with floral patterns*   *Goddess in the attitude of worship*

Cases 6 and 7   Grave goods from various sites: stone vases, pottery (MM III to LM III).

Cases 8 and 9   LM III grave goods from Arméni and Apostóli: bronze double axes, imple-
                    ments, knives.
                        In the corner of the rooms are funerary stelae from Arméni (LM III).

Case 10   Important material from Arméni and Pegalokhorió (LM III): jewellery and
                    seal-stones. A unique item is a basket made of organic material with bronze
                    handles.

Case 11   LM III material from shrines and necropolises: goddesses with raised
                    hands.

Cases 12 and 13   Late Minoan and sub-Minoan pottery from various sites.

Case 14   Geometric material from the Elefthérna necropolis: pottery, terracotta
                    idols, bulls' heads from offering vessels.
                        In front of the cases are sarcophagi from the Mycenaean necropolis at
                    Arméni which are among the finest pieces in the museum. Particularly
                    interesting types of decoration are hunting scenes and horns of
                    consecration.
                        The marble statue of Dionysus with a satyr (c. A.D. 300) also comes from
                    Elefthérna.

Cases 15–18   Material from the Roman necropolis at Stavroménos: oil lamps, e.g. with
                    a love scene (15); cosmetic utensils and vases (16); marble vases and
                    jewellery (17); glass vessels (18).

Objects from a wrecked ship at Ayía Galíni: Roman bronze sculpture.	Case 19

Roman marble and alabaster heads of Greek gods; oil lamps from Aryiroúpoli.	Case 20

Coins of various periods. Of particular interest is a gold coin from Knossós with the representation of a labyrinth (illustration, p. 24).   Cases 21 and 22

Against the end wall is a marble statue of the goddess Artemis (2nd century B.C.). Opposite this, at the pillar, are (from right to left) a headless Roman figure of Dionysus from Réthymnon; an athlete with a dog, from Stavroménos (c. 460 B.C.); a child with a duck and fruit (c. 3rd century B.C.).

Terracottas, expressive female figures and heads of the Daedalic and Archaic periods from various sites.   Cases 23 and 24

On the wall are inscriptions. To the right is a funerary stele from Elef-thérna (6th century B.C.).

Hellenistic terracottas and vases from various sites.   Case 25

In front of this case is a marble basin with an inscription of the 3rd century A.D., found in Réthymnon.

Also in this part of the museum are numerous marble statues ranging in date between the 1st century B.C. and the 4th century A.D.: female statues with changeable heads; Faustina the Elder, from Lappa; an Aphrodite from Lappa with an elaborate coiffure and one foot on a duck; two Roman heads of children; a figure of Dionysus from Piyí.

Other Sights in Réthymnon

One of the town's principal sights is the Fortezza (open: 8am–8pm), situated on a hill from which there are fine panoramic views. It was built by the Venetians between 1573 and 1580. The best preserved parts of the fortress are the outer walls; most of the buildings within the walls have   ★Fortezza

The mosque in the Fortezza with its massive dome

been destroyed, either by earthquakes or by Second World War bombing. After the Turkish capture of Réthymnon the church of Áyios Nikólaos in the centre of the fortress was converted into a mosque (after 1646) and capped with a large dome. The mosque with its beautiful mihrab (prayer niche) can still be seen, together with the remains of a chapel and numerous cisterns.

In summer there are open-air performances of various kinds in the Fortezza.

Kara Mousa Pasha Mosque

The little Kara Mousa Pasha Mosque (Odós Arkadíou; open: Mon.–Fri. 11am–1pm) has remains of earlier painting in the mihrab and contains old Turkish gravestones.

Veli Pasha Mosque

The 17th century Veli Pasha Mosque, with several domes, has a doorway decorated with arabesques. From the minaret there is a fine view of the town.

Public gardens

In the public gardens, a green oasis between the old and the modern town, visitors can see Cretan wild goats and other animals living in freedom in small enclosures. During the second half of June Crete's biggest wine festival is held in the gardens.

Surroundings of Réthymnon

Pánormos
(Πάνορμος)

Pánormos (22km/14 miles east of Réthymnon) was the port of the Greek city of Eleutherna, and there are scanty remains of the ancient town on the coast. Above the village are the foundations of the Early Byzantine basilica of Ayía Sophía (5th century), which was destroyed in the 7th century. The church is three-aisled, with a central apse and a narthex. To the west is a walled courtyard with a square cistern in the middle. There are also a few fragments of columns and capitals.

Melidóni Cave
(Σπήλαιο του
Μελιδονιού)

The Melidóni Cave, 11km/7 miles south of Pánormos near the village of Melidóni, is well signposted from the coastal expressway. The cave, which is open and accessible, consists of several chambers.

Like Arkádi monastery, the Melidóni Cave featured in the story of Greek resistance to the Turks. In 1824 some 340 Greek women and children and 30 men of the Cretan resistance who had hidden in this stalactitic cave were discovered and ruthlessly killed or burned alive. This atrocity is commemorated by an altar and a memorial tablet.

In Classical times Hermes was venerated in the cave.

Báli
(Μπάλι)

The former fishing village of Báli (illustration, p. 206) lies in a beautiful bay 31km/19 miles east of Réthymnon. It has now been transformed into a holiday resort with several large hotels and numbers of holiday bungalows, preserving something of its original atmosphere only round the tiny harbour. The best bathing is on a small sandy beach in a rocky cove north of the village.

Episkopí
(Επισκοπή)

At Episkopí, 47km/29 miles east of Réthymnon, are the impressive remains of a 13th century cross-in-square church of Áyios Ioánnis, known as the Frangoklisá (the "Frankish church", a name which also means Roman Catholic church). Built on the site of an earlier church, it was much altered in later times: the date 1568 above the north doorway marks one such rebuilding.

Of the original five domes two have survived. The narthex at the west end has almost completely disappeared. An unusual feature is the central apse, with the lower part four-sided and the upper part triangular, decorated with blind arcading and a beautiful triple-arched window.

There are remains of frescos (the Mother of God with angels, the Descent of the Holy Ghost); on the south wall is a tomb and in the central apse a bench for the priests.

The village of Maroulás, lying near the coast 10km/6 miles south-east of Réthymnon, in the foreland of the Mount Ida range, has preserved many Venetian and Turkish buildings. It is now being converted, with European Union aid, into a large holiday village. The owners of old and dilapidated houses are given financial assistance to restore them in their original style and equip them with modern amenities, and in return are required to make them available for letting to holiday visitors by the state.

Maroulás
(Μαρουλάς)

10km/6 miles east of Réthymnon, at Piyí, is the largest olive grove in the Mediterranean area, with one and a half million olive-trees.

Olive grove,
Piyí

★ Arkádi monastery (Μονή Αρκάδιου)

23km/14 miles south-east of Réthymnon, commandingly situated on a 500m/1640ft high plateau, is the fortress-like monastery of Arkádi, a Cretan national shrine and one of the island's principal sights.

Situation

The monastery was probably founded in the 10th or 11th century. The present buildings date from the 17th century and were restored after the 1866 catastrophe.
  The monastery played an important role in the 18th and 19th centuries as a centre of resistance to Turkish rule. A decisive date in the history of the Cretan struggle for liberation was November 8th 1866, when 1000 patriots, including 300 armed fighters, under the leadership of Abbot Gavriíl, entrenched themselves in the monastery against an attack by 15,000 Turks. When the defenders rejected the Turkish commander's demand for their surrender the Turks blew up the gate and broke into the monastery, and a bloodbath ensued. At last, seeing that resistance was hopeless, the abbot and Yiamboudákis, commander of the Cretan forces, blew up the powder magazine, to which most of the defenders had retreated. Only 114 men survived the explosion. The incident aroused horror throughout Europe. Since then November 8th has been the Cretan national day.

History

Arkádi Monastery

185

The monastery buildings are in the form of a rectangle, with entrances on all four sides, enclosing an inner courtyard in which is the church (1587). The imposing façade of the church shows a charming mix of Renaissance and Baroque features. The church is entered through the two side doorways; what seems to be the central doorway is merely a niche. The façade is articulated by fluted double columns with Corinthian capitals, heavy cornices and curved pediments and topped by a tall double-arched bellcote. The church is two-aisled, with apses at the east end. The interior dates mostly from the early 20th century, the carved olive-wood iconostasis from 1927.

In the west range of buildings, through which visitors enter, are storerooms, the guest-house, refectory and kitchen, and at the north end the powder magazine which was blown up during the siege and never rebuilt. The monks' cells are in the east wing, and in the south wing are more store-rooms and a small museum with a relief model depicting the 1866 siege, as well as icons, liturgical utensils and vestments, portraits of freedom fighters and the banner of the 1866 rebellion.

Other Sights in the Surroundings of Réthymnon

At the village of Eléftherna, 5km/3 miles north-east of Arkádi monastery, is the site of ancient Eleutherna, which was a place of some consequence in the Dorian period. The most striking feature of the site, on the summit of a rocky hill, is the ruin of a massive tower of the Roman and Early Byzantine period. On the terraces beyond this are the foundations of houses, and on the west side of the hill are two large cisterns with massive pillars.

1km/¾ mile north of the site is a picturesque Hellenistic bridge.

Margarítes, the best known potters' village in Crete, lies 6km/4 miles north-east of Eléftherna in a lush green setting on a hill. It is mainly occupied by young craftsmen and potters. Large *pithoi* like those of Minoan times are still produced here.

The village has a number of Byzantine churches, among them the church of Áyios Ioánnis, which has good frescos of 1383.

11km/7 miles south of Réthymnon is the unspoiled hill village of Prasiés, where visitors can enjoy a stroll through the village and a meal of good home cooking in the local taverna.

In the village of Méronas, 24km/15 miles south-east of Prasiés, is the three-aisled church of the Panayía, which has an attractive decoration of blind arcading and pilasters on the apses. It has numerous frescos of high artistic quality; others are still covered by whitewash applied during the Turkish period. The poorly preserved icon of the Panayía (late 14th century) is the second oldest panel painting in Crete.

Close to Méronas is Thrónos (22km/14 miles south-east of Prasiés), which has an interesting church of the Panayía. It has frescos of the 14th and 15th centuries, the older ones in the sanctuary and the later ones in the naos. The mosaic pavement inside the church, with some fragments outside it, is from an Early Christian basilica.

Thrónos occupies the site of ancient Sybrita, probably founded in the Dorian period. There are some remains of the ancient city above the village.

This monastery, 43km/27 miles south-east of Réthymnon, is now an agricultural college. Built in the 17th century, it shows Venetian influences. The little church has a magnificent iconostasis.

Lambiótes, 5km/3 miles south of the Asómaton monastery, has a one-room chapel of the Panayía with frescos of the second half of the 14th century.

Eléftherna
(Ελεύθερνα)

Margarítes
(Μαργαρίτες)

Prasiés
(Πρασιές)

Méronas
(Μέρωνας)

Thrónos
(Θρόνος)

Moní Asómaton
(Μονή Ασώματων)

Lambiótes
(Λαμπιότες)

◄ *Arkádi monastery, a Cretan national shrine*

Réthymnon (Rethimnon)

Vizári
(Βιζάρι)

1km/¾ mile west of Vizári (3km/2 miles south-east of Lambiótes) is one of the most important sights in the area, the remains of an Early Christian episcopal basilica. It is reached by taking a road opposite the post office, turning sharp right off this and following a stream, crossing it and continuing for another 500m/550yd. This large 7th century church has three aisles ending in arches and a narthex. In the apse of the south aisle is a stepped font.

Apodoúlou
(Αποδούλου)

1km/¾ mile before Apodoúlou (13km/8 miles south of Vizári), above the road on the left, is a Mycenaean domed tomb.

In the village is the church of Áyios Yeóryios, which is notable for its large arcades. It has frescos in popular style of the mid 14th century.

Ayía Paraskeví
(Αγία Παρασκευή)

18km/11 miles south of Vizári is the village of Ayía Paraskeví, with the church of the Panayía, which has fine frescos of 1516.

Mýli
(Μύλοι)

The modern village of Mýli lies to the right of the road 8km/5 miles south-east of Réthymnon. 1.5km/1 mile beyond this, in the valley below the road on the left, is the old village, abandoned because of constant rockfalls, which can be reached in a 20-minute walk. Visitors can stroll through the empty lanes of this picturesque old village, passing flower-gardens and overgrown courtyards, see the waterfall beside the church which flows from autumn to spring and listen, undisturbed, to the birds.

Khromonastíri
(Χρομοναστήρι)

The village of Khromonastíri, 3km/2 miles south of Mýli, has preserved a number of Venetian and Turkish buildings. It also has two small Byzantine churches.

From the north end of the village a track runs east to the 10th century church of Áyios Eftýkhios, one of the most important churches in Crete, showing a transition between the basilica and the cross-in-square church. There are scanty fragments of frescos in the apse.

The other church is the cross-in-square church of the Panayía Kerá, which was built in different phases between the 11th and the 14th century. It has an iconostasis reaching right up to under the dome and well preserved frescos; particularly fine is the Deesis on the vaulting of the apse.

Arméni
(Αρμένοι)

To the north of Arméni (9km/5½ miles south of Réthymnon), just off the main road, is a large Mycenaean necropolis with over 100 tombs, some of which can be entered. They are small rock-cut chamber tombs with dromoi (sometimes stepped) between 3 and 5m (10 and 16ft) long. Material from the tombs, including painted larnakes (ash-urns), can be seen in the archaeological museums in Réthymnon and Chaniá.

Kourtaliótiko Gorge
(Κουρταλιώτικο Φαράγγι)

The road to the Préveli monastery branches off the main Réthymnon–Ayía Galíni road at Koxaré and runs south through the wild and impressive Kourtaliótiko Gorge. Half way through the gorge a road runs down to the valley bottom, where there are a church of Áyios Nikólaos and a number of springs.

Préveli monastery
(Μονή Πρέβελη)

A visit to the monastery of Préveli, 28km/17 miles south of Arméni, is particularly to be recommended for the grandiose scenery and the monastery's imposing situation.

Turkish bridge

On the way to the monastery, 3km/2 miles after the village of Asómatos, the road crosses a stream on a picturesque single-arched Turkish bridge of 1850 with its original paving.

Káto Moní Préveli

Soon afterwards can be seen the ruins (not accessible from the road) of Káto Moní Préveli, the lower monastery of Préveli, dating back to the 16th century. The older name is Moní Méga Potamó, the "monastery on the great river".

Préveli monastery, a centre of resistance to foreign rule

1km/¾ mile farther on, to the left, in the gorge, is the one-room chapel of Ayía Photiní, with good frescos of around 1500. Note particularly the fine figures of female saints on the south wall.

Ayía Photiní

3km/2 miles beyond this is the main monastery, Píso Moní Préveli (open: 9am–7pm). The monastery may be as much as 1000 years old, though the present buildings are later. With extensive holdings of land, it was one of the leading monasteries in central Crete. It played a part in many rebellions against Turkish rule in the 18th and 19th centuries, and during the Second World War it was a centre of resistance to the German occupation, helping many British, Australian and New Zealand soldiers to escape to Egypt by submarine.

★Píso Moní Préveli

From the cemetery, with two burial chapels, in front of the monastery (to left) there is a good general view of the monastery; prominent features are the chimneys of the cell block with their pointed tops.

Passing through the gate of the monastery, we come into a courtyard on a lower level, with a fountain bearing an inscription dated June 15th 1701 – the earliest date in the present monastery. The church of Áyios Ioánnis, which dates from 1836, has two aisles with apses and a bell-cote at the west end.

The most notable features of the interior are the iconostasis, with many old icons, the carved pulpit and the lecterns, also bearing icons. On the altar in the south aisle is a magnificently decorated gold cross containing a fragment of the True Cross which is credited with healing powers.

To the west of the church are the guest-house and, lower down, a small museum in which are displayed valuable liturgical vestments and utensils, bishops' crowns, including one richly decked with diamonds and emeralds, and votive offerings. The most important document in the museum is a charter of 1798 making the monastery directly subordinate to the Patriarch of Constantinople.

Réthymnon (Rethimnon)

The beautiful beach of Préveli

Préveli Beach

At the mouth of the Megálos Potamós, on the south coast of Crete is the beautiful and very popular Préveli Beach, enclosed by rocks and shaded by palms. It is reached by returning about a kilometre on the road to the monastery and taking a road which runs across a plateau and down into the gorge.

Plakiás
(Πλακιάς)

13km/8 miles north-west of Préveli monastery, in Plakia Bay, is the busy seaside resort of Plakiás, with a sandy beach 2km/1¼ miles long, which has been spoiled by overbuilding.

Lambíni
(Λαμπίνη)

Lambíni, 17km/11 miles south of Arméni, has a very beautiful 14th century cross-in-square church dedicated to the Panayía (key in kafeníon in Mixórrouma). The façade and the drum of the dome are decorated with delicate blind arcading. At the entrance to the church is a plaque commemorating a rising against the Turks in 1827, when the Turks set fire to the church, in which the local people had gathered for safety, and burned them alive.

Spíli
(Σπήλι)

The large hill village of Spíli (5km/3 miles farther along the main road to Ayía Galíni), where there is a seminary for the training of priests, is famed for its numerous springs. During the day large numbers of excursion coaches and hired cars stop here, but in the evening there are only local people. The village's principal sight is a Venetian fountain with lion's-head water-spouts.

Ayía Galíni
(Αγία Γαλήνη)

24km/15 miles south-east of Spíli, on the Gulf of Mesará, is Ayía Galíni, once an idyllic village but now a busy tourist resort with hotels and apartment blocks extending on to the slopes of the hill. It is now to be recommended only to holidaymakers looking for plenty of noisy activity and lots of people.

Roústika

The picturesque little hill town of Roústika, 16km/10 miles south of Réthymnon, has preserved many Venetian buildings, as well as the two-aisled church of the Panayía, which has fine frescos of 1381–82 in the north aisle and a wonderworking icon.

At the upper (south) end of the village is the 19th century monastery of Prophítis Ilías, set in a luxuriant garden.

The village of Yeoryioúpolis is named after Prince George of Greece, appointed High Commissioner for independent Crete in 1898. Once a quiet little place centred on its large *platía* with an idyllic fishing harbour at the mouth of a stream and beautiful sandy beaches, it is now a small tourist resort with several new hotels.

Yeoryioúpolis
(Γεοργιούπολις)

Lake Kournás, Crete's only inland lake, lies amid hills near Yeoryioúpolis Bay. In the lake live snakes and fish up to 7kg/15lb in weight. It offers visitors good bathing, pedalos and several tavernas.

Lake Kournas
(Λίμνη Κουρνάς)

Samariá Gorge

D 4

Φαράγγι τής Σαμαριάς

Nomós: Chaniá
Chief town of nomós: Chaniá

Some 42km/26 miles south of Chaniá is the village of Omalós ("level, flat"), on the edge of the fertile Omalós plain (alt. 1050m/3445ft). 6km/4 miles beyond this, where the road ends at the Xylóskalo pass (1227m/4026ft), is the head of the famous Samariá Gorge in the White Mountains (Léfka Ori).

Situation

The Samariá Gorge, the longest in Europe, is one of the scenic highlights of Crete, visited by innumerable tourists (on some days up to 2000 or 3000). It is 18km/11 miles long, up to 600m/2000ft deep and at the "Iron Gates" (Sidiróportes) only 3–4m (10–13ft) wide.

★★Topography

In 1965 the gorge was declared a National Park, with an area of 4500 hectares (11,000 acres), in order to preserve the Cretan wild goat (*kri-kri*), which was already being depicted in Minoan art. These shy creatures are hardly ever to be seen: almost the only goats visitors are likely to encounter are domestic goats which have gone wild.

The gorge is also the habitat of numerous plants (pines, planes, kermes oaks, cedars, field maples and cypresses with a girth of up to 7m/23ft) and birds (eagles, falcons, barn owls). In addition there are a number of endemic plants (i.e. species found nowhere else in the world).

The gorge is open from 6am to 4pm. Visitors are not allowed to spend the night there, and after 4pm they must not go farther into the gorge, from either end, than 2km/1¼ miles. From November to April the gorge is closed because of the danger from rockfalls and flash floods.

The walk through the Samariá Gorge from the end of the road to the Libyan Sea, a distance of 18km/11 miles, takes about 6 hours. Essential requirements are stout boots or shoes, protection against the sun and supplies of food and particularly water.

Through the
gorge

The best plan is to join a walking party organised by a travel agency. The group will then be taken by coach to the starting-point of the walk on the Omalós plain and met at the end of it, at Ayía Rouméli, and taken by boat to Khóra Sphakíon or Palaiókhora, where buses for the return journey will be waiting.

For those who balk at the long walk through the gorge there is an alternative way of reaching the Iron Gates. The travel agencies offer trips which take visitors to and from Ayía Rouméli by boat, leaving them only with a 6km/4 mile walk, mainly on level ground.

Those who want to do the walk on their own can take the earliest service bus from Chaniá to Xylóskala, or spend the night in the small hotel there. Rooms can also be had in private houses in Omalós. From Khóra Sphakíon and Palaiókhora there are service buses back to Chaniá.

The walk begins at Xylóskala ("wooden steps"), from which there are impressive views down into the gorge and of the surrounding hills. Just before this a path on the left climbs to the Kalérgi mountain hut (1680m/5510ft), belonging to the Greek Climbing Club (EOS), which offers overnight accommodation.

The steep (formerly "wooden") path winds its way down through cypresses and pines, with views of Mt Gíngilos (2080m/6825ft). On the way down can be seen, depending on season, white lilies, white peonies, alpine violets and on the rock walls, often rising vertically above the abyss, various endemic plants. After a quarter of an hour the path comes to a small rest area above a precipitous rock face, and half an hour later to the Neroutsiko ("Little Water"; 940m/3085ft) spring, under an ancient plane-tree. The walk continues steeply down, between ever higher rock walls, to the floor of the gorge, through which flows a small stream. The next rest area is at the Ríza Sykiás ("Root of the Fig-Tree") spring.

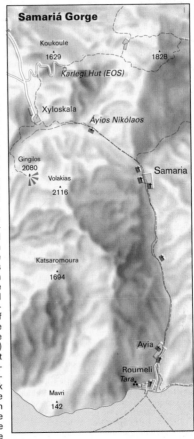

Samariá Gorge

The path continues past a patch of pastureland, with the church of Áyios Nikólaos (alt. 660m/2165ft), set amid cypresses, the mightiest of which has a girth of over 7m/23ft. Lower down is the abandoned village of Samariá (300m/985ft), which the inhabitants had to leave when the gorge became a National Park. Here there is a shady rest area with a fountain. The walk then continues past the chapel of Osía María (1379), whose name, contracted to Sa María, was given to the village and the gorge.

Thereafter the gorge becomes steadily narrower until, at the "Iron Gates", it is only 3–4m (10–14ft) wide. This is the most impressive part of the gorge, with rock walls rising vertically to almost 600m/2000ft. The last 3km/2 miles to Ayía Rouméli are over a wide, barren and shadeless coastal plain.

From Ayía Rouméli, at the mouth of the Samariá Gorge, there are boats to Palaiókhora to the west and Khóra Sphakíon to the east.

Ayía Rouméli (Αγία Ρουμέλη)

◀ *The Iron Gates in the Samariá Gorge*

Sitía

This was the site of the ancient city of Tarra. The church of the Panayía was built in 1500 on the site of an ancient temple. On the west side of the hill are the ruins of a Turkish fort.

Áyios Pávlos
(Άγιος Πάυλος)

From Ayía Rouméli it is well worth while taking a footpath which runs just above the beach for 4km/2½ miles to the church of Áyios Pávlos (10th/11th century), finely situated by the sea. This architecturally harmonious cross-in-square church, built of dressed and undressed stone, has a number of frescos, including scenes from the life of Christ.

Legend has it that the Apostle Paul landed here and baptised the local people in a nearby spring, though there is no mention of this in the Acts of the Apostles.

Sitía

D 17

Σητεία

Nomós: Lassíthi
Chief town of nomós: Áyios Nikólaos
Population: 7000

Situation and characteristics

The little country town and port of Sitía, the most easterly town in Crete, is picturesquely situated at the south-west corner of Sitía Bay, with its predominantly modern buildings extending up the slopes of a low hill. From the east end of the town, at a good sandy beach, the coast road runs round the harbour. In the inner harbour are fishing boats and pleasure craft, while the outer harbour is used by cargo boats and ferries. The main shipping connections are with the islands of Kárpathos and Rhodes and the Cyclades.

The town's main square is the Platía Iróon Polytekhníou, which with its palm-trees and cafés is an ideal place to absorb the tranquil atmosphere of the little town. Round here are all the principal shops and tavernas.

History

The Sitía area was settled as early as Minoan times. The ancient city was known as Eteia, though it is not clear whether it occupied the site of the present town or lay farther inland. It was destroyed by earthquakes in 1303 and 1508 and by the Turkish admiral Khaireddin Barbarossa in 1538, when the men captured by the Turks were forced to man their galleys and the women and children were sold into slavery. After the town was again destroyed by the Turks in 1651 it was abandoned by the Venetians and was not reoccupied by the Turks until 1870. As a result most of the houses in the old town date from the turn of the century.

Sitía was the birthplace of Vitzéntzos Kornáros (see Famous People), author of the epic poem "Erotokritos" (published 1713) which is still well known in Greece.

Sights in Sitía

Kazárma fort

The Kazárma fort (from Italian "casa di arma"), the only building of importance in Sitía, dates in its present form from 1631. The surviving parts of the fort are its battlemented walls and three-storey tower. From the fort there are wide views. In summer plays and concerts are performed here.

Roman fish-tanks

On the shore below the fort, just under the water, are horseshoe-shaped tanks in which the Romans kept fresh fish.

Archaeological Museum

For the dating of the Early Minoan (EM I–III), Middle Minoan (MM I–III) and Late Minoan (LM I–III) periods see the table on p. 34.

A picturesque lane in Sitía ▶

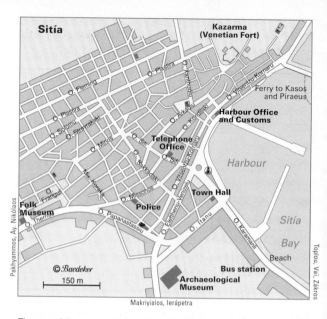

Makriyialos, Ierápetra

Tour of museum	The tour of the museum (open: Tues.–Sun. 8.30am–3pm) goes in a clockwise direction. The numbering of the cases corresponds with the numbers on the plan and in the museum.
	In the centre of the entrance lobby is an ivory statuette from Palaíkastro.
Case 27	Neolithic stone axes and sherds of pottery from the Pelekíta cave.
Cases 1 and 2	EM II material from the Ayía Photiá necropolis: pottery, obsidian blades.
Case 3	Human and animal idols from various peak sanctuaries in the Sitía area.
Case 4	Minoan pottery from various sites.
Case 5	Finds from Palaíkastro: two fine *rhytons* with bull's head motifs.
Case 6	Pottery from various sites.
Cases 7–9	Material from various sites, including the necropolis on the island of Mókhlos.
	Between cases 8 and 9 is an unnumbered case displaying recent finds from Petrás.
Case 10	Material from the Zákros palace and surrounding area.
	To the left of case 10 is a wine-press from Zákros.
Cases 11, 15, 16, 12, 17, 13, 18, 14	Material from the Zákros palace: pottery with relief decoration and octopus motifs, cups, jugs and stone vessels; fine bull's horn (18).
Case 19	Material from Sitía.

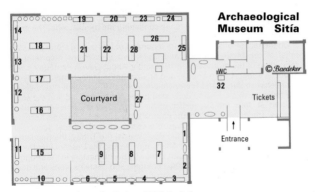

Archaeological Museum Sitía

Archaic material from the Roússa Ekklisía shrine.

Case 20

Geometric material from Áyios Yeóryios and Tourtoulí: grave goods.

Case 21

Votive terracottas from the Archaic and Geometric shrine at Sitía.

Case 22

Hellenistic material from Zíros, Xirókambos and Sitía: coins (28), fragments of a bronze discus (26).
   Between cases 23 and 24 is a grain mill of the Hellenistic period.

Cases 28, 23, 26

Roman material from various sites.

Cases 24 and 25

In this part of the museum are a terracotta model (Hellenistic) from Tripitó, an ancient marble head and, along the wall, underwater finds from round the island of Kouphonísi. Below the windows looking into the inner courtyard are Late Minoan sarcophagi. Opposite the entrance is a statue base from Itanos (1st century A.D.) with a dedicatory poem.

Other Sights in Sitía

In Odós Therisou is an interesting little Folk Museum (open: Tues., Thur., Fri. 9am–1pm and 5–8pm, Wed. 5–8pm, Sat. 9am–1pm) with a collection of domestic equipment, costumes, implements, embroidery and needlework displayed in rooms furnished in traditional Cretan style.

Folk Museum

Surroundings of Sitía

To the north of Ayía Photiá (5km/3 miles east of Sitía) is an Early Minoan necropolis with numerous shaft graves and chamber tombs. Ask in the potter's workshop in the main street for directions to the site.

Ayía Photiá
(Αγία Φωτιά)

16km/10 miles east of Ayía Photiá, through rugged country with a certain charm of its own, is the fortress-like Toploú monastery (open: 9am–1pm and 2–6pm), which dates back at least to the first half of the 14th century. The name of the monastery contains the Turkish word *top* ("cannon"), indicating that in Venetian times the monastery had a cannon for defence against pirates. The monastery, which originally was called the Panayía Akrotirianí (Mother of God of the Promontory), was several times destroyed, in particular by a severe earthquake in 1612. It was a centre of resistance against the Turks and a refuge from the Germans during the Second World War.
   Passing through a handsome round-arched gateway into a forecourt and then through the doorway in the bell-tower (1558), visitors come into the

Toploú monastery
(Μονή Τοπλού)

picturesque inner courtyard, surrounded by three-storey galleried buildings. Here they can enter the range containing the monks' cells. The architecture shows clear Venetian influence.

On the façade of the church are a number of interesting stone tablets: a
relief of the Mother of God and Child, two inscriptions recording the
rebuilding of the monastery in 1612 under Abbot Gavriíl Pantógalos with
financial support from Venice, and an inscription concerning a treaty (70
B.C.) between Itanos and Hierapytna (Ierápetra). The church is two-aisled,
the older north aisle being dedicated to the Mother of God and the south
aisle to St John the Evangelist. In the north aisle are fine 14th century
frescos. The most notable of the church's icons is one by Ioánnis Kornáros
(1770) with numerous miniature representations of Biblical scenes, including particularly (from the top downwards) the Trinity, the Baptism of
Christ, the Mother of God with Adam and Eve and the Descent into Hades.

The museum illustrates the part played by the monastery in the struggles
for liberation in the 19th and 20th centuries, and contains icons and documents on church history as well as rifles, submachine guns and coins.

Vái Beach
(Βάι
Φοινικοδασός)
(illustration,
pp. 202/03)

Near the little village of Vái, 9km/5½ miles north-east of Toploú monastery,
is Vái Beach, in a beautiful sandy cove flanked by Crete's only palm grove.
The beach tends to be overcrowded in summer, but it is well worth a visit
for the sake of the unusual scenery. There is no accommodation for visitors, nor facilities for camping. From the restaurant, higher up, there is a
good view of the beach and the rocky coast.

Vái is said to owe its palm grove to the Arabs, who camped here in 824
and after a meal of dates left the stones, which then grew into palms.

Ítanos
(Ἴτανος)

3km/2 miles north, at Erimoúpolis, are the remains of ancient Ítanos
(recommended only to those with a particular interest in archaeology).
Ítanos was of importance in antiquity as a port engaged in trade in the

Remains of ancient Ítanos

Mediterranean. In the 2nd century B.C. it had an alliance with Hierapytna (Ierápetra) and these two cities then controlled eastern Crete. The town was rebuilt after an earthquake in A.D. 795. It was finally abandoned in the 15th century because of pirate raids.

The acropolis was on a crag above the sea, from which there is a fine view of the coast. Below can be seen the remains of buildings. On the slopes of the acropolis are the foundations of a three-aisled basilica (5th/6th century), incorporating stone from ancient buildings. In Middle Byzantine times a small cruciform church was built in the central aisle.

To the north of the site is a large necropolis with a well preserved Hellenistic tomb.

Three beautiful and unfrequented beaches of coarse sand offer good bathing.

23km/14 miles east of Sitía is Palaíkastro, the most easterly village of any size in Crete and a favourite resort for young individual travellers. The unspoiled village square is a scene of lively activity.

Palaíkastro
(Παλαίκασρο)

Near the beach is the site of a Minoan town known as Rousolákkos ("red cave"), where the foundations of houses and the lines of streets have been brought to light. Like Ítanos, this is a site for those with a special interest in archaeology.

Rousolákkos

The heyday of Rousolákkos, the most important Minoan town in Crete after Gourniá, was in MM III; in LM III it declined. The town was known in Classical times as Heleia. Much of the site, which was excavated in the early 20th century, was destroyed during the Second World War.

To the south is the hill of Petsophás, on which there are remains of a peak sanctuary. From the top of the hill there are magnificent views.

Petsophás

This idyllic little village between Palaíkastro and the sand and shingle beach of Khióna is an ideal place for a restful holiday.

Angáthia
(Αγκάθια)

At Akhládia, 8km/5 miles south of Sitía, is a completely preserved Late Minoan tholos tomb. A steep dromos leads into the tholos, 4m/13ft high, at the back of which is a small tomb chamber. The tomb is difficult to find: it is reached on a track which goes off on the left 1km/¾ mile east of the village and climbs gently.

Akhládia
(Αχλάδια)

In Káto Episkopí, 3km/2 miles south of Sitía, is the interesting 11th century episcopal church of the Áyii Apóstoli. It is a three-bay structure with short lateral arms which are semicircular internally and triangular externally. Over the central bay is a dome borne on an octagonal drum with squinches. The apse is recessed within the thick east wall and is not visible from outside. The church is said to have had two altars, one for the Latin and one for the Orthodox rite.

Káto Episkopí
(Κάτω Επισκοπή)

Just before the village of Zou (2km/1¼ miles south), above the road on the right, are the remains of a Minoan villa (MM III). Among other features is a room with a bench seat.

Zou
(Ζου)

14km/8½ miles south of Sitía are the remains of the ancient city of Praisós, half an hour's walk from the quiet village of that name. It was of importance as a place of retreat for the Minoan population, who were thus able to preserve their language into the Greek period.

Praisós
(Πραισός)

Two notable features of the site are a tholos tomb and a number of chamber tombs hewn from the rock. There are remains of buildings to be seen on three hills; the city, which was walled, lay on two of them. On the hill outside the city, known as the Altar Hill, are remains of a sanctuary. On the highest hill are well preserved walls of dressed stone and a Hellenistic house with a basin for catching rainwater and an olive-press.

Khandrás plateau

From Néa Praisós the road continues south on to the Khandrás plateau, a sultana-growing area. The villages on the plateau have preserved their original character.

Khandrás
(Χανδράς)

1km/⅗ mile north of the village of Khandrás, on the slopes of a hill, are the ruins of the destroyed medieval village of Voilá, which can be reached only on foot. The remains include the tower house of a Venetian noble family who converted to Islam, the 16th century church of Áyios Yeóryios, which has a fine fresco, and a number of handsome Turkish fountains.

Zíros
(Ζίρος)

In Zíros, 4km/2½ miles east of Khandrás, are the church of Ayía Paraskeví, with frescos of 1523, and an ossuary containing the remains of the inhabitants of Skaliá, a village to the south-west which was destroyed by the Turks in the 17th century.

Etiá
(Ετιά)

At the hamlet of Etiá, 4km/2½ miles west of Khandrás, is a three-storey Venetian palazzo built by the de Mezzo family at the end of the 15th century and destroyed by the Greeks during the 1897 revolution. Some rooms have been preserved in the partly restored house.

Makriyialós
(Μακρυγιαλός)

29km/18 miles south of Sitía is the seaside resort of Makriyialós, now joined up with the neighbouring Análipsis, which attracts many package holidaymakers. It has a long but narrow sandy beach.
  From the main road a signpost points the way to the remains of a Late Minoan villa; the site is unenclosed.

Near the village church are the remains, fenced in and now surrounded by modern houses, of a Roman villa of the 1st century A.D., with numerous rooms laid out round a courtyard.

Kapsá monastery
(Μονή Καψά)

35km/22 miles south of Sitía, at the mouth of a gorge, is the lonely monastery of Kapsá, now occupied only by two monks. Probably built in the 15th century, it is dedicated to John the Baptist; the church has a fine icon with scenes from his life. Within the monastery is the grave of a monk named Josíf Yerondoyánnis, who performed miraculous healings.
  From the monastery there is a fine view of the island of Kouphonísi.

Phaneroméni monastery
(Μονή Φανερομένη)

2km/1¼ miles from Sitía on the road to Áyios Nikólaos a gravel road goes off on the right to a little cove which offers good bathing from the shingle beach or from shelving rocks.
  From the little taverna it is a half hour's walk to the abandoned Phaneroméni monastery, in an almost empty village of trim houses, occupied only at the time of the grape and olive harvests.

Khamézi
(Χαμέζι)

In the unspoiled hill village of Khamézi, 10km/6 miles west of Sitía, is an interesting little private folk museum (enquire in the kafeníon below the museum). Housed in a one-roomed cottage, it displays a wide variety of everyday objects.

From the road to Áyios Nikólaos a field track goes off on the left just outside the village, below the stumps of two windmills at the top of a pass, and ends in 700m/765yd at a hill on which are the remains of a Middle Minoan villa with an unusual oval ground-plan.

Mókhlos
(Μόχλος)

The fishing village of Mókhlos, on the coast 30km/19 miles west of Sitía, has preserved its original character. It is difficult to reach by public transport, boat trips are possible from Áyios Nikólaos.

On the island of the same name, 150m/165yd offshore, numerous chamber tombs were found, containing utensils and grave offerings of the Early
Minoan period (now in the Archaeological Museums of Iráklion and Sitía).

46km/29 miles west of Sitía is Kavoúsi, 3.6km/2¼ miles from which is the   Kavoúsi
little sand and shingle beach of Paralía Thólou, a gently shelving and   (Καβούσι)
unfrequented beach very suitable for children.

**Practical
Information
from A to Z**

Accommodation

See Camping and Caravanning; Hotels; Private Accommodation; Self-Catering Accommodation; Youth Hostels

Air Services

International flights

Crete is linked with the international network of air services, both by Olympic Airways, the Greek national airline, and numerous international airlines.

Airport tax

The recently introduced airport taxes (6400 Dr. for international flights and 3200 Dr. for domestic flights) are intended to finance the new international airport in Athens.

Domestic services

Greece has a dense network of domestic services. Olympic Airways and its domestic subsidiary Olympic Aviation (information from Olympic Airlines: addresses, see below) have daily flights from Athens to all the principal Greek islands, including Crete.

Since Greek domestic timetables cannot be implicitly relied on, it is essential to check before departure that the advertised services will actually depart at the times stated.

From Athens there are services to Iráklion, Chaniá and Sitía.

From Salonica there are services to Iráklion and Chaniá.

From Iráklion there are services to Rhodes, Santorini, Salonica and other airports.

Charter flights

There are numerous charter flights during the main holiday season to Crete and elsewhere in Greece. Information from travel agents.

Special flights

There are also special cheap flights for students and campers. Information from specialist travel agents.

Airlines

Olympic Airways

UK

11 Conduit Street
London W1R 0LP
tel. (0171) 409 2400 and 409 3717

USA

647 Olympic Towers
645 Fifth Avenue, 6th Floor
New York NY 10022
tel. 212 838 3600

168 North Michigan Avenue
Chicago IL 60601
tel. 312 329 0400

526 Statler Office Buildings
20 Park Plaza, Suite 937
Boston MA 02116
tel. 617 451 0500

624 South Grand Avenue, Suite 1709
The One Wilshire Building
Los Angeles CA 90017
tel. 213 624 6441

◄ *The palm-fringed beach of Vái*

120 McGill College Avenue
Suite 1250, Montreal
Quebec H3B 4G7; tel. (514) 878 9691

Canada

80 Bloor Street, Suite 502
Toronto, Ont. M5S 2V1; tel. (416) 964 2720

Áyios Nikólaos: Plastira 20, tel. 0841 2 20 33 and 2 82 99
Chaniá: Stratigou Tzanakaki 88, tel. 0821 5 80 05 and 5 77 01
Ierápetra: Elefthériou Venizélou, tel. 0842 2 24 44 and 2 29 08
Iráklion: Ethnikis Antistasis Square, tel. 081 22 91 91
Réthymnon: Koumoundourou 5, tel. 0831 2 22 57, 6 32 19 and 2 73 53
Sitía: Elefthériou Venizélou 56, tel. 0843 2 22 70 and 2 25 96

Crete

Antiquities

The export of antiquities and works of art (e.g. icons) is prohibited and is subject to heavy penalties. Information about exceptions from the rule can be obtained from :
Ministry of Culture and Science
Odós Aristidou 14, GR-10186 Athens, tel. 01 3 24 30 15–20

There is no difficulty about taking out copies of antiquities and works of art in museums (frescos, icons, jewellery, etc.) such as are sold in the museum shops in Iráklion.

Bathing Beaches

Crete has many sandy beaches (some with coarse sand and shingle) and beautiful coves and inlets. The bathing season lasts from April to November; between June and September average water temperatures range between 19°C/66°F and 23°C/73°F (lower on the north coast, higher on the south). Since there are quite cool evening breezes on the coast it is advisable to have some warm clothing with you.

There are a number of excellently equipped beaches run by the Greek National Tourist Organisation (EOT), which in addition to the usual facilities such as cabins, kiosks and play areas also offer a wide range of sports facilities, restaurants and discothèques. They are mostly round the larger towns and were established primarily to cater for local people.

EOT beaches

Particularly in July and August the strong north winds known as the meltemi (see When to Go) can give rise to a heavy swell which may make bathing difficult or even dangerous and litter the beaches with seaweed and flotsam.

Heavy seas

Hotel beaches are subject to strict state control and are accordingly well equipped and well cared for. Not all of them have first aid posts and a beach supervisor.

Hotel beaches

The north coast has long sandy beaches and little coves and inlets; one of the longest and finest is at Yeoryioúpolis, 33km/21 miles east of Chaniá. Near Kastéli Kisámou in north-western Crete is the beach of Phalásarna, one of the finest on the island. In the Gulf of Mirabéllo, 75km/47 miles east of Iráklion, is the popular Eloúnda Beach, in a sheltered situation which makes bathing possible until late autumn. Some 30km/20 miles east of Sitía, at Vái, is Crete's famous palm beach (illustration, pp. 202/03).
An idyllic bay of fine sand is Evita Bay, at the fishing village of Balí, on the north coast 32km/20 miles east of Réthymnon. On the south coast, below

Sandy beaches

A beautiful cove near Balí, between Iráklion and Réthymnon

the medieval fort of Frangokastello to the east of Khóra Sphakíon, is a beach of particularly fine sand.

Shingle beaches   At the west end of the island, under limestone cliffs, are sheltered shingle beaches.

Rocky coasts   On the south side of Crete there are stretches of rocky coast, in many of which are beautiful little coves with good bathing.

Buses

Crete has a dense network of bus services. The hub of the long-distance services is Bus Station A, near the ferry terminal at Iráklion harbour, where there are also the central information bureaux of KTEL, the bus company: tel. 081 28 39 25 (city) 24 50 19 (Lassithi, long distance), and 22 17 65 (Chaniá, long distance).

Bus timetables in English can be obtained in the larger tourist information offices (see Information) and at bus stations in Áyios Nikólaos, Chaniá, Ierápetra, Iráklion, Kastéli Kisámou, Réthymnon and Sitía. Chaniá, Iráklion and Réthymnon have several bus stations. (Where a town has more than one bus station the various services may start from different stations: you should check, therefore, which is the right station for the particular service you want.) Buses will usually stop between the official bus stops if you hail them.

Tickets must be bought in advance at the bus station; in smaller places en route they can be bought on the bus.

Excursions by coach   Many travel agencies in Crete organise coach trips, either round the sights of a town or to some particular tourist attraction. From Iráklion and Chaniá, for example, there are excursions to Knossós, the Samariá Gorge and Réthymnon, and from Iráklion to Phaistós, Górtys and Mátala (a whole-day trip), to Áyios Nikólaos and Kritsá and to the Lassíthi plain. Information about other excursions can be obtained at hotel reception desks and local tourist offices (see Information).

Business Hours

Statutory shop closing times were abolished at the end of 1992, and shopkeepers are now free to decide how long to stay open. Shops can be open round the clock on weekdays, and also on Sundays and public holidays in tourist areas.

See Currency	Banks
See entry	Chemists
See entry	Museums
See Postal Services and Telecommunications	Post offices
Restaurants are normally open from noon to 4pm and from 8pm to midnight.	Restaurants
In the larger towns retail shops are usually open Mon., Wed. and Sat. 8.30am–2.30pm, Tues., Thur. and Fri. 8.30am–1.30pm and 5.30–8.30pm. Foodshops and supermarkets in the larger towns are open Mon.–Fri. 8.30am–8pm, Sat. 8.30am–4pm. Souvenir shops are usually open from the morning until late evening.	Shops

Camping and Caravanning

Greek Camping Association
Solonos 76, GR-10680 Athens, tel. 01 3 62 15 60

Information

Information can also be obtained from the information bureaux of the Greek National Tourist Organisation, local tourist offices and the Greek Automobile Club (ELPA) office in Athens; for information on camping sites the address is Mesoyion 2, GR-11527 Athens, tel. 01 7 79 16 15–19.

The great majority of Greek camping sites are subject to supervision by the tourist authorities. They are classified in three categories according to the standard of facilities and amenities provided: A (first-class), B (good) and C (satisfactory).
    In addition to the sites managed by the Greek National Tourist Organisation there are others run by the Greek Touring Club or privately owned. Some of the sites have small chalets which can be hired.

Classification of sites

Trailer caravans are subject to the following limits on size and weight: maximum height 3.8m/12ft 6in.; maximum width 2.5m/8ft 3in.; maximum length 12m/39ft; maximum axle weight 9 tons; maximum length of car and trailer 15m/49ft.

Trailer caravans

Camping outside authorised sites – by the roadside, in parking places and in the open country – is officially prohibited.

"Wild" camping

A list of camping sites can be obtained from the Greek National Tourist Organisation.

List of sites

Car Ferries

Visitors travelling by car to Greece and Crete cannot at present drive down through former Yugoslavia but must use one of the many ferry services between Italy and Greece. From the Italian Adriatic ports of Venice, Ancona, Bari and Brindisi there are ferries to Patras. The shortest and cheapest crossing is from Brindisi in Apulia to Igoumenitsa in western Greece.

From Ancona there are ferries direct to Iráklion, there are daily services from Athens (Piraeus).

Ferry Services to and from Crete

SERVICE	FREQUENCY	COMPANY
Italy to Crete		
Ancona–Iráklion	weekly in season (end Jun.–mid Sept.)	Marlines
Piraeus to Crete	daily (all year)	ANEK Lines
Piraeus–Iráklion	daily (all year)	Minoan Lines
Piraeus–Chaniá	daily (all year)	ANEK Lines
Piraeus–Réthymnon	four times a week	Rethymniaki Shipping

Since the shipping companies accept no responsibility for losses, no objects of value should be left in your car during the crossing. It is advisable to take out insurance covering loss or theft during transport by sea.

Owners of trailer and motor caravans should check with the shipping line or with a travel agent that their outfit is within the permitted limits of size. (On limits of size in Greece, see Camping and Caravanning.)

Agents in the United Kingdom

ANEK Lines
Marlines

Viamare Travel Ltd
Graphic House
2 Sumatra Road, London NW6 1PU
tel. (0171) 431 4560

Minoan Lines

Magnum Travel Ltd
747 Green Lanes, Winchmore Hill
London N21 3RZ
tel. (0181) 360 5353

Car Rental

Car rental is now a major service industry in Crete. In addition to the international car rental organisations there are numerous local firms, particularly in Áyios Nikólaos, Iráklion, Chaniá and Réthymnon.

The main car rental companies have desks at Greek international airports. Arrangements for car hire can also be made through hotel reception desks. Rental tariffs are relatively high. In addition to cars (including jeeps and minibuses seating 5 to 7 people) the local firms also hire out motorcycles, motor scooters, mopeds, mountain bikes and ordinary bicycles.

The minimum age for hiring a car is 21. National driving licences (with a minimum of one year to run) are usually accepted, though it may sometimes help to have an international driving licence.

It is advisable to take out passenger accident insurance.

Rental firms
Áyios Nikólaos
(dialling code 0841)

Avis, Akti Koundourou, tel. 2 84 97
Europcar, Akti Koundourou 23, tel. 2 43 43, 2 52 39, 2 53 66
Hertz, Akti Koundourou 17, tel. 2 83 11, 2 88 20
Sixt/Budget, Akti Koundourou 31, tel. 2 81 23

There are rental firms round the Venetian Harbour.
Avis, tel. 5 05 10
Europcar, tel. 5 68 30
Hertz, tel. 4 51 61, 4 03 66

Chaniá
(dialling code
0821)

There are many rental firms, particularly in Odós 25 Avgoustou.
Avis, tel. 22 94 02
Europcar, tel. 24 61 86, 22 25 05, 22 52 91
Hertz, tel. 22 97 02, 22 98 02
Sixt/Budget, tel. 24 39 18, 22 13 15, 24 10 91

Iráklion
(dialling code 081)

Avis, tel. 2 31 46, 2 03 57
Hertz, tel. 2 62 80

Réthymnon
(dialling code
0831)

Caves

Crete has a number of caves (mostly stalactitic caves) which can be entered:

Show caves

Bear Cave at Gouvernéto monastery (Chaniá)
Diktaean Cave at Psykhró (Lassíthi), 48km/30 mile east of Iraklio and
    52 km/33 mile west of Áyios Nikólaos
Eileithyia Cave near Iráklion, 1km/¾ mile south of Amnissós
Gerani Cave, 6km/4 mile from Réthymnon
Idaean Cave on Mount Ida, 20km/12 mile south of Anogia
Kamáres Cave on Mount Ida, 57km/35 mile from Iraklio
Melidóni Cave, 26km/16 mile from Réthymnon
Sentoni Zoniana Cave, 13km/8 mile west of Anogia in Réthymnon district
Skotinó Cave, 22km/12½ mile from Iráklion

Chemists

Chemists' shops are identified by a round sign with a cross and the name ΦΑΡΜΑΚΕΙΟΝ (Pharmakeion).

Mon. and Wed. 8.30am–3.30pm, Tues., Thur. and Fri. 8.30am–2pm and 5–8pm.

Opening times

Every chemist's shop displays a notice giving the address of the nearest pharmacy which is open outside the normal hours. The English-language daily "Athens News" also lists, under the heading "Chemists/Pharmacies", pharmacies which are open at night and on Sundays and public holidays.

Out-of-hours
service

Dial 100 (the police, who will pass on the message).

Emergency
telephone

Consulates

See Diplomatic and Consular Offices

Cruises

See Shipping Services.

Currency

Unit of currency	The Greek unit of currency is the drachma (Dr.), which is divided into 100 lepta. There are banknotes for 50, 100, 500, 1000, 5000 and 10,000 Dr. and coins in denominations of 1, 2, 5, 10, 20 and 50 Dr.; lepta have now practically disappeared from use.
Exchange rates	Exchange rates are subject to considerable fluctuation. Current rates are published in national newspapers and can also be obtained from banks and tourist offices.
Import of currency	Visitors may take into Greece a maximum of 100,000 Dr. in Greek currency. There are no restrictions on the import of foreign currency in cash or travellers' cheques. Foreign currency amounting to more than US $1000 should be declared on entry into Greece so that any unspent amount can be taken out again.
Export of currency	Visitors may take out up to 20,000 Dr. in Greek currency, in notes of no higher value than 1000 Dr. Foreign currency to the value of US $1000 may be taken out, or a higher amount if declared on entry.
Opening hours of banks	Banks (identified by the sign ΤΡΑΠΕΖΑ – Trapeza) are normally open Mon.–Thur. 8am–2pm, Fri. 8am–1.30pm. The airport branches of banks usually have longer opening hours.
Changing money	As is usual in countries with weak currencies, it is best to change money in Greece rather than outside it. Some post offices also change money. Some hotels will change money at the reception desk, though the rate of exchange is likely to be less favourable than in a bank. When you change money you should keep the receipts, since you may be asked to produce them when leaving the country.
Cheques	Eurocheques may be drawn for sums of up to 45,000 Dr., and can be cashed, on production of the drawer's cheque card (a passport or other form of identification may also be asked for), at banks in the larger towns and tourist centres. This applies also to travellers' cheques. Ordinary cheques will be honoured only after reference back to the drawer's home bank, a process which may take some days.
Credit cards	In Crete, as in the rest of Greece, the principal credit cards are widely accepted.
Loss of cheques or cards	In the event of loss or theft of eurocheques and/or cheque cards, travellers' cheques or credit cards, the bank or other organisation which issued them should be informed at once by telephone, with confirmation in writing.

Customs Regulations

Prohibited imports	The import of the following articles is strictly prohibited: firearms and ammunition (other than sporting guns and cartridges: see below); narcotics and drugs; bulbs, flowers, fruit and plants; fuel in spare cans.
Restricted imports	Portable television sets and valuable electrical apparatus may be imported temporarily against deposit of duty; otherwise the importation will be noted in the visitor's passport.
Import of personal effects	Visitors may bring in personal effects, including clothes, jewellery, etc., and also a portable camera, with films; a cine-camera, with film and projector; a record-player; a tape-recorder or dictating machine; portable musical instruments; a pair of field glasses and a pair of binoculars; a bicycle; camping equipment showing signs of use; equipment for skiing, golf, surfing and wind-surfing (to be noted in the visitor's passport); fishing

tackle; and a sporting gun showing signs of use and covered by a permit issued at the customs office, together with 200 cartridges.

There is no limit on the import of tax-paid goods from an EU country provided that they are intended for the visitor's personal use. The customs authorities have, however, laid down indicative limits on the import of alcohol and tobacco. Beyond these limits the visitor must be able to prove that the goods are for his personal use.

Imports from EU countries

For tobacco products the limits are 800 cigarettes or 400 cigarillos or 200 cigars or 1 kilogram of tobacco.

For alcoholic drinks the limits are 10 litres of spirits over 22° proof, 20 litres of spirits or fortified wine under 22° proof, 90 litres of wine (including a maximum of 60 litres of sparkling wine) and 110 litres of beer.

There are no limits for perfume and toilet water.

For goods bought duty-free (e.g. at the departure airport or on board a ship or aircraft) there are fixed limits: 200 cigarettes or 100 cigarillos or 50 cigars or 250 grams of tobacco; 1 litre of spirits over 22° proof, or 2 litres of spirits or fortified wine under 22° proof, or 2 litres of wine and 2 litres of still table wine; 50 grams of perfume and 250 millilitres of toilet water; 500 grams of coffee or 200 grams of coffee extract; 100 grams of tea or 40 grams of tea extract; and other goods to the value of 48,000 Dr.

Duty-free goods

Visitors under 18 may not import alcohol or tobacco products bought duty-free. Visitors under 15 may not import coffee bought duty-free, and their limit for "other goods" bought duty-free is 25,000 Dr.

The limits on the import of tobacco, alcohol, etc. bought in non-EU countries are the same as for goods bought duty-free in EU countries.

Imports from non-EU countries

Private cars (and trailers, motorcycles, sidecars and mopeds) may be taken into Greece without payment of duty for up to 6 months (with the possibility of extension for another 6 months), but must be registered in the visitor's passport if entering Greece via a non-EU country.

Cars and boats

Similar regulations apply to small motorboats and sailing boats brought in by road. Yachts (i.e. boats with cabin, galley, lavatory, etc.) must put in at a port with customs facilities and obtain a transit log (valid for 6 months, with the possibility of unlimited extension). The yacht's equipment may include one Very pistol and one flare pistol.

Further information can be obtained from local customs offices or from the Customs Investigation Department at Amvrosiou Fratzi 14, Neos Kosmos, Athens, tel. 01 9 22 73 07 and 9 22 73 15.

Cycling

Cycling is a very pleasant way to explore Crete, giving easy and leisurely access to remote villages, areas of unspoiled natural beauty and secluded beaches round the coast.

Information about cycling in Crete can be obtained from the Kastro Bicycling Club in Iráklion, Averof 19 (3rd floor), tel. 081 24 34 45 (office open: 8am–2pm), and specialist travel agencies on the island, e.g. Hellas Bike Travel.

Information

From Kastéli Kisámou, on the north coast of Crete, a road runs 24km/ 15 miles north-east, with few hills to climb, via Plakálona and Kolymbári to Tavronítis.

Suggested tours
From Kastéli Kisámou

From Réthymnon a level road runs north-east along the coast to Stavroménos; then eastward, with some hills, via Alexándrou to Pérama and Mourtzana; then, skirting the Kouloukonas hills, to Apladianá. The road (total distance 40km/25 miles) runs through beautiful scenery.

From Réthymnon

Diplomatic and Consular Offices

From Spíli   Spíli, south-east of Réthymnon, is the starting-point of an easy 22km/
14 mile trip, through scenery of great beauty, via Mixórrouma, Koxaré and
Asómatos to Plakiás.

From Plakiás   The route from Plakiás via Sellía, Kato Rodakino, Argoulés, Frangokastello
and Vouvás to Khóra Sphakíon (48km/30 miles) has a number of hills but
offers beautiful views of the coastal hills and the sea.

From Iráklion   Iráklion is the starting-point of a trip to the largest wine-growing area in
Crete. The route (49km/31 miles) runs south-east, with some hills to climb,
via Voútes, Áyios Mýron, Pýrgou, Káto Asítes and Priniás to Ayía Varvára
and Áyii Déka.

From Ierápetra   From Ierápetra there is an easy trip (28km/17 miles) eastward via Phérma
and Ayía Photiá to Análipsi through moderately hilly country, past beautiful
bathing beaches.

Mountain biking   Mountain bikes can be hired at the Grecotel Rithymna Beach for western
Crete and the Grecotel Creta Sun for eastern Crete.
     A helmet is usually supplied along with the bicycle. Essential items of
equipment are cycling trousers and gloves, a windproof top and stout
sports shoes. There is endless scope for attractive trips, for example
through the mountain world of Crete (White Mountains) or from the north
to the south coast.

Diplomatic and Consular Offices

Greek Embassies

In UK   1A Holland Park, London W11 3TP
tel. (0171) 229 3850

In USA   2221 Massachusetts Avenue NW
Washington DC 20008; tel. (202) 667 3169

In Canada   76–80 Maclaren Street
Ottawa Ont. K2P 0K6; tel. (613) 238 6271

Consulate in Crete

United Kingdom   Odós Papalexandrou 16, Iráklion, tel. 081 22 40 12

Distances

See page 213.

Diving

See Sport

Drinks

See Food and Drink

Distances in kilometres between selected towns in Crete	Áyios Nikólaos	Chaniá	Ierápetra	Iráklion	Kastéli Kisámon	Khóra Sphakíon	Palaiokhóra	Réthymnon	Sitía
Áyios Nikólaos	•	225	36	86	268	236	300	167	69
Chaniá	225	•	272	139	43	64	75	58	294
Ierápetra	36	272	•	122	304	237	347	203	64
Iráklion	86	139	122	•	182	150	214	81	155
Kastéli Kisámon	286	43	304	182	•	107	72	101	339
Khóra Sphakíon	236	64	237	150	107	•	139	69	305
Palaiokhóra	300	75	347	214	72	139	•	133	369
Réthymnon	167	58	203	81	101	69	133	•	236
Sitía	69	294	64	155	339	305	369	236	•

Electricity

Electricity is normally 220 volts AC; on ships it is frequently 110 volts AC.
Power sockets are mostly of normal European type. Adaptors are necessary for British or American plugs; they can sometimes be hired in hotels.

Embassies

See Diplomatic and Consular Offices

Emergency Services

The most useful source of assistance for visitors is the Tourist Police (Astynomía Alladapón), which has offices in many towns of tourist interest and can give general information and advice about accommodation. | Tourist Police

Áyios Nikólaos: tel. 0841 2 22 51
Chaniá: tel. 0821 9 88 88
Iraklio: tel. 081 24 65 39
Réthymnon: tel. 0831 2 22 89

Dial 100	Police
Dial 166	First aid
Dial 199	Fire service
Dial 191	Forest fires
See Motoring in Crete	Breakdown service
See Currency	Loss of eurocheques, etc.
See entry	Medical aid
See Sailing	Medical aid for yachts

213

Events

Seasonal events	The Greek National Tourist Organisation (see Information) runs a series of events of tourist interest during the summer season, including various festivals and folk performances.
Patronal and folk festivals	In many Cretan villages the feast day of the local saint is celebrated with traditional music and folk dances. There are numerous patronal and folk festivals all over the island, particularly between July and September. Information from local tourist offices (see Information).
January 1st	New Year's Day. Feast day of St Basil, with the cutting of the *vasilopitta* (New Year's Cake): there is often a coin hidden in the cake, bringing luck to the person who finds it. Processions of children (and sometimes adults), with *kalanda* (house-to-house) singing, the singers being rewarded with money and/or cakes (see also December 31st).
January 6th many places	Epiphany. Blessing of the waters, when a cross is held in lakes, rivers and the sea.
February/March many places	Carnival (particularly in Iráklion and Réthymnon).
Kathari Deftéra (Shrove Monday) everywhere	Kite-flying; preparation for the Fast (Lent), with meals of unleavened bread, fish, seafood, salads and wine.
March 25th	National Day, with military parades.
April 23rd many places	St George's Day. Particular celebrations in Asi-Gonia (Chaniá), with sheep-shearing (*koura*).
Easter everywhere	The Greek Orthodox Easter, by far the most important Greek church festival often falls on a different date from the date on which Easter is celebrated in the Roman Catholic and Protestant churches because it is based on the date of the real full moon and not an imaginary "ecclesiastical" moon according to the orthodox calendar. The colour for Easter is red (e.g. Easter eggs are dyed red), symbolising Christ's blood. On Good Friday there are processions of the faithful carrying lighted candles. On the eve of Easter Day, services culminate at midnight with the cry "Christós anésti!" ("Christ has risen!"). Easter is celebrated with the ringing of bells, the firing of cannon and fireworks, the traditional Easter soup (*mayiritsa*), the cracking of Easter eggs and the exchange of gifts. The Easter meal consists of spit-roasted lamb, and the typical Easter cake is the *tsouréki*, which is decorated with a red egg. Easter Day in 1997 is on April 27th.
May 1st everywhere	Labour Day, celebrated with parades, flower festivals and trips into the country.
May 27th–29th Chaniá	Dance festival, commemorating the battle for Crete.
June Akhládes	Apricot Festival at Akhládes (north of Pérama).
End of June Lassíthi	Performances of the prophecy play "Klidonas" in the villages of Pisko-képhalo and Kroustás.
Summer months Iráklion	Iráklion Summer Festival: opera, drama, ballet, classical music, folk singing and dancing, exhibitions, lectures, symposia (July/August).

Crete: the Principal Sights

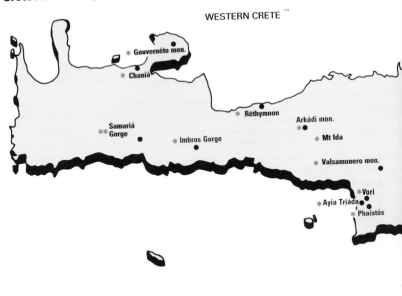

WESTERN CRETE

* Gouvernéto mon.
* Chaniá
* Réthymnon
Arkádi mon. **
* Mt Ida
** Samariá Gorge
* Imbros Gorge
* Valsamonero mon.
* Vori
* Ayia Triáda
* Phaistós

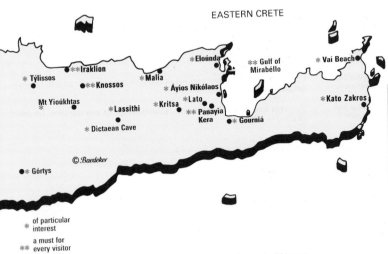

EASTERN CRETE

** Iraklion
* Týlissos
* Eloúnda
** Gulf of Mirabéllo
* Vai Beach
* Malia
** Knossos
* Áyios Nikólaos
* Mt Yioúkhtas
* Lassithi
* Kritsa
* Lato
* Kato Zakros
** Panayia Kera
* Gourniá
* Dictaean Cave

© Baedeker

* Górtys

* of particular interest

** a must for every visitor

For the principal sights at a glance, in alphabetical order and with page references, see p. 254.

July–August Áyios Nikólaos	Lato Festival, run by the municipal Cultural Centre: folk dancing, songs, concerts of modern music. Sea Festival, with boat races, swimming and wind-surfing competitions and fireworks in the harbour.
July–September Sitía	Kornareia cultural festival – theatre, music and dance.
July Réthymnon, Sitía	Cretan Wine Festival in Réthymnon (lasts two weeks), with music and dancing and free samples of Cretan wines. Sultana Festival in Sitía.
August/Sept. Réthymnon	Renaissance Festival (two weeks) in the Venetian fortress: open-air theatre, folk music and dancing, concerts, films and other entertainments by companies and groups from Greece and Europe. Detailed information from the Réthymnon municipal authorities and the Erophilí Theatre.
August Chaniá	"Musical August" – exhibitions, songs and concerts.
August 6th Anóyia	Fair, with folk performances.
August 15th many places	Feast of the Dormition of the Mother of God, celebrated with particular ceremony at Neápolis.
2nd half of August Kritsá	Cretan Wedding in Kritsá (Lassíthi)
August–September Chaniá (Palískhora)	"Summer" – traditional and classical music, dance and puppet shows.
October 28th everywhere	Ókhi Day: national holiday, with military parades (see Public Holidays).
November 8th Réthymnon	Commemoration of the 1866 rebellion and the destruction of Arkádi monastery by the Turks.
November 21st Réthymnon	Feast of the Presentation of the Virgin in the Temple.
December 24th everywhere	Christmas Eve, with processions of children (and sometimes adults) and *kalanda* (house-to-house) singing.
December 31st everywhere	The year ends, as it began, with *kalanda* singing: see January 1st and December 24th.

Ferries

See Car Ferries

Folk Traditions

Costumes	In recent years Greek traditional costumes have become rarer, but in some areas they are still part of everyday life. Thus in Crete men still occasionally wear the characteristic baggy breeches (*vráka*) and black head-scarf.
Customs	Long-established and deeply rooted traditional customs still find expression in the many church festivals (particularly at Easter and on the feast days of local saints) and in family celebrations in country areas.

Greek folk music, with its characteristic rhythms and unusual intervals, has in recent years become better known in western Europe, and it has also been a major influence on contemporary light music in Greece. — Folk music

See Art and Culture, Music and Dance — Folk dancing

Food and Drink

Food

Cretan food is, in general, the same as in the rest of Greece. Hotel restaurants usually offer the standard international cuisine, with some Greek dishes to add an extra touch of colour. In restaurants the national cuisine predominates, showing strong Eastern (mainly Turkish) influence and making much use of olive oil, garlic and herbs. Fruit and vegetables feature prominently on the menu. Fish and meat are almost always grilled.

Visitors requiring special diets should discuss this with the hotel management. Those with stomach or liver conditions should wherever possible choose grilled food, preferably without sauce (*khoris salsa*). Caution should be used in drinking iced water.

Essential items in the table setting are bread (*psomí*), salt (*aláti*), pepper (*pipéri*) and sugar (*zákhari*).

See Restaurants — Times of meals

There is a wide choice of hors d'œuvres. In addition to the appetisers (*mese*) which are served with ouzo or other aperitif the range includes prawns, seafood, vine-leaves stuffed with rice (*dolmádes*) and salads (*salátes*). — Hors d'œuvres (orektiká)

Greek soups are usually very substantial, and are often made with egg and lemon juice. *Fasolada* is a popular thick bean soup; other favourite soups are pepper soup (*pipéri soúpa*), with the addition of vegetables and meat, and clear bouillon (*somós kreátos*). There are also excellent fish soups (*psárosoupes*). Hand-ground wheat in the form of a coarse meal (*khondro*) is also used to make soup. — Soups (soúpes)

The favourite kind of meat is lamb (*arnáki* or *arní*), usually roasted or grilled. Also popular is *yíros,* meat grilled on a vertical spit; *souvlákia* (kebabs) are less commonly found in Crete than elsewhere in Greece. *Kokorétsi* are lamb entrails roasted on a spit. — Meat (kréas)

Popular entrées are *pastítsio* (macaroni with minced meat) and *mousaká* (minced meat and aubergines with a cheese sauce). — Entrées (entrádes)

Typical Greek vegetables are artichokes (*angináres*), aubergines (*melitsánes*), courgettes (*kolokythákia*), peppers (*piperiés*), zucchini and vine or cabbage leaves, usually stuffed with minced meat, rice and herbs and cooked in oil, accompanied by celery, spinach and leeks. — Vegetables and salads (lakhaniká, salátes)

Salads include lettuce (*maroúli*), tomatoes (*tomáto saláta*), asparagus (*sparángia saláta*) and "village salad" (*khoriatíki*) of tomatoes, cucumbers, olives and feta cheese, scattered with herbs..

Herbs are much used in Cretan cooking, including particularly mint, dill and oregano. Many dishes are given additional flavour by garlic, onions and lemons. — Herbs, etc.

Fish and seafood feature prominently on Greek menus. The commonest species are sea-bream (*synagrída, tsipoúra*), sole (*glóssa*), red mullet (*barboúni*) and tunny (*tónos*), together with lobsters (*astakós*), mussels (*mýdia*), squid (*kalamária*), octopus (*oktapódes*) and others. — Fish (psári)

Wedding bread

Desserts (dessér)

The most common desserts are fruit or an ice cream (*pagotó*). There is a wide variety of fruit, depending on the time of year: water-melons (*karpoúsia*), musk melons (*pepónia*), peaches (*rodákina*), pears (*akhládia*), apples (*míla*), oranges (*portokália*, grapes (*staphýlia*) and figs (*sýka*). Other desserts are rice puddings (*rizógalo*), custards, tarts and a kind of cake called *bougátsa, baklava* filo pastry with almonds and honey.

Cakes, bread

On the great church festivals such as Easter and Christmas and for family celebrations traditional kinds of bread are baked: Easter cake or egg cake for Easter, Christ's bread or cross bread at Christmas. Popular too are special wedding bread and christening bread in a variety of patterns.

Cheese (tyrí)

Most Greek cheeses are made from ewe's milk or goat's milk (*feta*), which are also used to make delicious yoghourt (*yaoúrti*). Cretan specialities made with cheese are the Sphakía pasty (lamb with cream cheese in pastry dough, baked in the oven) and *kalitsounia* (small hand-made pasties filled with cream cheese and cooked in oil).

Drinks

Wine

The commonest drink is wine (*krasí*), which has been made in Crete for more than 3000 years. Different types of grape are grown for red wine (*mávro krasí*) and white wine (*áspro krasí*); both dry and sweet wines are produced.

Wines of high quality are made from grapes grown in the vineyards round Arkhánes and Peza, to the south of Iráklion. The Peza Union in Iráklion produces the following brands: Mantiko (a dry red wine), Regalo (a dry white wine) and Logado (dry rosé, white and red wines). One of the

Market stalls, Iráklion ▶

oldest wine-making firms in this region is Minos Wines, among whose wines is San Antonio, a red wine comparable to claret. Good light wines for summer drinking are Minos Palace rosé and white wines.

Among wines produced by the Olympias firm in Iráklion are Cava d'Oro (rosé and white), Peza (red and white) and Gala White.

Retsina

Some Greek country wines are resinated to improve their keeping quality (*retsína, krasí retsináto*). This gives them a characteristic sharp taste which may not appeal to everyone at first; but resinated wines, once the taste has been acquired, are very palatable and stimulating to the appetite. The Greek liking for resinated wine dates back to ancient times, as is shown by the remains of resin found in some of the earliest amphoras. The resin is added to the wine during fermentation.

You should make sure that the wine comes from the wooden casks stored in the tavernas.

Unresinated wines

There are also unresinated wines, both white and red, which meet European Union regulations; they are identified by the letters VQPRD on the label.

Wine terms

emphiálosis	bottling
epitrapézio krasí	table wine
inopolíon	wine-shop
ínos	wine
ínos erythrós	red wine
ínos lefkós	white wine
ínos mávros	red wine
kambanítis	sparkling wine
krasí	wine
mávro krasí	red wine
paragoyí	production
pinetaí droseró	to be drunk chilled
retsína	resinated wine
rozé	rosé
sampánya	champagne
xirós	dry

Beer
(*bíra*)

The brewing of beer in Greece dates from the reign of King Otto I, who came from Bavaria, and the popular Fix brand is still made to a Bavarian recipe. There are also various international brands of beer (e.g. Henninger, Kronenbourg) brewed under licence.

Spirits
(*pnevmatódi potá*)

The most common aperitif is *ouzo*, an aniseed-flavoured spirit, usually diluted with water, which turns it milky. It is a favourite drink to accompany the famous Greek *mezedes*, appetizers taken by way of *hors d'œuvres* before lunch or dinner.

Raki – not to be confused with the Turkish schnaps of the same name – is distilled from wine marc and is fairly strong. You should beware of the cheap imitations sometimes sold in tourist shops.

Mastikha is a liqueur made from the bark of the mastic tree.

Greek brandy (*konyák*) is fruity and fairly sweet.

Soft drinks

In addition to water (*neró*) and mineral water (*metallikó neró*) the most popular soft drinks are orangeade (*portokaláda*), lemonade (*lemonáda*) and freshly pressed fruit juices (*portokaláda fréska,* orange juice).

Coffee (*kafés*)

"Greek" coffee comes in a range of different strengths and degrees of sweetness – e.g. *kafés glykós vrastós* made with plenty of sugar, *varys glykós* strong and sweet, *elafrós* light. A popular version is *métrios* medium strong and medium sweet. If you want milk ask for *gala*.

Tea (*tsái*)

Tea is of different kinds – *mávro tsái* black tea, *tsái ménda* peppermint tea, *kamoumillo* camomile tea and *tsái tou vounoú* an infusion of mountain herbs.

Getting to Crete

There are daily flights by Olympic Airways from Athens to Iráklion and **By air**
Chaniá; from Salonica there are several flights weekly to Iráklion and a
weekly flight to Chaniá. The best international connections are via Athens.
   There are also numerous charter flights to Crete during the holiday
season from London and other United Kingdom airports.

Information about special fares for children, students and senior citizens   Special rates
and Apex, etc., flights can be obtained from travel agents and airlines.

The route to Greece through former Yugoslavia is no longer open, and the   **By car**
longer route through Hungary, Romania and Bulgaria is not recommended
because of long delays at frontiers and filling stations, shortages of fuel,
poor roads and the difficulty of getting technical or medical aid in the event
of an accident or breakdown. Before venturing on this route you should
seek information on the current situation from the AA or other motoring
organisation.
   The best route to Greece is by way of Italy and one of the many car ferries
between Italy and Greece. In view of the increased pressure on these
services advance booking is essential, and weekends should be avoided.
   On ferry services between Italy and Greece, between mainland Greece
and Crete and between the Greek islands, see Car Ferries and
Island-Hopping.

The frontier crossing points into Greece are open 24 hours a day.   Frontier crossings

For information about bus services from London to Athens apply to: **By bus**
Eurolines (UK) Ltd, 23 Crawley Road
Luton, Beds LU1 1HX; tel. (01582) 404511

The rail journey to Greece is slow (3½ days from London) and is not   **By rail**
therefore to be recommended, except perhaps for young people, who can
get a cheap InterRail pass. There is no through service from Britain to
Greece, and it is necessary to travel via Germany and Austria and find a
connection there.

Health

The hot climate and unaccustomed food and drink may upset some people.
It is advisable, therefore, to avoid undue exertion or too much exposure to
the sun during the first few days of your holiday. You should also be careful
about eating raw food, unpeeled fruit and ice-cream and should drink only
bottled drinks.

A well equipped first aid kit should be included in your luggage, containing   First aid kit
such items as a thermometer, scissors, tweezers, cotton wool, gauze ban-
dages, dressings, sticking plasters, ointment, pain-killers, remedies for
diarrhoea and constipation, tablets against travel sickness and sun cream.
If you are regularly taking medicine you should of course ensure that you
have a sufficient supply.

It is advisable to have an anti-tetanus inoculation. Even small cuts should   Inoculation
be washed and disinfected to avoid inflammation.

See entry   Chemists

See Medical Aid   Doctors

Help for the Handicapped

Since the official list of hotels published by the Greek Chamber of Hotels (see Information) does not indicate which hotels have special facilities for the handicapped, you should write direct to your selected hotel – preferably in one of the higher categories – and enquire about their suitability for disabled persons.

The best means of transport for handicapped visitors to Crete are taxis.

Hotels

Booking	Visitors who plan to go to Crete at Easter or during the main holiday season (June to September) should be sure to book their rooms in plenty of time. Information about hotels and reservations can be obtained from the Greek Chamber of Hotels (see Information).
Prices	During the main holiday season hotel tariffs in Greece are not much below those in other European countries. During the off season they are considerably lower.
Hotel categories	Greek hotels are officially classed in six categories: L (luxury), A, B, C, D and E. Prices quoted for D category hotels exclude private shower and breakfast. Most are open from April to October The following list is based on the official list published by the Greek Chamber of Hotels, with a Baedeker star (★) for hotels of particular quality; (b=beds).
Holiday clubs, holiday villages	Holidays in holiday clubs and holiday villages are becoming increasingly popular, since they offer a wide range of leisure activities, particularly water sports, and lay on special events of all kinds. Information from travel agents.

List of Hotels (a selection)

Ammissós (Iráklion)	Minoa Palace, A, 124 rooms
Amoudára (Iráklion)	Candia Maris, L (28 bungalows, 221 hotel rooms) Agapi Beach, A, 391 b. Creta Beach (hotel and bungalows), A, 262 b. Dolphin Bay (hotel and bungalows), A, 498 b. Santa Marina Beach, A, 220 b. Zeus Beach, A, 72 rooms Alcyon, B, 58 b. Lambi, B, 108 rooms Marilena, B, 61 rooms Minoas, C, 67 b.
Amoudára (Lassíthi)	Virginia (apartments), B, 36 b. Stella (apartments), C, 29 b.
Ayía Galíni (Réthymnon)	Andromeda, B, 40 beds Sunningdale, B, 36 b. Acropolis, C, 32 b. Adonis, C, 39 b. A family-run hotel in a quiet situation Astoria, C, 42 b. Galini Mare, C, 48 b.

Irini Mare, C, 69 b.
  At the foot of a hill, 100m from the shingle beach; terrace with beautiful
  view of Ayía Galíni Bay
Areti, D, 74 b.

Alexia Beach, B, 17 rooms
Amalthia (hotel and bungalows), B, 115 b.
  On outskirts of town, on main road; mountain bike station
Santa Marina, B, 120 b.
  On sandy beach; rooms furnished in Cretan style
Apladas (furnished apartments), C, 32 b.

Ayía Marína
(Chaniá)

Capsis Beach (hotel and bungalows), L, 1229 b.
Alexander House, A, 109 b.
  Comfortable house near beach; buffet meals with wide choice
Peninsula (hotel and bungalows), A, 367 b.
  On cliffs, 50m from sand and shingle beach; evening events twice weekly
  in high season
Panorama, B, 156 b.
Stelios, B, 76 b.

Ayía Pelayía
(Iráklion)

Aghia Roumeli, B, 13 b.

Ayía Rouméli
(Chaniá)

★Minos Beach (hotel and bungalows), L, 233 b.
  Beautiful, quiet situation on a small peninsula; gardens, pool
★Minos Palace (hotel and bungalows), L, 276 b.
★Mirabello Tennis Resort Hotel Village (hotel and bungalows), L, 251 b.
St Nicholas Bay, L, 96 rooms
Archontikon (apartments), A, 20 b.
Candia Park Village, A, 186 rooms
Cretan Village (apartments), A, 22 b.
Hera Village (apartments), A, 88 b.
Hermes, Akti Koundourou, A, 379 b.
  Comfortable hotel near bathing cove with sandy beach, pool
Ammos, B, 56 b.
Ariadni Beach (apartments), B, 142 b.
Coral, B, 323 b.
  Superior middle-range hotel
Domenico, Aryiroupoulou 3, B, 46 b.
El Greco, Akti Themistokleous Milos, B, 87 b.
Leventis, M. Sfakianaki 15, B, 17 b.
Libritis (apartments), B, 30 b.
Miramare Gargadoros, B, 100 b.
Olga, Ergatikis Estias 20, B, 54 b.
Ormos, B, 86 b.
Rhea, Marathonos/Milatou 10, B, 220 b.
Sand Apartments, Yiamboudaki 6, B, 56 b.
Acratos, 28th October St 19, C, 59 b.
Alcestis, Akti Koundourou 30, C, 45 b.
Alfa, Tselepi 23, C, 74 b.
Almyros Beach, C, 87 b.
Apollon, Minoos 9, C, 114 b.
Astoria, C, 50 b.
Creta, Kitroplatia, C, 50 b.
Cronos, Arkadiou 2, C, 68 b.
Du Lac, 28 October St 17, C, 60 b.
Elena, Minoos 15, C, 77 b.
Europa, Ayiou Athanasiou 12, C, 64 b.
Kamara, Minoos 8, C, 51 b.
Kouros, Ethnikis Anistaseos-Koritsas 17, C, 47 b.
Lato, C, 48 b.

Áyios Nikólaos
(Lassíthi)

Minos Beach Hotel, Áyios Nikólaos

Lito, Havania, C, 71 b.
Myrsini, Akti Koundourou, C, 60 b.
Pangalos, Tselepi 17, C, 43 b.
Panorama, Akti Koundourou/Sarolidi 2, C, 50 b.
Pergola, Sarolidi 20, C, 50 b.
Sgouros, N. Pangalou Kitroplatia, C, 48 b.
Zephyros, Idomeneos 6, C, 48 b.

Chaniá
(Chaniá)

Amfora (pension), Parodos Theotokópoulou 20, A, 30 b.
   Historic 13th century building on old harbour; restaurant with traditional
   Cretan cuisine
Creta Paradise Beach Resort, A, 186 rooms
Kydon, Platía Agoras, A, 188 b.
Panorama, Kato Galates, A, 167 rooms
Doma, El. Venizélou 125, B, 56 b.
Porto Veneziano, Akti Enoseos, B, 108 b.
Samaria, Kydonias/Zimvrakakidon, B, 110 b.
Xenia, Theotokópoulou, B, 88 b.
   Fine view of harbour; beautiful garden
Aptera Beach (bungalows), Paralia Ayion Apostolon, C, 92 b.
Astor, El. Venizélou/A. Arkhontaki 2, C, 68 b.
Candia, Malaxis-Skiner-Nea Hora, C, 33 b.
Canea, Platía 1866 16, C, 94 b.
Diktynna, D. Episkopou 1, C, 61 b.
Kriti, N. Phoka/Kyprou 10, C, 189 b.
Lucia, Akti Koundourioti, Palaio Limani, C, 72 b.
Omalos, Kydonias 71, C, 63 b.
   In the elegant district of Khalepa, near beach
Halepa, El. Venizélou 164, 94 b.
   Country house furnished in 19th century style

★Astir Palace Eloúnda (hotel and bungalows), L, 551 b.
★Eloúnda Bay (hotel and bungalows), beside Eloúnda Beach Hotel
  Gardens; member of Leading Hotels of the World
★Eloúnda Beach (hotel and bungalows), L, 578 b.
  Building in local style, charmingly situated on Gulf of Mirabéllo; member
  of Leading Hotels of the World
★Eloúnda Mare (hotel and bungalows), L, 200 b.
  Quiet, terraced holiday complex on a small artificial beach
Eloúnda Marmin, A, 295 b.
  Large and well-equipped hotel complex on the sea
Driros Beach, B, 36 b.
Akti Olous, Shisma, C, 95 b.
Aristea, Shisma, C, 62 b.
Calypso, Shisma, C, 30 b.
Selena Village, C, 98 b.
Maria, D, 16 b.

Eloúnda
(Lassíthi)

Dafni (hotel/pension), B, 35 b.
Creta Maria (apartments), C, 29 b.
Vachos, C, 44 b.

Galatás
(Chaniá)

Erato (hotel/pension), C, 46 b.

Goúrnes
(Iráklion)

Aphrodite Beach, A, 500 b.
  Two linked complexes; entertainments (for children as well); weekly
  Cretan or barbecue evenings with music and dancing, swimming pools
Grecotel Club Creta Sun (rooms and bungalows), A, 568 b.
  Club hotel with amphitheatre, taverna (dancing) and discothèque
Marina (hotel and bungalows), A, 728 b.
  Family hotel in well cared for garden, swimming pools
Pantheon Palace, A, 310 rooms
Astir Beach, B, 161 b.
  Family hotel on a long sandy beach
Mon Repos, C, 70 b.
Sonia, C, 35 b.

Goúves
(Iráklion)

Bella Maris (hotel and bungalows), 121 rooms, 26 suites
Best Western Knossós Royal Village (apartments and bungalows), L,
  Anisaras, A, 661 b. First-class restaurants; sports facilities
★ Creta Maris (hotel and bungalows), L, 1014 b.
  Popular, spacious and comfortable complex in beautiful gardens; fitness
  centre, diving centre, entertainments, tennis courts, etc.
Belvedere (hotel and bungalows), A, 547 b.
  Rustic-style rooms, dancing, folk presentations
Best Western Cretan Village, A, 442 b.
  Large holiday complex in Cretan-style architecture; wide range of sports
  and leisure facilities
Hersonissos Palace, A, 145 rooms
King Minos Palace (hotel and bungalows), A, 253 b.
  Quiet situation; daily programme of entertainments during main season
Lyttos, A, 601 b.
Nana Beach (hotel and bungalows), A, 450 b.
  Extensive hotel complex in Cretan style
Silva Maris (hotel and bungalows), A, 401 b.
  Elegant hotel in Cretan style
Glaros, B, 270 b.
Hersonissos, Zotoú Street, B, 168 b.
Hersonissos Maris, B, 133 b.
Maragakis, B, 92 b.
Nora, B, 344 b.
Oceanis, 17 Minoos Street, B, 62 b.
Sergios, B, 149 b.

**Hersonissos Limín
Chersonísou**
(Iráklion)

Hotels

Venus Melena, B, 92 b.
  In town centre, 200m from beach
Albatros, 1 Dedalou Street, C, 182 b.
Anna, El. Venizélou 148, C, 82 b.
  House in Cretan, near harbour
Avra, Ayías Paraskevís 131, C, 32 b.
Blue Sky, C, 44 b.
Diktina, C, 72 b.
Eva, Yiamboudaki 1, C, 62 b.
Ilios, El. Venizélou 1, C, 139 b.
Iro, Evangelistrias 72, C, 94 b.
Melpo, C, 77 b.
Miramare, C, 67 b.
Nancy, Ayías Paraskevís 15, C, 49 b.
  Centrally situated, family-run
Niki, C, 57 b.
Oassis, Annisaras, C, 35 b.
Palmera Beach, C, 123 b.
Pela-Maria, Eletheriou Venizélou 177, C, 168 b.
Thalia, C, 93 b.
Zorbas, Navarhou Nearhou, C, 40 b.

Ierápetra
(Lassíthi)

Cretan Houses (apartments), A, 39 rooms
Eden Rock Beach Hotel, A, 75 rooms
Koutsounari Traditional Cottages (apartments), A, 39 b.
Lyktos Beach Resort, A, 421 b.
Petra-Mare, A, 405 b.
Blue Sky, B, 45 b.
Minoan Prince, B, 105 b.
Camiros, M. Kothri 17, C, 75 b.
Creta, C, 50 b.
Kyrva, C, 56 b.
Zakros, Eleftherias Zakhros 1, C, 89 b.

Iráklion
(Iráklion)

Astoria, Platía Elefthérias 11, A, 273 b.
Atlantis, Iyias 2, A, 296 b.
Creta Beach, A, 262 b.
Galaxy, Odós Dimokratías 67, A, 264 b.
  In town; inner courtyard with pool and sun terrace
Xenia, S. Venizélou 2, A, 156 b.
Atrion, K. Palaiologou 9, B, 117 b.
Esperia, Idomeneos 22, B, 92 b.
Kastro, Theotokópoulou 22, B, 63 b.
  Centrally situated; fine view of sea from roof terrace
Mediterranean, Platía Daskaloyánni 1, B, 105 b.
Petra, Dikaiosinis 55, B, 64 b.
Apollon, Minoos/Anoyion 63, C, 96 b.
Athinaikon, Ethnikis Anastaseos 89, C, 77 b.
Blue Sky, 62 Martyron 105, C, 50 b.
Castello, Platía Koraka, C, 120 b.
Daedalos, Dedalou 15, C, 115 b.
Domenico, Almirou 14, C, 73 b.
El Greco, Odós 1821 4, C, 165 b.
Evans, Ayiou Phanouriou 146, Néa Alikarnassos, C, 48 b.
Gloria, Aigeou Poros 15, C, 95 b.
Gorgona, Gazi Amoudara, C, 73 b.
Grabelies, Skordilon 26, C, 80 b.
Heraklion, Kalokeirinou/Delimarkou 128, C, 72 b.
Irene, Idomeneos 4, C, 105 b.
Knossós, 25 Avgoustou 43, C, 46 b.
Kronos, S. Venizélou, C, 28 b.
Lato, Epimenidou/Lavrinthou 15, C, 99 b.

Marin, Beaufort 12, C, 83 b.
Metropole, Karterou 48, C, 75 b.
Mirabello, Theotokópoulou 12, C, 42 b.
Olympic, Platía Kornarou, C, 135 b.
Santa Elena, 62 Martyron 372, C, 104 b.
Selena, Androyeo 11, C, 52 b.
Egyptos, Kalokairinou 172, D, 48 b.
Hellas, Kandanoleontos 11, D, 23 b.
Hermes, 62 Martyron 11, D, 69 b.
Ikaros, Kalokairinou 202, D, 83 b.
Palladion, Khandakos 16, D, 45 b.
Phaestos, Tsakiri 8, D, 41 b.
Porto, D, 32 b.
Rea, Kalimeraki/Khandakos 4, D, 37 b.

★Istron Bay, Pilos Kalo Khorio, L, 215 b.   **Kalo Khorio**
Mistral, B, 128 b.   (Lassíthi)
Elpida, C, 168 b.
Golden Bay, C, 49 rooms

Amnissos (bungalows), B, 108 b.   **Karteros**
Karteros, B, 105 b.   (Iráklion)
Xenios Dias (apartments), C, 10 b.

Arina Sand (hotel and bungalows), A, 452 b.   **Kokkiní Kháni**
Knossós Beach (hotel and bungalows), A, 206 b.   (Iráklion)
Rinela Beach, A, 298 rooms
Themis Beach, A, 229 b.
Prima (pension), B, 13 rooms
Xenia Ilios, B, 205 b.
Akti, C, 37 b.
Danae, C, 34 b.
Kamari, C, 62 b.

Corakies Village, B, 34 b.   **Korakies**
                                                          (Chaniá)

Pirgos (hotel/pension), B, 33 b.   **Kounoupidiana**
                                                          (Chaniá)

Happy Days Beach, B, 66 rooms   **Kourna**
Kavros Beach, C, 80 rooms   (Chaniá)

Cretan Houses (studios and apartments), A, 78 b.   **Koutsounári**
  Painting and drawing courses   (Lassíthi)

Apollonia Beach (hotel and bungalows), A, 590 b.   **Linoperamata**
  Extensive holiday complex on sandy beach; full programme of   (Iráklion)
  entertainments
Zeus Beach, A, 717 b.

Grecotel Malia Park, A, 364 b.   **Mália**
  Bungalow complex round main house; theme dinners   (Iráklion)
Ikaros Village, A, 326 b.
  Picturesque hotel and bungalow complex in Cretan village style, set in
  gardens; ideal for activity or convalescent holiday
Kernos Beach, A, 519 b.
  On gently shelving sandy beach
Mália Bay (hotel and bungalows), A
  On sandy beach, near centre of picturesque village
Sirens Beach, A, 466 b.
Alexander Beach, B, 137 rooms
Anastassia, B, 43 rooms
Ariadne, B, 59 b.
Calypso (bungalows), B, 78 b.
Costas, B, 64 b.

Hotels

Gramnatikaki, B, 50 rooms
Maha Beach, B, 186 rooms
Phaedra Beach, B, 167 b.
Artemis, C, 45 b.
  Small family-run hotel
Elkomi, C, 55 b.
Florella, C, 56 b.
Mália Holidays, C, 162 b.
  Central, but quiet situation
Sofokles Beach, C, 64 b.
Sterling, C, 34 b.
Armonia, D, 39 b.
Drossia, D, 34 b.
Drossia II, D, 59 b.

Mátala
(Iráklion)

Armonia, B, 25 rooms
Frangiskos, C, 69 b.
  Family atmosphere
Mátala Bay, C, 104 b.
  Near the famous Mátala caves
Chez Xenophon, D, 43 b.

Missiria
(Réthymnon)

Grecotel Creta Palace (hotel and bungalows), A, 162 rooms, 204 bungalows

Mókhlos
(Lassíthi)

Aldiana Club, B, 262 b.

Mýrtos
(Lassíthi)

Esperides, C, 112 b.
Mýrtos, C, 32 b.

Palaiokhóra
(Chaniá)

Aghas (pension), B, 13 rooms
Aris (pension), B, 25 rooms
Elman (apartments), B, 41 b.
Polydrosos, C, 24 b.
Rea, C, 23 b.
  Well kept rooms; simple breakfast

Palaiokástro
(Iráklion)

Rogdia, C, 42 b.

Pánormos
(Réthymnon)

Europa, B, 84 b.
Panormo Beach, C, 61 b.

Perivolia
(Réthymnon)

Anita Beach, C, 44 b.
Eltina, C, 71 b.
Silver Beach, C, 100 b.
Zantina Beach, C, 33 b.

Phérma
(Lassíthi)

Corina Village (hotel and bungalows), B, 69 b.
Porto Belissario, B, 40 rooms

Piskopiano
(Iráklion)

Kalimera (apartments), B, 44 b.
Panorama (apartments), B, 14 b.
Stelva Villes (apartments), B, 22 b.
Villes Mika (apartments), B, 24 b.

Plakiás
(Réthymnon)

Calypso Cretan Village (bungalows), Plevraki 19, A, 204 b.
Alianthos Beach, Ag. Vassiliou, B, 88 rooms
Neos Alianthos, B, 173 b.
  Hotel in Cretan style with family atmosphere
Alianthos, Platía Ayiou Nikolaou, C, 35 b.
Myrtis, C, 39 b.

Orizon Beach, C, 39 b.
Plakias Bay, C, 51 b.
Sophia Beach, C, 48 b.
  Informally run hotel near harbour

Aegean Palace, A, 45 rooms
Louis Maleme Beach Hotel, A, 420 rooms
Geraniotis Beach, B, 146 b.
Santa Elena, B, 134 b.
  Apartments with children's playground; suitable for families with
  children
Villa Platanias, B, 32 b.

Platánias
(Chaniá)

Passiphae, Naxou 1, C, 32 b.
Poseidon, Posidonos 46, C, 49 b.
Prince, Konitsis 7, C, 50 b.
Vines (hotel/pension), Koritsas 13, C, 40 b.

Poros
(Iráklion)

Grecotel Rithymna Beach (hotel and bungalows), A Superior, 1114 b.
  Diving centre; tennis camp; children's camp
Adele Mare, A, 212 b.
  Architecturally attractive complex on a mile-long sand and shingle beach
Atlantis Beach, A, 90 rooms
Creta Palace, A, 710 b.
  Luxury hotel in the style of a Cretan village directly on a broad sandy
  beach; environment-friendly management; water sports centre
Creta Star, A, 591 b.
  Comfortable hotel in beautiful gardens on beach
Grecotel El Greco, A, 652 b.
  Large and well-equipped complex with main house and bungalows laid
  out on terraces; smoking and non-smoking areas in dining room;
  children's club; surfing and sailing school
Grecotel Porto Rethymno, A, 400 b.
Minos Mare, A, 120 rooms
Rethymno Bay, A, 129 b.
  Cretan-style bungalow complex in spacious grounds with old trees
Rethymno Mare, A, 135 b.
  11km/7 miles from town; regular bus services to town centre; occasional
  evening entertainments
Theartemis Palace, A, 175 rooms
Adele Beach Bungalows, B, 101 b.
Brascos, Kh. Daskali/Th. Moátsou 1, B, 156 b.
Dias, Kambos Adele, B, 100 b.
Eva Bay, Adele, B, 55 b.
Fortezza, Melisinou 16, B, 102 b.
Gortyn, B, 37 rooms
Idaeon, B, 141 b.
Jo-An, Dimitrakaki 6, B, 93 b.
Kriti Beach, S. Venizélou/Papanastasiou, B, 100 b.
Olympic, Moátsou/Dimokratías, B, 123 b.
Orion, Kambos Adele, B, 138 b.
Xenia, N. Psarrou 30, B, 54 b.
Astali, Koundouriotou 172A, C, 63 b.
Golden Beach, Adele, C, 299 b.
  6km/4 miles west of Réthymnon
Ionia, Yiamboudáki 62, C, 50 b.
Katerina Beach, Adele, C, 92 b.
Kyma Beach, Platía Iróon, C, 64 b.
Miramare Beach (apartments), Papanastasiou 18, C, 45 b.
Steris Beach, Konstantinoupoleos 1, Kalithea, C, 83 b.
Valari, Koundouriotou 84, C, 42 b.

Réthymnon
(Réthymnon)

Minoa, Arkadiou 60, D, 57 b.
  1km/¾ mile from town, 150m from beach
Minos, B, 254 b.
  Two pools, cafeteria, snack bar, tennis court, children's play area

Sissi
(Lassíthi)

Hellenic Palace, A, 179 b.
Porto Sissi (apartments), A, 30 b.

Sitía
(Lassíthi)

Hotel Club Sitía Beach, Karamanli, A, 310 b.
Sunwing (hotel and bungalows), A, 276 b.
Maresol (bungalows), B, 47 b.
Crystal, Kapetan Sifi 17, C, 75 b.
Helena, C, 42 b.
Itanos, Karamanli 4, C, 138 b.
Mariana, Misonos 67, C, 47 b.
Vai, C, 84 b.

Stalida
(Iráklion)

Anthussa Beach, A, 259 b.
Creta Solaris (apartments), A, 30 b.
Alkyonides, B, 54 b.
Blue Sea (bungalows), B, 371 b.
Cactus Beach, B, 116 b.
Horizon Beach (hotel and bungalows), B, 106 b.
  View of Stalida Bay
Palm Beach, B, 40 b.
Sunny Beach, B, 133 rooms
Zephyros Beach, B, 101 b.
Electra (apartments), C, 38 b.
Heliotrope, C, 156 b.
Stalis, D, 76 b.

Yeoryioúpolis
(Chaniá)

Mare Monte, A, 195 b.
Pilot Beach, A, 164 rooms

Information

Ellinikós Organismós Tourismoú (EOT)
Greek National Tourist Organisation (GNTO)
GNTO Offices Abroad

United Kingdom

4 Conduit Street, London W1R 0DJ
tel. (0171) 734 5997; fax (0171) 287 1369

USA

Olympic Tower, 645 Fifth Avenue
New York NY 10022
tel. (212) 421 5777; fax (212) 826 6940

168 North Michigan Avenue, Suite 600
Chicago IL 60601
tel. (312) 782 1084; fax (312) 782 1091

611 West Sixth Street, Suite 2198
Los Angeles CA 92668
tel. (213) 626 6696/9; fax (213) 489 9744

Canada

1300 Bay Street, Toronto, Ont. M5R 3K8
tel. (416) 968 2220; fax (416) 968 6533

1233 rue de la Montagne, Suite 101
Montréal, Qué. H3G 1Z2; tel. (514) 871 1535

Local Information Offices

Municipality Akti Koundourou 20, tel. 0841 2 23 57	Áyios Nikólaos
Information Bureau in Pantheon Building Odós Kriari 40, tel. 0821 9 29 43 and 9 26 24	Chaniá
Communal Authority Ipokratous, tel. 0897 2 27 64	Hersonissos/Limín Khersonísou
Municipality Ierápetra Museum Odós K. Andrianou 2, tel. 0842 2 22 46	Ierápetra
Directorate of Tourism for Crete Odós Xanthoulidou 1, tel. 081 22 82 25 and 22 82 03	Iráklion
Communal Authority Palaiokhóra, tel. 0823 4 15 07	Palaiokhóra
Municipality Sofokli Venizélou, tel. 0831 2 91 48 and 2 41 43	Réthymnon
Municipality Iróon Polytekhniou, tel. 0843 2 49 55	Sitía

Other Sources of Information

Rooms cannot be booked through EOT offices or information bureaux. **Booking rooms**
Written requests for reservations can be addressed to:

Xenodokhiako Epimelitrio (XENEPEL)   Greek Chamber
Stadiou 24, GR-10564 Athens   of Hotels
fax 01 3 22 54 49 and 3 23 69 62

Hotel rooms can also be booked on application in person to the Greek
Chamber of Hotels desk in Athens:

2 Karayeoryi Servias (inside the National Bank of Greece)
tel. 01 3 23 71 93
Mon.–Thur. 8.30am–2pm, Fri. 8.30am–1.30pm, Sat. 9am–12.30pm.

Information can also be obtained from the tourist police (Astynomia   **Tourist police**
Allodapon): see Emergency Services. If there is no tourist police office in
the town, apply to an ordinary police station.

Insurance

See Health Insurance under Medical Aid.

Island-Hopping

Some visitors will want to use Crete as a base for visits to other Greek
islands. There are boat services (ferries, hydrofoils) from Crete to numerous other islands; many of them can also be reached by air.

Boat services

Services to the Aegean Islands mostly depart from Athens (Piraeus). Connections between the islands are not always direct: it may sometimes be necessary to return to Piraeus for a connection.

Since departure times are frequently changed because of wind conditions or for other reasons, it is advisable to confirm timings before setting out and to arrive punctually at the departure point.

If you are travelling by car, motor caravan or trailer caravan you should arrive at the ferry at least two hours before departure.

Information about domestic Greek shipping services can be obtained from National Tourist Organisation offices (see Information).

See also Shipping Services.

Air services
Olympic Airways

There are daily flights by Olympic Airways (see Air Services) to the main islands.

Air Greece

Air Greece (head office in Iráklion) flies Seven Islands air tours from and to Iráklion (Crete – Kárpathos – Rhodes – Kos – Sámos – Mýkonos – Santorini – Crete) and Western Aegean air tours from and to Athens (Kýthera – Crete – Santorini – Mýkonos).

Air taxis

Air taxis, enabling you to fly in your own time, can be hired in Athens. Information from Olympic Airways (see Air Services) or Aegean Aviation Air Taxis at the East Terminal of Ellinikon Airport, Athens (tel. 01 9 95 03 26, 9 95 09 53 and 9 95 09 62).

Jeep Safaris

A wide range of jeep safaris, usually starting and finishing in Iráklion, are offered in Crete: for example through the Mount Ida range, to the Lassíthi plain, to Chaniá, through the White Mountains and to Phódele. For detailed information about accommodation available, English-speaking guides, jeeps (for four persons), insurance and events organised en route (e.g. Cretan evenings, barbecues), etc., apply to travel agents.

Language

In most parts of Greece visitors are likely to come across local people with some knowledge of another European language; but in country areas it is helpful to have at least a smattering of modern Greek.

Modern Greek

Modern Greek is considerably different from ancient Greek, though it is surprising to find how many words are still spelt the same way as in Classical times. Even in such cases, however, the pronunciation is not the same. The difference in pronunciation is found in both the divergent forms of modern Greek, which also differ in grammar and vocabulary: *dimotiki* (demotic or popular Greek) and *katharévousa* (the "purer" official or literary language).

All official announcements, signs, timetables, etc., and the political pages in newspapers were formerly written in *katharévousa*, which approximates more closely to Classical Greek and may be deciphered (with some effort, perhaps) by those who learned Greek at school. The ordinary spoken language, however, is demotic, which has been the officially accepted version of the language since 1975. This form, the result of a long process of organic development, had long established itself in modern Greek literature and in the lighter sections of newspapers.

The Greek Alphabet

Ancient Greek			Modern Greek	Pronunciation
A	α	alpha	alfa	a, semi-long
B	β	beta	vita	v
Γ	γ	gamma	gamma	g; y before e or i
Δ	δ	delta	delta	th as in "the"
E	ε	epsilon	épsilon	e, open, as in "egg"
Z	ζ	zeta	zita	z
H	η	eta	ita	ee, semi-long
Θ	θ	theta	thita	th as in "thin"
I	ι	iota	iota	ee, semi-long
K	κ	kappa	kappa	k
Λ	λ	lambda	lamvda	l
M	μ	mu	mi	m
N	ν	nu	ni	n
Ξ	ξ	xi	xi	x
O	o	omicron	ómikron	o, open, semi-long
Π	ρ	pi	pi	p
P	π	rho	ro	r, lightly rolled
Σ	σ, ς	sigma	sigma	s
		(σ is used in the middle of a word, ς at the end)		
T	τ	tau	taf	t
Y	υ	ypsilon	ípsilon	ee, semi-long
Φ	ζ	phi	fi	f
X	χ	chi	khi	kh, ch as in "loch"; before e or i, somewhere between kh and sh
Ψ	ψ	psi	psi	ps
Ω	ω	omega	oméga	o, open, semi-long

Accents
The position of the stress in a word is very variable, but is always shown in the Greek alphabet by an acute accent: formerly there were three accents (acute, grave and circumflex), but since in modern Greek there was no difference in practice only the acute accent is now used.

The diaeresis (¨) over a vowel indicates that it is to be pronounced separately, not as part of a diphthong.

Punctuation
Punctuation marks are the same as in English, except that the semicolon is used in place of the question-mark and a point above the line in place of the semicolon.

Numbers

Cardinals

0	midén	14	dekatésseris, dekatéssera
1	énas, myá, éna	15	dekapénde
2	dyó, dío	16	dekaéksi, dekáksi
3	tris, tría	17	dekaëftá
4	tésseris, téssera	18	dekaokhtó, dekaoktó
5	pénde	19	dekaënyá, dekaënnéa
6	éksi	20	íkosi
7	eftá	21	íkosi énas, myá, éna
8	okhtó	22	íkosi dyó, dío
9	enneá	30	triánda
10	déka	40	saránda
11	éndeka	50	penínda
12	dódeka	60	eksínda
13	dekatrís, dekatría	70	evdomínda

80	ogdónda, ogdoínda	500	pendakósi, -ies, -ia
90	enenínda	600	eksakósi, -ies, -ia
100	ekató(n)	700	eftakósi, -ies, -ia
101	ekatón énas, myá, éna	800	okhtakósi, -ies, -ia
153	ekatón penínda tris, tría	900	enneakósi, -ies, -ia
200	diakósi, diakósies, diakósia	1000	khíli, khílyes, khílya
300	triakósi, -ies, -ia	5000	pénde khilyádes
400	tetrakósi, -ies, -ia	1,000,000	éna ekatommíryo

Ordinals

1st	prótos, próti, próto(n)	10th	dékatos, dekáti
2nd	défteros, -i, -o(n)	11th	endékatos, endekáti
3rd	trítos, -i, -o(n)	20th	ikostós, -í, -ó(n)
4th	tétartos, -i, -o(n)	30th	triakostós, -í, ó(n)
5th	pémptos	100th	ekatostós, -í, -ó(n)
6th	éktos	101st	ekatostós prótos
7th	évdomos, evdómi	124th	ekatostós ikostós tétartos
8th	ógdoos	1000th	khilyostós
9th	énnatos, ennáti		

Fractions

½	misós, -í, -ó(n), ímisos
⅓	tríton
¼	tétarton
¹⁄₁₀	dékaton

Everyday Expressions

Good morning, good day!	Kaliméra!
Good evening!	Kalispéra!
Good night!	Kalí níkhta!
Goodbye!	Kalín andámosi(n)!
Do you speak	Omilíte
English?	anglaká?
French?	galiká?
German?	yermaniká?
I do not understand	Den katalamváno
Excuse me	Me sinkhoríte
Yes	Ne, málista (turning head to side)
No	Okhi jerking head upwards)
Please	Parakaló
Thank you	Efkharistó
Yesterday	Khthes
Today	Símera, símeron
Tomorrow	Ávrio(n)
Help!	Voíthia!
Open	Anikyó
Closed	Klistó
When?	Póte?
Single room	Domátio me éna kreváti
Double room	Domátio me dío krevátia
with bath	me loutró
What does it cost?	Póso káni?
Waken me at 6	Ksipníste me stis éksi
Where is	Pou iné
the lavatory?	to apokhoritírion?
a pharmacy?	éna farmakíon?
a doctor?	énas yatrós?
a dentist?	énas odontoyatrós?
. . . Street?	o odós (+ name in genitive)?
. . . Square?	i platía (+ name in genitive)?

Aerodrome, airfield	Aerodromíon
Aircraft	Aeropláno(n)
Airport	Aerolimín
All aboard!	Is tas thésis sas!
Arrival	Erkhomós
Bank	Trápeza
Boat	Várka, káiki
Bus	Leoforíon, búsi
Change	Allásso
Condom	Kapóta, profiláktika
Departure (by air)	Apoyíosis
(by boat)	Apóplous
(by train)	Anakhórisis
Exchange (money)	Saráfiko
Ferry	Férri-bóut, porthmíon
Flight	Ptísis
Hotel	Xenodokhíon
Information	Pliroforía
Lavatory	Apokhoritírion
Luggage	Aposkevé
Luggage check	Apódixis ton aposkevón
Non-smoking compartment	Dya mi kapnistás
Porter	Akhthofóros
Railway	Sidiródromos
Restaurant car	Vagón-restorán
Ship	Karávi, plíon
Sleeping car	Vagón-li, klinámaxa
Smoking compartment	Dya kapnistás
Station (railway)	Stathmós
Stop (bus)	Stásis
Ticket	Bilyétto
Ticket-collector	Ispráktor
Ticket window	Thíris
Timetable	Dromolóyion
Train	Tréno
Waiting room	Ethousa anamonís

Address	Diéfthinsis
Air mail	Aeroporikós
Express	Epígousa
Letter	Epistolí
Letter-box	Grammatokivótio(n)
Package	Dematáki
Parcel	Déma, pakétto
Postcard	Takhidromikí kárta
Post restante	Post restánt
Post office	Takhidromíon
Registered	Sistiméni
Stamp	Grammatósimo(n)
Telegram	Tilegráfima
Telephone	Tiléfono(n)
Telex	Tilétipo(n)

Sunday	Kiriakí
Monday	Deftéra
Tuesday	Tríti
Wednesday	Tetárti
Thursday	Pémpti
Friday	Paraskeví
Saturday	Sávvato(n)
Day	(I)méra
Weekday	Kathimeriní
Holiday	Skholí

Holidays	New Year's Day	Protokhroniá
	Easter	Páskha, Lambrá(i)
	Whitsun	Pendikostí
	Christmas	Khristoúyenna
Months	January	Yanouários, Yennáris
	February	Fevrouários, Fleváris
	March	Mártios, Mártis
	April	Aprílios
	May	Máyos, Máis
	June	Yoúnios
	July	Yoúlios
	August	Avgoustos
	September	Septémvrios
	October	Októvrios, Októvris
	November	Noémvrios, Noémvris
	December	Dekémvrios
	Month	Min, mínas
Terms in a Greek menu	See Food and Drink	

Maps

Visitors planning to explore the remoter parts of Crete will find it useful to have additional maps to supplement the general map enclosed with this guide.

The following is a selection of road maps available outside Greece:
1:300,000 Globetrotter: Crete
1:275,000 Bartholomew: Holiday Map of Crete
1:250,000 GeoCenter: Euro-Holiday Map of Crete
1:200,000 Mair: Crete
1:200,000 Freytag & Berndt: Crete
1:200,000 Nelles: Crete
1:200,000 Hildebrand: Crete
1:200,000 Berndtson and Berndtson: Crete
1:80,000 Harms-Verlag: Crete Tourist Map (5 maps for walkers)

The Greek Statistical Office publishes maps for the various Greek *nomoi*, including:
1:240,000 Chaniá
1:230,000 Iráklion
1:240,000 Lassíthi
1:200,000 Réthymnon

Medical Aid

Medical care is provided in Crete through hospitals and health centres (*kentra iyias*). The addresses of English-speaking doctors can be obtained from the British consulate in Iráklion.

Emergency calls	Dial 100 for the police, who will call the emergency services.
	For first aid dial 166.
	Other emergency services: see Emergency Services.
Health insurance	British citizens, like nationals of other European Union countries, are entitled to obtain medical care under the Greek health services on the same basis as Greeks. Before leaving home they should obtain the booklet

"Health Advice For Travellers" from a post office, public library, travel agent or doctor's surgery. They should complete the E111 application form which is included in it and return it to the post office to be stamped. Remember to take form E111 to Greece with you. The booklet includes detailed advice on what to do if you need hospital treatment or medicines in Greece.

It is nevertheless advisable, even for EU nationals, to take out some form of short-term health insurance, providing full cover and possibly avoiding bureaucratic delays. Nationals of non-EU countries should certainly have insurance cover.

Motoring in Crete

Most roads in Crete are asphalted, but in the hilly interior of the island they are often narrow and winding, and in some areas are unsurfaced.

Roads

Road signs and traffic regulations are in line with international standards. Traffic goes on the right, with overtaking on the left. There are heavy penalties for traffic offences.

Traffic regulations

The use of the horn is prohibited in built-up areas.

Safety belts must be worn.

In well lit built-up areas only sidelights are normally used at night. (Some drivers switch their lights off altogether when meeting another vehicle!)

Parking is prohibited on marked "priority streets".

The blood alcohol limit is 0.5 per 1000 (lower than Britain's 0.8).

The speed limit for cars (including cars with trailers) is 50km/31 miles an hour in built-up areas, 90km/56 miles an hour on ordinary roads, 110km/69 miles an hour on national highways (expressways) and 120km/75 miles an hour on motorways. For motorcycles over 100 cc the limits are respectively 40km/25 miles an hour, 80km/50 miles an hour, 90km/56 miles an hour and 120km/75 miles an hour.

Speed limits

Drivers exceeding the speed limit may have their driving licences confiscated and the car's licence plates removed.

When driving at night on country roads you should keep a good lookout for animals and vehicles without lights.

Policemen with a knowledge of foreign languages bear an arm-band labelled "Tourist Police".

Tourist Police

For the maximum permitted dimensions of trailers see Camping and Caravanning.

Trailers

Unleaded petrol (premium grade, 95 octane) is available almost everywhere in Crete. Standard grade petrol is 90 octane, premium grade 96 octane. Diesel fuel is widely available.

Fuel

The carrying of cans of spare fuel is prohibited on car ferries.

Assistance in Case of Breakdown or Accident

Dial 100

Police

Dial 166

First aid

The Greek Automobile and Touring Club (ELPA) has offices in Iráklion and Chaniá:

ELPA

Chaniá: Apokoronou/N. Sloula, tel. 0821 9 66 11 and 9 71 77

Iráklion: Knossou/Y. Papandreou, tel 081 28 94 40

ELPA's Athens office (dial 01 174) supplies tourist information in English and French (as well as Greek); the service operates daily (including Sundays and public holidays) from 7.30am to 10pm.

OVELPA
(breakdown
service)

The main tourist routes are patrolled by the yellow vehicles of ELPA's breakdown service, OVELPA, marked "Assistance Routiére".

Drivers in need of assistance should indicate this by raising the bonnet of their car or waving a yellow cloth.

Help can be summoned from OVELPA depots, which operate round the clock, by dialling 104 preceded by the appropriate dialling code (Áyios Nikólaos 0841, Chaniá 0821, Iráklion 081, Réthymnon 0831, Sitía 0843).

OVELPA patrols normally give assistance free of charge, though there are call-out and tow-away charges.

ELPA has a list of lawyers who provide free legal information to motorists.

Repair garages

There are authorised garages for well-known makes of car (Audi, Ford, BMW, Mercedes, Opel, Peugeot, Renault, Volkswagen, etc.) in Chaniá, Iráklion, Réthymnon and other towns.

Museums

Opening times

Museums and archaeological sites have varying opening times, which are given in the Sights from A to Z section of this guide. As a general rule they are open between 9am and 3pm. Many museums are closed at the beginning of the week (usually on Monday, sometimes also on Tuesday). They are open only in the mornings on January 6th, Shrove Monday, Easter Saturday, Easter Monday (of Greek Orthodox Easter), Whit Sunday, August 15th and October 28th. Most museums and archaeological sites are closed on January 1st, March 25th, Good Friday (until noon), on Easter Sunday, May 1st and Christmas and Boxing Days. Museums open 8.30am–12.30pm on January 2nd, the last Saturday of Carnival, Maundy Thursday, December 24th and December 31st.

Charges

With only a few exceptions there are admission charges in museums and at archaeological sites. On Sundays there is no admission charge at state museums and sites.

Information about possible reduced charges or free admission can be obtained from the Greek National Tourist Organisation or local offices of the Antiquities Service (Ephories Arkhaiotiton).

Newspapers and Periodicals

English-language newspapers and periodicals are available in Crete – usually a day late – in Ayía Galíni, Ayía Pelayía, Áyios Nikólaos, Chaniá, Daphnila, Goúves, Iráklion, Limín Khersonísou, Linoperamata, Mália, Mátala, Réthymnon, Sitía, Stalida and sometimes elsewhere.

The English-language "Athens News", a daily, contains both Greek and international news. A special European version of the Greek publication "This Month Crete", in English and German, can be obtained from information bureaux of the Greek National Tourist Organisation and Olympic Airways offices.

Foreign newspapers, periodicals and books can be bought not only in international bookshops (e.g. International Press, El. Venizélou/Petikhaki, Réthymnon, tel. 0831 5 16 73) but also in newspaper kiosks and souvenir shops.

Night Life

Particularly popular with foreign visitors are the local tavernas with their bouzouki music, clubs featuring Cretan music, "music tavernas" (*kritiká kentrá*) in which you have a good meal and enjoy Cretan music at the same time (see Restaurants) and other restaurants with folk or art shows.

There are also night clubs and piano bars in some of the large hotels and in jazz clubs. Discothèques are to be found mainly in tourist areas, in the older parts of towns and along the seafront promenade. Where hotels put on special evening entertainments (Cretan evenings, barbecues, etc.) there is usually an additional charge.

Nude Bathing

Nude bathing is tolerated in Greece in areas set apart for that purpose and not open to the general public.

Visitors should have regard to Cretan sensitivities and make sure that on beaches outside these areas they are appropriately clad. If local people object to naked bathers the offenders may be subject to police action and severe penalties.

Opening Times

See Business Hours

Photography

Photography is usually permitted in museums; a fee is payable for the use of flash or a tripod.

On archaeological sites photography is also normally permitted. Special permission is required for the use of a tripod and a charge is payable, at different rates for amateurs and professionals and varying according to the size and type of film used. Application should be made for a permit and the appropriate fee paid in advance. Information can be obtained from the Greek National Tourist Organisation (see Information) or the Ministry of Culture and Science in Athens (see Antiquities).

It is forbidden to photograph or film military installations (e.g. the NATO airport at Chaniá).

Films are dear in Greece, so you should take a sufficient supply with you. It is advisable to take out special insurance for valuable photographic equipment.

Ports

See Car Ferries; Sailing

Postal Services and Telecommunications

In places of some size the post offices of the Greek postal administration ELTA (Ellinniká Takhydromía) are normally open: Mon.–Fri. from 7.30am to 2 or 3pm; in the larger towns they may stay open on weekdays until 6pm and also open until 1pm on Saturdays. In villages their opening times are shorter. Post-boxes are coloured yellow and are cleared daily.

General

Since postage rates are frequently raised it is advisable to enquire at your hotel reception desk or in a post office about the current rates. It is best to

Postage rates

buy stamps in post offices, since elsewhere (e.g. at a newspaper kiosk) they cost more.

Telephoning

Most places in Greece, including Crete, are connected with the international direct dialling network. There are no public telephones in post offices; to make a call it is necessary to go to a telephone and telegraph office (OTE). There are also payphones at newspaper kiosks, in tavernas and in hotels (though in this case the charge is higher).

Telephone cards are now in use; they can be obtained from OTE offices.

Information

Telephone information (directory enquiries):
Crete: dial 131
Rest of Greece: dial 151
Abroad: dial 161

International dialling codes

From Britain to Greece: 00 30
From the United States or Canada to Greece: 011 30
From Greece to Britain: 00 44
From Greece to the United States or Canada: 00 1

When telephoning to Greece or Britain the initial zero of the local dialling code should be omitted.

Complaints

Dial 135

Speaking clock

Dial 141

Weather

Dial 149

Telephoning a telegram

Within Greece: dial 155

Private Accommodation ("Bed and Breakfast")

A room in a private house is the cheapest form of holiday accommodation in Crete. All over the island, in the country as well as in towns, visitors can find modest but clean rooms available for an overnight stay. Addresses can be obtained from the tourist police or the local tourist information office.

Public Holidays

Statutory public holidays

New Year's Day (January 1st)
Epiphany (January 6th)
Independence Day (March 25th)
Labour Day (May 1st)
Ókhi Day (October 28th: "No Day", commemorating the Greek rejection of the Italian ultimatum in 1940)
Christmas Day (December 25th)
Boxing Day (December 26th)

Religious feast days

In addition to the statutory holidays there are a series of religious festivals, the most important of which are:

Katharí Deftéra (Shrove Monday);
Good Friday;
Easter Sunday and Monday (see Events, Easter);
Whitsun Monday (Pentecost) also called Day of the Holy Spirit;
Feast of the Annunciation; and
the Dormition of the Mother of God (Assumption Day, August 15th)

On January 2nd and 5th, the Saturday before Carnival, Maundy Thursday, Good Friday, Easter Monday, May 1st and Whit Sunday most public offices and shops are closed all day or open only in the morning.

There are also numerous local patronal festivals (*paniyiri*).

Radio and Television

The National Radio and Television Corporation, Ellinikí Radiofonía Tileórasis (ERT, in Greek lettering EPT) consists of Greek Radio (ERA/EPA) and Greek Television (ET/ET, with three channels: ET 1, ET 2 and ET 3).

ERT

Short news bulletins in English (Mon.–Sat. 1.30, 3.40, 8.40 and 10.40am and 12.30, 3.30, 6.40, 7.20 and 11.35pm; Sun. 8.40 and 10.40am and 12.35pm), French (7.30pm) and German (7.40pm) are broadcast by ERA 5, the "Voice of Greece" on medium wave (792 kHz, Kavála).

ERA 5

There are also a number of private television stations, including the Mega Channel and Antenna TV. One of the most popular of the numerous local private radio channels is Sky, on 100.4 kHz.

Private companies

It is also possible, with luck, to pick up the BBC World Service, the Voice of America and the US Forces radio.

British and US radio

Special weather reports and warnings for sailing craft: see Emergency Services and Sailing

Weather advice for sailing craft

Railways

There are no railways in Crete, but some visitors may like to travel by rail to Greece on their way to Crete (see Getting to Crete).

Information on railway services in Greece can be obtained from:
Organismos Siderodromon Ellados (OSE)
(Greek Railways)
Odós Karolou 1–3 and Odós Sina 6, Athens
tel. 01 5 24 06 01–05 and 5 24 06 46–48

Information

Timetable information can also be obtained by telephoning 01 8 23 77 41.

Restaurants

Restaurants are classified in categories, and their prices are monitored by the market police.
   The better-class hotel restaurants in the larger towns offer international cuisine. Visitors can sample local specialities in the ordinary Greek restaurants (*estiatório*) and tavernas. For a quick meal at a (*mayériko*) restaurant, guests can choose the dishes they want in the kitchen or on the hotplate, numerous pizzerias have now sprung up. There are also "ouzerias" (*oúzeri*) in which ouzo is the main drink, accompanied by small *hors-d'œuvres*.
   Visitors who want a good meal accompanied by music and perhaps dancing are catered for tavernas with music (*kritiká kéntra*).

The kafeníon or coffee-house plays an important part in Greek daily life (see Baedeker Special, p. 22). It is not only a place to get a drink: it is also a place for meeting your friends, for conversation, for playing games and for doing business. A cup of coffee is always accompanied by a glass of water (*neró*),

Kafeníon

ouzo, the popular aniseed-flavoured aperitif, by various bits and pieces (cheese, olives, nuts, etc.), known as *mese*.

Times of meals | Breakfast (*próyevma*), of the usual continental type, is usually taken between 8 and 10am. Lunch (*yévma*) is usually served between noon and 3pm, dinner (*dípno*) between 8 and 11pm. During the summer many restaurants stay open until midnight.

The menu | The menu is often written in another European language (often English) as well as Greek, but in more modest establishments will usually be only in Greek. Except in restaurants of the higher categories it is quite normal to go into the kitchen and choose your meal for yourself.

Pâtisseries | The Greek equivalent of the French pâtisserie is the *zakharoplastío*, which serves French coffee, tea and other drinks and also pastries and sweets, usually considerably sweeter than in northern Europe.

Restaurants (a selection)

Áyios Nikólaos | Itanos (frequented by local people; also terrace restaurant), Odós Kyprou 1

Chaniá | Aeriko (seafood, poultry), Akti Miaouli
Tamam (in a former Turkish bath; Cretan dishes), Odós Zambeliou 49
Nicola's Pizza Restaurant
Pazoli'a Pizza

Ierápetra | Konaki (taverna)
Regina (café, bar), on seafront

Iráklion | Amygdalies (reasonably priced Cretan taverna), Akadimias 89
Chinese Restaurant, Daidalou
Faros (fish taverna), Meteoron 12
(Other fish tavernas round harbour and in Alikarnassos)
Kiriakos (wide selection, wine from the barrel), Dimokratías 45
Knossós (good plain cooking), El. Venizélou
La Parisienne (French cuisine; antique-style interior), Ayiou Titou 7
Lukullos (Italian cuisine), Odós Korai
Pizza di Roma, Knossou 145
Pizza Tartufo, Dimokratías 83

Réthymnon | Avli (restaurant in medieval courtyard in old town; French cuisine; fish and seafood), Odós Xanthoudidou 22/Odós Radamanthyos
Cavo d'Oro (top-class restaurant on Old Harbour; fish and seafood, grills), Nearkhou 42–43
Paradise (British cuisine; selection of beers), Soph. Venizélou 66
Othonas (taverna, restaurant), Petikhaki 27
Toscana (Greek and Cretan specialities; steak with herbs, pizzas), near Old Harbour, on sea
Ziller's (elegant restaurant with sea view; international and Greek cuisine; grills a speciality), beside Ideon Hotel, Nikolaou Plastira 8
Zorba (restaurant, cocktail bar, steak house), Platanes

Safety and Security

In general Crete is a relatively safe place for a holiday: the Cretans attach great importance to hospitality and honesty. Nevertheless it is well to remember the proverb "Most thieves are opportunists".

It is advisable, therefore, to keep any valuables you carry (passport, money, credit cards, etc.) in an inner pocket or belt, to carry as little cash as possible and to deposit any large amounts of money and traveller's cheques in the hotel safe.

It is also a good idea to have photocopies of important documents (see Travel Documents).

Loss of Eurocheques, etc. See Currency

Emergency services. See entry

Sailing

The passengers and crew of a yacht sailing in Greek waters are officially classed as visitors in transit. On entering Greek waters a foreign yacht must put in at a port with customs facilities for entry and exit (the "port of entry"). In Crete the ports of entry are Chaniá (Port Authority; tel. 0821 28888) and Iráklion (Port authority: tel. 081 22 60 73).

The port authorities will then issue a transit log entitling it to free passage in Greek waters for up to six months. During their stay in Greece the passengers and crew must spend the nights on board; any who propose to spend one or more nights ashore or to leave Greece by some other means of transport must have official entry and exit stamps entered in their passport. The transit log must be kept on board during the vessel's stay in Greece and must be produced to the port authorities on request.

After the first six months the owner of the yacht may apply to the customs authorities for an extension for a further year, and may repeat the process as often as required.

Small pleasure craft which are brought in by road are subject to broadly the same customs regulations as private cars. They may remains in Greece without payment of duty for up to four months.

There are numerous marinas with servicing and supply facilities, run by the Greek National Tourist Organisation, local authorities and sailing clubs.

Entry into Greece

Information about sailing in Greek waters (sailing schools, port taxes, etc.) can be obtained from the Greek National Tourist Organisation (see Information) and from:

Information

Athens Sailing Association
  Xenophontos 15A, Athens, tel. 01 3 23 68 13
Hellenic Yachting Federation (HYF)
  Akti Navarkhou Koundourioti 7, Kastela, 18534 Piraeus, tel. 01 4 13 73 51.
  The Federation can also supply information about regattas.
Harbourmaster's Office, Piraeus, tel. 01 4 51 13 11, 4 11 47 85 and
  4 52 09 11

Charter boats sailing in Greek waters must be officially authorised and must sail under the Greek flag. A copy of the charter contract and a list of the passengers and crew must be lodged with the port authorities at the port of departure, and the person in charge of the boat must carry copies of these documents.

Chartering boats

Harbours in Crete

243

A boat may be chartered without a crew only if the charterer and another member of the party can produce a sailing certificate or letter of recommendation from a recognised sailing club or can demonstrate their competence.

Further information about chartering (charter firms, types of boat, rates, etc.) can be obtained from the Greek National Tourist Organisation (see Information).

Weather forecasts

Weather forecasts for Greek sea areas can be obtained from the National Meteorological Service in Athens, 24 hours a day, by telephoning 01 9 69 93 06.

Special weather reports and gale warnings (6–7 and over on the Beaufort scale), in Greek and English, are broadcast by Hellas Radio (ERA) on VHF channel 16 daily at 7.03, 9.03 and 11.33am and 11.03pm. There are also weather reports for shipping, in English, on medium wave (729 kHz) and VHF at 6.30am Monday to Friday.

The First Programme of Greek television (ET 1) gives weather forecasts daily at 8pm and midnight and on Monday also at 5.30pm. ET 2 and ET 3 give forecasts daily at 9pm and midnight. Although the forecasts are given in Greek, the international meteorological symbols on the weather maps are easy to understand.

Medical emergency service

Greek radio telephone stations also transmit instructions on medical aid. Medical emergency services (English-speaking) are available 24 hours a day through Athens Radio (callsign SVN) on medium wave (2182 kHz).

Self-Catering Accommodation

Self-catering accommodation can be found in many places in Crete. Lists of such accommodation can be obtained from local tourist offices (see Information) and from travel agencies.

The following are merely some suggestions:

Koutsounari

At Koutsounari, on the south coast of Crete near Ierápetra, there is a choice between old peasant houses, well restored, and Naku Village (new houses built in traditional style), with magnificent sea views. Information from:
Koutsounari Traditional Cottages and Naku Village
P.O. Box 32, GR-72200 Ierápetra
tel. 0842 6 12 91 and 2 57 38

Zorbas

15km/9 miles from Chaniá, on the sea (sandy beach suitable for children), are the Zorbas holiday apartments. Information from:
Apostolos Lagonikakis
Platía Metropoleos, GR-73100 Chaniá
tel. 0821 5 25 25

Minotours Hellas, Rethimno Tours, Kalamaki Travel

Minotours Hellas (Istro), Rethimno Tours (Réthymnon) and Kalamaki Travel (Chaniá) have available for letting selected holiday apartments furnished in traditional Cretan style.

Shipping Services

During the main holiday season Greek domestic shipping lines (car ferries) sail one or more times weekly from Iráklion, Sitía and Kastéli Kisámou to various Greek islands and from Iráklion, Chaniá and Réthymnon to Piraeus. There are also day cruises from Iráklion to Santorini. On alternate days a ship coming from Piraeus and the Cyclades calls in at Áyios Nikólaos and continues to Rhodes. On the south coast of Crete there are daily services from April to October between Ayía Rouméli, Loutró and Khóra Sphakíon and between Palaiokhóra, Soúyia and Ayía Rouméli. In the main summer holiday season there are boats to the island of Gávdos one or more times weekly from Khóra Sphakíon and once weekly from Palaiokhóra (via Soúyia and Ayía Rouméli).

A list of shipping lines which run cruises can be obtained from the Greek National Tourist Organisation (see Information).

One very attractive cruise is from Iráklion to Santorini with a guided tour of the sites, Rhodes, Kuşadasí (Turkey). Detailed information can be obtained from travel agencies.

The fare for day cruises usually includes trannsfer from your hotel to the port and back and a buffet lunch. For longer trips it includes full board (with reduced fares for children).

Detailed information can be obtained from local tourist offices (see Information) or from:
Paleologos Shipping Agency, Travel Bureau
25 Avgoustou 5, Iráklion, tel. 081 24 61 85 and 24 62 08 | Information

Shopping and Souvenirs

Crete offers plenty of opportunities for acquiring interesting souvenirs. In recent years, however, mass production has taken over, and it is not always easy to find articles of good quality.

A good idea of the range of folk art and craft products can be obtained from visits to one or two craft shops. In some villages it is possible to see craftsmen actually at work. For information apply to local tourist offices (see Information). | Folk arts and crafts

Much sought after are the knotted woollen *flokáti* rugs, looking like long-haired sheepskins, which come either in natural wool or in a wide range of colours. | Flokáti rugs

Visitors will be tempted by the great variety of gold jewellery, particularly in the tourist areas. They will often find rings, chains and bracelets considerably cheaper than at home. | Gold jewellery

Icons are much prized by art-lovers. It is possible to have a particular icon painted to order by a Cretan painter. | Icons

Pottery can be bought in all price ranges – poor imitations of antique vases, good copies and ceramic products of the highest quality.
Caution is required in buying pottery. Most ware is not really washable, since the colours have usually not been fired into the material.
There is a potter's workshop worth visiting in the village of Margarítes (nomós of Réthymnon). | Pottery

Freshly picked herbs, sometimes offered as herb teas or recommended for their medicinal value, can be bought in special herb shops. | Herbs

In certain streets in Iráklion are cutlers who make the traditional Cretan knives. | Cretan knives

Typically Cretan leather goods are the traditional high boots (*stivania),* which can be bought, for example, in *stivanadika* shops in Chaniá. Other good buys are hand-made handbags and leather sandals (very reasonably priced; good quality products in Réthymnon, Chaniá, Kávros and Yeoryioúpolis). | Leather goods

Other favourite souvenirs are macramé purses. Beautiful examples can be found, for example, at Phódele, 30km/20 miles west of Iráklion. | Macramé work

Social Conduct

Raki	Cretan supermarkets sell a variety of local specialities, including raki (see Food and Drink).
Stone and metal articles, woodcarving	Many visitors are tempted by articles made from marble, onyx or alabaster, copper or pewter, or carved from olive-wood.
Sweets, nuts, drinks	Crete offers a wide range of sweet things (aromatic Cretan honey, fig cakes soaked in ouzo, chocolate, nut pastries, etc.), dried fruit, walnuts, almonds, pistachios, and a variety of wines and spirits.
Textiles	Other popular purchases are Greek traditional costumes, Réthymnon embroidery (including embroidered blankets, table linen, handkerchiefs and slippers) and lace. Kritsá is famed for its delicate embroidery.
Woven fabrics	Beautiful hand-woven fabrics can be bought, for example, in Anóyia, Zoniana (Réthymnon nomós) and Zarós (Iráklion nomós).

Social Conduct

The people of Crete are polite and helpful to visitors without being intrusive. They show a lively interest in world events, but visitors will be well advised to be discreet in discussing political matters and above all to avoid thoughtless criticism of conditions in Greece.

Dress   As in many southern countries, Cretans attach importance to correct dress, even though with the increase in tourism there has been a less rigid attitude in this respect.

Souvenirs

See Shopping and Souvenirs

Sport

Crete offers visitors a wide range of facilities, especially during the main holiday season, for every kind of sport, particularly water sports.

Star Waterpark   The luxury hotels listed under Hotels, above, offer a variety of sports facilities. An even wider range is offered by the Star Waterpark at Limín Chersonísou, which in addition to every kind of water sport (water-skiing, wind-surfing; swimming pool, water slide; diving school; boat hire) offers billiards, minigolf, parasailing, volleyball, electronic games, a children's play area, a restaurant and a bar on the beach.

Ball games   There are large sports halls for basketball, volleyball and handball in Chaniá, Iráklion, Sitía and other places.

Bathing beaches   See entry

Bowling   Bowling enthusiasts should visit Candia Bowling in Iráklion.

Climbing   There is good climbing and rock-climbing in the Mount Ida range and the White Mountains. Further information can be obtained from the Greek Climbing Club (EOX) in Iráklion, Dikaiosinis 53, tel. 081 22 76 09 (office open 7–9pm). There are other sources of information (EOS climbing club) in Chaniá, Tzanakaki 90, tel. 0821 2 46 47, and Réthymnon, tel. 0831 2 27 10,

2 22 29 and 2 36 66. The climbing clubs maintain mountain huts in the mountains (see Walking).

See Cycling

Cycling, mountain biking

In order to protect underwater archaeological remains, diving with breathing apparatus is prohibited both in Greek coastal waters and in inland lakes and rivers, with only a few exceptions. Areas excepted from this ban – are Eloúnda (information in Eloúnda Beach Hotel) and Ayía Pelayía (information in Peninsula Hotel) – where divers must strictly observe the regulations issued by the Directorate of Marine Antiquities of the Ministry of Culture and Science.

Diving

Information about areas where diving is permitted and about current regulations on diving and underwater fishing, together with a list of compressed air filling stations, can be obtained from the Greek National Tourist Organisation (see Information). It is in any event advisable to enquire about local conditions in the nearest harbourmaster's office.

Information also from:
Scubakreta Diving Centre
Limín Chersonísou, tel. 0897 2 23 68, 2 23 91, 2 29 50 and 2 29 51

A permit is required for fishing. Information can be obtained from the harbour authorities, e.g. at Iráklion, tel. 081 22 42 07. At many places fishing boats can be hired.

Fishing

Information about flying can be obtained from the Aeroclub at Iráklion International Airport, tel. 081 28 42 24 and 24 55 92.

Flying

Other sources of information: in Chaniá, Venizélou, tel. 0821 2 95 92; in Sitía, Phountalidou 18, tel. 0843 2 83 76.

There are football grounds in Chaniá and Iráklion, and well over a hundred elsewhere in Crete.

Football

Information about motocross events can be obtained from the Racing Club, Kalama 2, Iráklion.

Motocross

In addition to the well known Karteros Riding Club in Iráklion, tel. 081 28 20 05, which also runs pony and pony-cart treks, and Finikia in Iráklion, tel. 081 25 31 66 and 28 54 44 (Amoudára), there are the following riding centres:
Flamoriana/Lakonia Riding Centre, Áyios Nikólaos, tel. 0841 2 69 43
Deres Riding Centre, Chaniá, tel. 0834 3 13 39
Tsicalaria Riding Centre, Chaniá, tel. 0821 8 98 06
Platanes/Tharavis Riding Centre, Réthymnon. tel. 0831 2 89 07

Riding

Rowing boats can be hired at most rowing clubs. Information in Iráklion: Café Marina, Venetian Harbour, tel. 081 22 11 28. There are other rowing clubs at Áyios Nikólaos, Chaniá and Réthymnon.

Rowing

See entry

Sailing

Information in Iráklion:
Yachting Club, Harbour, tel. 081 22 81 18
and from specialised travel agencies.

Swimming is possible not only in the sea (see Bathing Beaches) but in hotel swimming pools. Iráklion has a swimming pool of Olympic standard.

Swimming

There are numerous tennis courts (mostly hard courts) attached to hotels and in seaside resorts. There are private club courts in Chaniá, Iráklion and other places.

Tennis

See entry

Walking

Surfing

Water-skiing, wind-surfing
There are a number of water-skiing and wind-surfing schools in Crete, and instructors at Mália, Limín Chersonísou, Ayía Pelayía, Eloúnda and other resorts.

Winter sports
Winter sports can be practised in the Mount Ida range and elsewhere in Crete. Information can be obtained from climbing clubs (see Climbing, above) in Chaniá, Iráklion and Réthymnon, which also maintain mountain huts.

Surfing

See Sport, Wind-surfing

Taxis

Taxis have the word "Taxi" on their roof and can be hailed in the street or picked up at taxi ranks. In towns they are to be found in considerable numbers in busy areas (airports, bus stations, etc.) and outside large hotels and museums. Fares are lower than in western Europe.

Extra charges
There are additional charges for taxis picked up at bus stations, airports and ports, for each piece of luggage over 10kg/22lb in weight and for night journeys (between 1 and 5am). Fares are also higher at Easter and Christmas.

Communal taxis
An even cheaper alternative to the ordinary taxis is provided by the communal taxis which ply in many holiday centres. They take as many passengers as there is room for.

Excursions by taxi
When a taxi is hired for an excursion the fare should be agreed on before departure.

Telephones and Telecommunications

See Postal Services and Telecommunications

Television

See Radio and Television

Tennis

See Sport

Time

During the winter months Crete is on East European Time (Greenwich Mean Time + 2 hours). From the end of March to the end of September Summer Time is in force (GMT + 3 hours).

Tipping

Hotels
Hotel prices are usually inclusive of service. Pages are usually given 100 Dr for carrying luggage, etc., chambermaids 200–300 Dr.

In restaurants and cafés it is usual to give a tip of 15% of the bill. In addition the amount is usually rounded up, and a small sum may also be left on the table.

Restaurants and cafés

Taxi-drivers usually get a 10% tip, and the amount is rounded up.

Taxis

At Easter taxi-drivers, hairdressers, etc., expect a small "Easter gift" (*paskha doro*), usually of 100 Dr.

Travel Documents

Although in principle passport controls for European Union citizens within the EU have been abolished, passports are still checked at EU airports and seaports. EU citizens, like nationals of other countries, must therefore produce their passport on entry into Greece.
EU citizens do not require a visa. Nationals of Canada, the United States and many other countries do not require a visa for a visit of up to three months.
Visitors whose passport contains a stamp or other entry by the authorities in (Turkish) North Cyprus may be refused entry into Greece.

Passports and visas

British driving licences and registration documents and those of other EU countries are accepted in Greece. Nationals of most other countries must have an international driving licence.
Cars entering Greece must bear the usual oval nationality plate.
An international insurance certificate ("green card") valid for Greece is required. Although third party insurance is compulsory in Greece it is advisable to take out temporary insurance giving comprehensive cover.

Car papers

See Sailing

Boat papers

No inoculations are required for visitors from Europe, North America and many other countries.

Inoculations

See Medical Aid

Health insurance

It is advisable to photocopy your travel documents, to have two extra passport photographs and to take these with you, keeping them separate from the documents themselves. This will simplify the process of getting new documents if the originals are lost or stolen.

NB

Walking

Walking is becoming an increasingly popular activity in Crete. But since there are no maintained or waymarked routes nor any suitable maps it is advisable to join an organised party or to take a local guide.

For hill walking the essential requirements, in addition to walking boots, a rucksack, jeans or trekking trousers, an anorak, rainwear and a pullover, are a sun hat, sun cream, insect repellent and a drinking flask.

Equipment

A brochure suggesting some good walks and giving the addresses of walking clubs can be obtained from the Greek National Tourist Organisation (see Information).

Information

A number of agencies in Crete organise one-day walks (for individuals or groups). Among them is the Happy Walker, Soph. Venizélou 21, Réthymnon, tel. 0831 2 24 46.

Agencies in Crete

The six-hour walk through the Samariá Gorge (see Sights from A to Z, Samariá Gorge) is one of the great experiences of a visit to Crete, though it

Some suggestions
Samariá Gorge

is a pleasure which must be shared with large numbers of other walkers. Walking through the gorge is prohibited from November to the end of April, and the gorge may also be closed because of bad weather.

Górtys – Phaistós – Mátala – Ayía Galiní – Spíli (about 200km/125 miles)
Zákros – Vái – Toploú monastery (about 60km/37 miles)
Réthymnon – Arkádi monastery (23km/14 miles)
Makriyialós – Ierápetra – Gourniá (about 180km/112 miles)

Kamáres Cave, Walks to the Kamáres Cave and the Idaean Cave: see Sights from A to Z,
Idaean Cave Mount Ida

Mountain huts From Chaniá 27km/17 miles on an asphalt road to Kambi Kydonias; from
Volikas hut there a 3-hour walk to the Volikas hut (1360m/4460ft) in the White Mountains (tel. 0821 5 45 60). Information from EOS climbing club in Chaniá.

Kalérgi hut From Chaniá 41km/25 miles on an asphalt road to Omalós (1580m/5185ft)
in the White Mountains; from Makhi, near Omalós, 5km/3 miles on a poor
country road to the Kalérgi hut; then on to the Samariá Gorge (see above).
Information from EOS in Chaniá.

Prinos hut From Iráklion 23km/14 miles on an asphalt road to the village of Ano Asites
Maleviziou; then 2km/1¼ miles on a country road to Melisses; from there
1½-hour walk to the Prinos hut (1100m/3610ft). Information from SOX
climbing club in Iráklion.

Hut on Either from the village of Kouroutes, near Réthymnon, on a country road to
Mt Psilorítis the chapel of Áyios Titos in the Pardi Forest, and from there 5km/3 miles to
the hut; or from the village of Lokhria Amariou on a country road to
Kouropito on Mt Psilorítis, and from there to the hut (1500m/4920ft). Information from EOS in Réthymnon.

Water Sports

See Sport

When to Go

The best times to go to Crete, with its Mediterranean climate (see Facts and
Figures, Climate), are in spring, from about the second half of March to the
end of May or beginning of July, and in autumn, in the months of September and October, sometimes extending into early November. Both spring
and autumn are ideal times for walking. The summer months (mid June to
the beginning of September) are very hot, and at this time of year insects
(midges, mosquitoes) can become troublesome. From the middle of
November to the end of March there is a good deal of rain.

March to May The months of March, April and May are mild, and nature is in all its
splendour of blossom. Moreover Easter falls in this period and is celebrated with impressive ceremonies all over the island (see Events, Public
Holidays).

Mid June to The summer months are hot, but as a result of the dryness of the air and the
early September constantly blowing *meltemi* (north wind) the heat is quite tolerable. In July
and August the *meltemi* can whip up a heavy swell, making the sea unsafe
for swimmers.
Summer is the time to visit Crete for the various festivals and folk
performances, as well as the wine festivals with their opportunities for
sampling Cretan wines.

Even in summer it is advisable to have a woollen jacket or pullover with you, since on the coast and in the mountains it is often quite cool in the evening; a raincoat is useful on boat trips; and stout footwear is necessary if you want to do a lot of walking. Protection against the sun and insect repellents are other essentials.

During the day it is best to have only a light meal: the main meal should be in the evening.

In October the weather becomes milder again, and good weather often continues into November, though there may be the first rainfalls of winter.

October and November

Youth Hostels

Youth hostels offer cheap accommodation, particularly for young people. Most youth hostels in Crete are open throughout the year. It is advisable, and during the main holiday season essential, to book your place in plenty of time: payment in advance is required, particularly for groups. There are limits on the number of days you can stay at the same hostel.

All hostellers must present their national youth hostel membership card.

There are youth hostels in Chaniá, Iráklion, Limín Chersonísou and Sitía.

Organosis Xenonon Neotitos Ellados
(Greek Youth Hostel Association)
Odós Dragatsaniou 4, GR-10559 Athens, tel. 01 3 23 41 07

Information

None of the above hostels is affiliated to the International Youth Hostels Association.

Index

Principal Sights of Tourist Interest

Map showing principal sights on page 215

Note: The places listed above are merely a selection of the principal sights – places of interest in themselves or for attractions in the surrounding area. There are, of course, innumerable other sights in Crete, to which attention is drawn by one or two stars.

mprint

01 illustrations, 14 special plans, 6 town plans, 5 general maps, 3 tables, 1 drawing,
large map of Crete

Original German text: Carmen Galenschovski, with contributions by Vera Beck, Rainer
Eisenschmid, Helmut Linde, Reinhard Strüber and Andrea Wurth

Editorial work: Baedeker-Redaktion (Carmen Galenschovski)

General direction: Dr Peter Baumgarten, Baedeker Stuttgart

Source of illustrations: Archiv für Kunst und Geschichte (1); Ehrenfried-Warme (4);
HB Verlags- und Vertriebsgesellschaft mbH (3); Henseler (18); Galenschovski (13);
Historia-Photo (3); Lade Fotoagentur (1); Mauritius Bildagentur (3); Schapowalow
Bildagentur (1); Schumann (2); Strobel (4); Strüber (43); Tzaferis (1).

English translation: James Hogarth

1st English edition 1996

© Baedeker Stuttgart
Original German edition 1995

© 1996 Jarrold and Sons Limited
English language edition worldwide

© 1996 The Automobile Association
United Kingdom and Ireland

Published in the United States by:
Macmillan Travel
A Simon & Schuster Macmillan Company
1633 Broadway
New York, NY 10019–6785

Macmillan is a registered trademark of Macmillan, Inc.

Distributed in the United Kingdom by the Publishing Division of the Automobile
Association, Fanum House, Basingstoke, Hampshire RG21 2EA

Licensed user:
Mairs Geographischer Verlag GmbH & Co.,
Ostfildern-Kemnat bei Stuttgart

Printed in Italy by G. Canale & C.S.p.A – Borgaro T.se –Turin

ISBN 0–02–861364–3 USA and Canada
    0 7495 1417 5 UK